John William. Ed Nutt

**Fragments of a Samaritan Targum**

edited from a Bodleian Ms. with an Introduction

John William. Ed Nutt

**Fragments of a Samaritan Targum**
*edited from a Bodleian Ms. with an Introduction*

ISBN/EAN: 9783741161063

Manufactured in Europe, USA, Canada, Australia, Japa

Cover: Foto ©Thomas Meinert / pixelio.de

Manufactured and distributed by brebook publishing software
(www.brebook.com)

John William. Ed Nutt

**Fragments of a Samaritan Targum**

# FRAGMENTS

OF A

# SAMARITAN TARGUM.

By the same Author.

TWO TREATISES ON VERBS CONTAINING FEEBLE
AND DOUBLE LETTERS: By R. Jehuda Hayug of
Fez. Translated into Hebrew from the original Arabic by
R. Moses Gikatilla of Cordova; to which is added, THE
TREATISE ON PUNCTUATION, by the same author, translated
by Aben Ezra; edited from Bodleian MSS., with an English
translation.

London, 1870, 8vo.

pp. xlii, and 147, English; pp. xv, and 132, Arabic and Hebrew.
Price 7s. 6d.

_____

In preparation.

A HEBREW COMMENTARY ON ISAIAH, by a French
Rabbi of the 12th century, edited from a Bodleian MS. with
an English translation.

# FRAGMENTS

OF

# A SAMARITAN TARGUM,

*EDITED FROM A BODLEIAN MS.*

## WITH AN INTRODUCTION,

CONTAINING A SKETCH OF

SAMARITAN HISTORY, DOGMA, AND LITERATURE,

BY

## JOHN W. NUTT, M.A.,

FELLOW OF ALL SOULS' COLLEGE, GRINFIELD READER ON THE LXX.
SUB-LIBRARIAN OF THE BODLEIAN LIBRARY, OXFORD.

TRÜBNER AND CO., LONDON.

1874.

# TABLE OF CONTENTS.

# INTRODUCTION.

More than two centuries and a half have passed away since the discovery was made at Damascus of a Hebrew Pentateuch, written in Samaritan characters, and with readings different from those of the Masoretic text in use among the Jews, and also of a complete translation of the same into the Samaritan idiom. The attention of learned Europe was thus directed to the literary remains of a people now languishing and well nigh extinct, but once the bitter and formidable religious opponents of the Jewish nation, and an interest was aroused in them which the labours of De Sacy, Gesenius, and others in the present century have again revived. The results, however, of these enquiries, extending as they do over so long a period, are in many cases buried in rare and costly volumes or hidden away in periodicals and long-forgotten dissertations. It has been thought, therefore, that a short sketch, embodying the latest information attainable with regard to the history, writings, and religious tenets of the Samaritans, may fitly

b

serve as an introduction to the interesting and
important fragment of their literature which is
here published.

I. The tide of Assyrian conquest which had begun
to overflow the land of Israel under Pul[1] about
770 B.C., and had continued its progress during
the reigns of Tiglath Pileser[2] and Shalmaneser[3],
reached its height in the time of Hosea, when, in
722, 'the king of Assyria[4] took Samaria, and carried Israel away into Assyria, and placed them in
Halah and in Habor by the river of Gozan, and
in the cities of the Medes[5],' supplying their place

---

[1] 1 Chron. v. 26; 2 Kings xv. 19.  [2] 2 Kings xv. 29.

[3] 2 Kings xvii. 3-5.

[4] *Ibid.* xvii. 6; xviii. 11. This appears to have been Sargon,
the successor of Shalmaneser. See the article 'Sargon' in
Smith's *Bible Dictionary*, iii. 1142, and George Smith's *Chronology of the Reign of Sennacherib* (1873), p. 12. On a cylinder
in the British Museum, Sargon is called the 'Punisher of wide
Beth-Omri;' and in a bull inscription of Khorsabad, 'Destroyer
of the city of Samaria, all Beth-Omri.' In the copy of his annals
he says, 'The city of Samaria I besieged and captured, 27,290
people dwelling in it I carried captive, 50 chariots in the midst
of them I arranged and the rest of them I took possession of,
my general over them I appointed, and the taxes paid by the
former king I fixed upon them.' Cf. Schrader, *Die Keilin-
schriften und das A. T.* (1872), p. 158 sq.

[5] 2 Kings xvii. 24. For an identification of these places see
Asahel Grant's *Nestorians* (1841), p. 129 sqq. Halah is probably the Calah of Gen. x. 11, 12, now Nimrūd. The Habor
flows S.W. into the Tigris from the mountains of Assyria (so

with colonists from 'Babylon, and from Cuthah,

---

Ewald, *Gesch.* (1866), iii. 638 ; but according to Schrader, p. 161, it is the greater stream of that name which flows into the Euphrates near Carchemish). Gozan=Zozan, the Nestorian name for pastures : the high lands on either side of the great Zâb river, W. of lake Ooroomiah. (Rages also near Teheran, Nineveh, and Ecbatana, are mentioned in the book of Tobit as settlements of Israelites : Elkosh, the home of the prophet Nahum, where his tomb is still shewn and greatly venerated, was north of Nineveh.) Dr. Grant brings forward several striking reasons for the identity of the independent Nestorian Christians inhabiting this almost inaccessible tract of country with some of the ten tribes. They call themselves Bene Israel ; the patriarch claimed to be of the tribe of Naphtali ; the neighbouring Jews allow that they are of the same stock as themselves, and speak almost the same dialect with them, though the two bodies hate each other and will not eat together. The Nestorians still offer peace-offerings, practise vows of Nazaritism, bring first-fruits, keep the Sabbath strictly, have a recess in their churches termed the Holy of Holies ; children may be baptized on the eighth day after birth ; the purification of women after childbirth extends for forty days in the case of a male, for sixty of a female infant ; they keep the Passover, but the holy Eucharist supersedes the Jewish sacrifice ; their physiognomy and names are Jewish ; their patriarch, both in his civil and religious capacity, strongly resembles the ancient high-priest ; they have 'avengers of blood,' the churches serve as 'cities of refuge.' The 'Chaldean' Church dates from A.D. 1681, when the Nestorian metropolitan of Diarbekir quarrelled with his patriarch, and had himself consecrated by the Pope patriarch of the converts to papacy from the Nestorian and Jacobite Churches who designate themselves by this title. Dr. Grant's conclusions are doubted by Ewald, *Gesch.* (1864), iv.

and from Ava, and from Hamath, and from Sepharvaim[1].'

---

120, who however does not bring forward reasons in support
of his view. He mentions, giving references, the journey of
Eldad the Danite in the ninth century in search of the ten tribes
described by Josephus (*Ant.* xi. 5. 2) as existing in great
numbers beyond the Euphrates, Benjamin of Tudela's description of them in the twelfth, and the various attempts made to
discover them among Afghans, Chinese, Parthians, Buddhists,
and North American Indians. For Talmudical traditions as
to their position see Neubauer, *Géographie du Talmud,* p. 372 ;
for other references to Josephus, St. Jerome, &c., Jnynboll, *Comment. in Hist. Gent. Sam.* p. 26 sq. ; also Chwolson's *Achtzehn Hebr.
Grabschriften aus d. K'rim* in *Mém. de l'acad. imp. de St. Péters-
bourg,* série 7, vol. ix. 7, for records of the ten tribes in the
Crimea and (p. 59) Caucasus ; and for their connection with the
legend of Prester John, cf. Oppert, *Der Presbyter Johannes*
(1864), p. 17. Benjamin of Tudela has found a successor in
' J. J. Benjamin II,' who went on the same quest in 1846–1855 ;
he corroborates Dr. Grant's statements ; see his 'Eight Years in
Asia and Africa' (Hanover, 1863), p. 124.

[1] For the position of Cuthah, see below, p. 9, note 4. That
of Ava is not known. Hamath was plundered by Sargon in the
second year of his reign, its inhabitants carried off, and others
settled in their place, Schrader, pp. 162–6. Ewald, *op. cit.* iii.
655 (1866), places Sepharvaim and Ava near Hamath. Sargon
in his first year transported colonists from Babylon to Samaria :
cf. Schrader, p. 162. Other colonists seem to have joined
them later. Sargon says in 715 B.C. : 'The Tamudi, Ibadidi,
Marsimani and Hayapa, remote Arabians [cf. 'Geshem the
Arabian,' Nch. ii. 19, iv. 7] dwelling in Bari whom the Akku
and Sapiru knew not of . . . in the service of Assur my lord
I destroyed them, and the rest of them I removed, and in

It has been much debated to what extent this
depopulation was carried out[1]. In the later conquest of Judah it is especially mentioned that the
'poorest sort of the people of the land'[2] were left
behind, and only the nobles, warriors, and artisans
carried away. And it seems most probable that
such had been the case with Israel also, for Josiah,
in 630, puts down idolatry in 'Manasseh and
Ephraim, and Simeon, even unto Naphtali[3],' and a
little later repairs the temple with money collected
for the purpose from 'Manasseh and Ephraim and
all the remnant of Israel[4],' as well as from Judah
and Benjamin. Again, after the ruin of Judah,
in 588, worshippers from Shechem and Shiloh and
Samaria are represented as coming with offerings

the city of Samaria I placed . . .' Vid. George Smith, *op. cit.*
p. 14, and Schrader, p. 163. Other tribes also are mentioned
in Ezra iv. 9, 10, as having been brought over by Asnapper
and settled in Samaria, (for their position see Ewald, iii. 727):
in iv. 2, the Samaritans ascribe their settlement to Esarhaddon.
Makrizi's account of this shifting of populations is to be found
in De Sacy, *Chrestomathie Arabe*, i. 302.

[1] For a reference to varying opinions on the subject see the
article 'Samaria' in Smith's *Bible Dict.* iii. 1105.

[2] 2 Kings xxiv. 14.   [3] 2 Chron. xxxiv. 6.

[4] 2 Chron. xxxiv. 9. The invitation of Hezekiah to the passover in 2 Chron. xxx. seems to have extended principally, if not
only, to the parts untouched by Assyria: the reference therefore
appears to be of no value for determining the question of what
Israelitish population was left behind by the conquerors.

to the temple at Jerusalem [1]. In all likelihood,
therefore, a considerable population of Israelites
remained behind, who were recruited after the
withdrawal of the Assyrian armies by returning
fugitives [2] and fresh drafts of foreign populations from the various countries which, in their
turn, came beneath the yoke of the kings of
Assyria [3].

At first the worship of Jehovah seems to have
been entirely overlooked amid that of the numerous deities [4] introduced by the new settlers, but
in consequence of the country being visited by a
plague of lions, it, or some modification of it [5], was
established by an Israelite priest [6] at Bethel, the

---

[1] Jer. xli. 5.

[2] Cf. Jer. xl. 7–12 for the similar case of Judah.

[3] The term ἀλλογενής as applied to a Samaritan in Luke xvii.
18 cannot fairly be pressed so as to exclude the notion of there
being an Israelitish element among the Samaritan population.

[4] 2 Kings xvii. 30, 31. Succoth-benoth, the deity of the
Babylonians, cannot be traced. Nergal signifies the 'lion-god,'
mentioned in cuneiform inscriptions as worshipped by the people
of Cutha. This source gives no information as to Ashima,
Nibhas, and Tartak. The burning of children by the inhabitants of Sepharvaim may have been connected with their worship of the sun, the name signifying the 'city of the sun.'
Schrader, 166–168.

[5] Possibly the old calf-worship was restored again, Bethel
having been the seat of it. Ewald, iii. 729.

[6] The priests, as being an educated and important class of the
community, would naturally have been among the captives.

former centre of state idolatry under Jeroboam and
his successors; each nationality meanwhile retaining its own peculiar divinity and religious rites.
Although, therefore, the influence of the sanctuary
at Bethel seems in time to have spread throughout the new immigrants and to have expelled the
various deities and rites introduced by them [1], still
Zerubbabel and his returning brethren may have
had good reason for declining the co-operation of
the 'lion-converts' [2] in the work of restoring the
ancient ritual and temple at Jerusalem. This
refusal roused the deep hostility of the Samaritans, and from this time the relations between the
two people became continually more and more
embittered, till an absolute separation ensued between them. Even now, when one common ruin
has for so many centuries involved them both,
they hold no intercourse with each other. From
this time forward one thought alone presented
itself to the Samaritans' mind, to depress by every
possible means, fair or foul, their hated rivals of
Jerusalem, to represent themselves as the true
disciples of the great prophet of Israel and Garizim as the sanctuary chosen of God on which the
first temple was at His command built by Joshua,
while Eli, Samuel, David, and Solomon were held

---

[1] Ezra iv. 2.　　　　[2] *Bab. Baba K'ama*, 38 b.

up to reprobation as the apostate leaders of a national and religious schism [1].

By the possession of a tract of country remarkable for its fertility, and venerable for its religious associations, the Samaritans were well qualified for maintaining an opposition to the rival state [2]. It extended, according to Josephus [3], from Ginaea or En-Gannim, on the south side of the great plain of Jezreel, to the borders of Benjamin, thus including the old territory of Manasseh and Ephraim. Its principal towns were Bethshan [4], famous for its fertility, known later under the name of Scythopolis; Abelmeholah [5], the home of Elisha; Jezreel [6], the residence of Ahab; Tirzah [7], proverbial for its beauty, where dwelt the kings of Israel from

---

[1] Yet, when it suited them, the Samaritans would deny all connection with the Jews and assert their heathen extraction: thus in the time of Darius Hystaspes they claim to be Persians (Josephus, *Ant.* xi. 4. 9), under Alexander the Great, Sidonians (*ib.* xi. 8. 6; xii. 5. 6).

[2] The old tribe of Ephraim, whose territory they possessed, had been of great political importance under the Judges; under Abimelech it gained the royal power, and later opposed Ishbosheth to David and Jeroboam to Rehoboam, always bearing with great unwillingness the supremacy of Judah: the Samaritans assumed exactly the same position.

[3] *B. J.* iii. 3. 4; but in the next chapter he makes Anonath or Durkin the frontier. Cf. Neubauer, *Géographie,* p. 57.

[4] 1 Sam. xxxi. 10.     [6] 1 Kings xix. 16.

[5] 1 Kings xviii. 46.     [7] Cant. vi. 4.

Jeroboam to Zimri; Shiloh, the resting-place of the ark [1]; Bethel, the scene of Jacob's visions [2].

But the principal events of Samaritan history gather round the two centres of Samaria and Shechem. Built originally by Omri in a commanding position of great fertility, strength, and beauty, on a hill some six miles north-west of Shechem [3], Samaria continued till the Assyrian captivity the capital of the kingdom of Israel, the centre of Ahab's Baal-worship, the scene of many of the miracles of Elijah and Elisha displayed in famines brought upon the land, in the sudden return of plenty, and in deliverance from Syrian invasions; the object of the bitter denunciations of Hosea and other prophets for luxury, idolatry, and oppression. Taken in 722, after a three years' siege [4], the city must have sunk for a

---

[1] Josh. xviii. 1.   [2] Gen. xxviii. 19.   [3] 1 Kings xvi. 24.
[4] 2 Kings xviii. 9, 10. For further references cf. Robinson, *Palestine* (1867), ii. 304, and Winer, *Bibl. Real-Wörterbuch* (1847), p. 369. The term שׁמְרוֹן is once (2 Kings xvii. 29) used in the Old Testament for the 'inhabitants of Samaria.' In later times the Samaritans designated themselves as שׁמרים, which, by a play upon the word, they interpreted 'observers' of the Law or Sabbath, or, according to others, 'guardians' of the land, senses recognised by Origen (*Comm. in Joan.* p. 355; *Hom. in Ezech.* ix. 1), Eusebius (*Chron.* ii. ad ann. Abrahami 1270), Hieronymus (*Onomastica*, ed. Lagarde, p. 66, cf. also p. 197), Epiphanius (*Haeres.* i. 9); cf. also De Sacy, *Not. et Extr.* xii. p. 175. They were termed by the Jews כותים, from Cutha, a

while into ruin, for it does not reappear in history
till the time of Alexander the Great, when it was
captured by him, part of the inhabitants put to
the sword, others removed to Shechem, and a new
colony introduced. Some frontier towns also were
lost to Judaea at this time[1]. It appears soon after
to have been rebuilt by Perdiccas, but in 311,
during the wars of Antigonus and Ptolemy Lagi, it
suffered the demolition of its walls : restored again
in a short time, it continued to exist till about B. C.
129, when it was taken and utterly destroyed by
John Hyrcanus, the Jews retaining possession of
the site[2]. It was restored by Pompey to its former

district in Asia of doubtful locality, whence colonists, perhaps
the most important, had been transplanted to Samaria by the
king of Assyria (cf. 2 Kings xvii. 24). Abulfath, in his Chronicle (ed. Vilmar, p. lix), explains that in a persecution under
Darius some Samaritan exiles fled from the Jews to the valley of
Cutha, hence the name was fixed upon them in order to deprive
the nation of that of 'Israelites.' On the position of Cutha, cf.
De Sacy, *Chrest. Arabe*, i. 331 ; Herzfeld, *Geschichte*, i. 473,
iii. 598 ; Ewald, *Gesch.* (1866), iii. 727 ; Neubauer, *Géogr.*
p. 379. According to Schrader, p. 164, it must be sought for
in Mid-Babylonia.

[1] Eusebius, *Chron. ad ann. Abrahami* 1684 ; cf. Munk, *Palestine*, p. 485. This was in revenge for the murder of Androma-
chus, the Macedonian governor of Coelesyria. Herzfeld, ii. 120.

[2] The 25th of Marheshwan was kept in memory of this ; the
15th and 16th of Siwan in memory of the annexation of Bethshan and the plain of Jezreel ; *Meg. Ta'anith*, 3, 8 ; Grätz,
*Gesch.* (1863), iii. 422.

owners, and rebuilt by Gabinius a few years B.C.,
and somewhat later again fortified, colonised, and
magnificently adorned by Herod the Great, receiving the name of Sebaste, in honour of Augustus,
to whom a splendid temple was erected within
the city. A Roman colony was planted there by
Septimius Severus early in the third century, and
coins are found extending from Nero to Geta, the
brother of Caracalla [1]. At what time Herod's mag-
nificent erections were laid waste is not known.
A bishop of Sebaste was present at the council
of Nicaea in 325, and another at the synod of
Jerusalem in 536. When the place fell into the
hands of the Crusaders, a Latin bishopric was
established there about 1155, the title of which
was still kept up by the Roman Church till the
fourteenth century. A small Arab village now
occupies the site of the old town, traces of whose
former grandeur are still visible in the stately
remains of the church of St. John Baptist [2] and
long rows of broken columns.

But more interest attaches to Shechem, the

---

[1] Or perhaps somewhat later to Alexander Severus, 222-235.
Cf. De Sauley, *Numismatique de la Terre Sainte* (1874), p. 281.

[2] St. Jerome gives Sebaste as the burial-place of St. John
Baptist, as also of Elisha and Obadiah: later a tradition sprang
up that it had been the scene of the Baptist's imprisonment and
death also, whereas Josephus, followed by Eusebius, places these
at Machaerus, on the east of the Dead Sea. Robinson, ii. 306.

modern Nablus [1], the principal centre of Samaritan
life after the decline of Samaria, where still lingers
on the feeble remnant of the last Samaritan community. Built upon a gentle slope at the foot
of Mount Garizim, at a point where the mountain
and the opposite height of Ebal enclose a valley
of some 500 yards in breadth, Shechem, with its
bright streams and luxuriant vegetation, has always
drawn forth the warmest admiration of travellers [2].
Its associations were especially sacred. Near it
stood the oak of Moreh (Gen. xii. 6), the resting-
place of Abraham; in the immediate vicinity of
which was the parcel of ground (xliii. 22) bought
by Jacob from Hamor and given by him as a possession to Joseph; it is marked still by Jacob's
well and Joseph's tomb. Here dwelt the patriarch
till compelled to leave in fear of the consequences

[1] There seems to be no good reason for the identification of
Shechem (in LXX, Συχέμ and Σίκιμα) with the Συχάρ of John,
iv. 5. Eusebius and the Bordeaux pilgrim expressly distinguish
them: see the reff. in Smith's *Bibl. Dict.*, art. 'Sychar,' iii. 1395;
Robinson, ii. 291; Neubauer, 169; Bargès, *Les Samaritains de
Naplouse*, 10 sqq. Raumer identifies the latter with Askar,
half an hour east of Nablus, whence apparently were named the
plain and fountain Sahl-el-Asgar, and Aiu-el-Asgar mentioned
by Berggren (in which case the derivation from שקר, the 'city
of lies,' cf. Hab. ii. 18, suggested by Ireland, or Lightfoot's from
שכור 'of drunkards,' cf. Isa. xxviii. 1, will fall through): but
Robinson (i'i. 133) demurs to this.

[2] See the interesting quotations in Smith's *Dict.* iii. 1236.

which might ensue from the vengeance taken
upon Shechem by Levi and Simeon for the insult
offered to their sister. Under the same oak which
gave shelter to Abraham he buried the gods
brought by his family from Mesopotamia (xxxv.
1-4). By the same, in all probability, was Abimelech made king[1]. Near Shechem Joseph and
his brethren fed their flocks[2]; from Ebal and
Garizim were pronounced the curses and blessings
of the Law[3]; on Ebal Joshua built an altar and
set up stones on which were written the words of
the Law[4]; at Shechem, which had been appointed
a city of refuge and possession of the Levites, he
gave his last warning to the assembled congregation of Israel, setting up as a witness a great
stone 'under an oak which was by the sanctuary
of the Lord[5];' on Garizim was delivered Jotham's
parable after Abimelech's slaughter of his brethren,

---

[1] Judg. ix. 6.    [2] Gen. xxxvii. 12.

[3] Deut. xxvii. 11. For the account of an interesting experi-
ment as to the acoustic capabilities of the spot, see Mills, *Nablus*
(1864), p. 57. The voice of a reader can with ease be heard
from one mountain to another, and there is ample space for the
accommodation of a crowd like the Israelites.

[4] Josh. viii. 30. The Samaritans charge the Jews with
having altered Garizim to Ebal in Deut. xxvii. 4 out of spite
to them, in order to rob Garizim of its honours. In the
neighbourhood of Sichem they shew the tomb of Eleazar,
Ithamar, Phinehas, Joshua, Caleb, the Seventy Elders, &c.
Bargès, p. 15.    [5] Josh. xxiv. 26.

the connivance of the inhabitants of Shechem in
this deed of blood soon after returning on their own
heads in the destruction of their city by Abimelech ;
hither came Rehoboam to receive the kingdom [1] :
and here for some time dwelt Jeroboam after his
accession [2]. The city no doubt suffered like others
during the Assyrian invasion, but is mentioned
as existing about 588 [3]. It gained in importance
by the erection of a temple on the neighbouring
height of Garizim in opposition to that of Jerusalem, which lasted from about the time of Alexander the Great to B.C. 129, when it was destroyed
by John Hyrcanus [4]. Later it acquired the name
of Mabortha [5] or Mamortha [6], and, apparently
under Vespasian, that of Flavia Neapolis [7], whence

---

[1] 1 Kings xii. 1.  ·  [2] 1 Kings xii. 25.  [3] Jer. xli. 5.

[4] The 21st of Khislew (or, according to *Bab. Yoma*, 69 a, the
25th of Tebeth) was long kept by the Jews in memory of this.
*Meg. Ta'anith*, cap. 9.

[5] Josephus, *B. J.* iv. 8. 1.

[6] Pliny, *H. N.* v. 13. Olshausen suggests מבירתא as the derivation of the name, Nablus being a halting-place between Jerusalem and Galilee; Neubauer, p. 172, מברכתא. Cf. 'Torberie,'
the 'blessed,' as a name of Garizim mentioned by Masudi and
Makrizi, De Sacy, *Chrest. Arabe.* i. 303, 343.

[7] Robinson (ii. 292) thinks the old city may have extended
further eastwards than Neapolis (hence Eusebius' statement
that Sichem was ἐν προαστίοις Νέας πόλεως), and now have disappeared entirely: to the same effect Ewald in *Götting. Gel.
Anz.* 1865, p. 1671. Coins of the city are found from Titus

its modern name of Nablus is derived. Here our
Lord made many converts[1], and here in all probability was founded a Church in apostolic times[2]:
Justin Martyr, who suffered at Rome about 163,
was a native of the place. A bishop of Neapolis
was present at the council of Ancyra and Neo-
caesarea in 314, of Nicaea in 325, and at the synod
of Jerusalem in 536[3]. After this brief survey of
the country occupied of old by the Samaritan
people, it is time to return to their history.

Disappointed in their wish to unite with the

---

(or Domitian) to Volusianus (A.D. 251–4), or Gallienus (253–68).
The year 72 was termed the 'era of Neapolis,' probably in
consequence of the ruin of Jerusalem and Judaea in 70-1. In
the time of Hadrian a representation of Garizim first occurs
on coins of the city, the temple having been rebuilt by him
(*Chron. Sam.* cap. 47). The mountain is of conical shape,
with two summits: on the one to the left appears a temple
with columns in front and a long flight of steps leading up
to it, as described by the Bordeaux pilgrim in 333; that on
the right has a small edifice on it, without columns. Neapolis
had received the 'Jus Italicum' under the Flavian family, hence
its name of 'Aurelia Flavia Neapolis.' Of this it was deprived
by Septimius Severus (193–211) for supporting the cause of
Pescennius Niger. Under the Emperor Philip (244–9) it became a Latin colony, receiving the title of 'Colonia Julia Sergia
Neapolis.' De Saulcy, p. 244 sq.

[1] John iv. 39–42.    [2] Acts viii. 25, ix. 31, xv. 3.
[3] Robinson, ii. 293. The portal and other remains of the
cathedral, which was dedicated to St. James the Less and is now
converted into a mosque, are still to be seen. Bargès, p. 93.

Jewish exiles on the return of the latter from
captivity in 536, the Samaritans succeeded in
preventing the erection of the Temple for twenty
years, and offered the same unrelenting opposition
to Nehemiah when, in 445, he set about rebuilding the walls of Jerusalem, which till now had
lain in ruins. They welcomed with open arms
any refugees from Jerusalem who, for crime or
to escape the strict Mosaic rule there established,
might wish to leave their country [1]. No doubt
the stern reforms introduced by Nehemiah on his
second visit (chap. xiii) were highly distasteful to
many who preferred the laxity which had crept
in during his absence, and to these an asylum was
always open at Shechem. The alienation between
the two nations was finally completed when the
Samaritans at last succeeded in erecting a rival
temple [2] on Garizim and endeavoured to transfer
thither the prestige of the older one of Jerusalem. The immediate occasion of the undertaking
was the refusal of Manasseh, brother of Jaddua the

---

[1] Josephus, *Ant.* xi. 8. 7.
[2] The date of the erection is doubtful. Josephus (*Ant.* xi.
8. 4) seems to place it in the reign of Darius Codomannus (335-
330), the last king of Persia, but if the Sanballat he mentions is
the same as in Neh. xiii. 28, the event should be placed under
Darius Nothus (413-10); cf. Winer, *op. cit.*, art. 'Nehemiah.'
Jost (*Gesch.* i. 48, note 2) thinks the temple must be much
earlier than Alexander.

high-priest and son-in-law to Sanballat the Samaritan governor, to dissolve his irregular marriage
in obedience to the admonition of the Jewish
elders. To reward him for his constancy, Sanballat exerted himself to erect a rival sanctuary,
and there established him in the high-priesthood[1].

On the troubled scene of politics which opened
after the death of Alexander the Samaritans suffered equally with the Jews from the cruelty and
ambition of their ever-changing masters. They
unfortunately served as the battle-field as well
as the prize of victory to the holders of Syria
and Egypt, and passed from the dominion of one
sovereign to that of the other according as the
tide of victory rolled hither or thither. From
the peaceful rule of Laomedon, the governor of
Syria, they passed into the hands of Ptolemy Lagi
in 320, to fall under the dominion of Antigonus
of Syria in 314. Three years later, by a sudden
incursion, Ptolemy repossessed himself of his former
conquest, but being compelled almost immedi-

---

[1] This temple the Jews termed שלמות (*Bereschith Rabba*,
c. 81), signifying, according to Reland (*Garizim*, c. 3), τελίθω
ναός, but the word is probably connected with πλάνος, i.e. the
שלוה of Gen. xxxv. 4; cf. Frankel, *L'influss d. palästin. Exegese*,
p. 248. The Samaritans in turn stigmatised that of Jerusalem
as קלפלתא בית or מבתש ב׳: by a play upon ירושלם they called
it אורי שלם 'the cursed Salem.' Neubauer's Chronicle, *Journ.
Asiat.* (1869), p. 402; see below, p. 125.

c

ately to retire, endeavoured to do as much mischief as possible to his enemy, and consequently
before his departure razed the walls of Samaria
and other fortified towns. In 301 he, by treaty,
entered again into peaceable possession of the
country, but, in 298, it underwent a cruel
ravaging at the hands of Demetrius Poliorcetes,
the son of Antigonus. Thenceforth, for many
years, Palestine enjoyed a respite from trouble
under the mild and beneficent rule of Egypt, and
nothing more is heard of Samaria except petty
squabbles with the neighbouring Jews during the
sway of the feeble and avaricious high-priest
Onias II, till the reign of Antiochus Epiphanes,
when a determined effort was made by this
monarch to root out the worship of Jehovah and
establish the ritual of Greece throughout his do-
minions. The conduct of the Samaritans at this
juncture formed a marked contrast to the noble
independence of the Jews in maintaining the faith
of their fathers: they abjured all connection with
Israel or its God, claimed to be Sidonians by
origin, and requested that their temple might
be dedicated to Zeus Hellenios[1]. To one principle of conduct however, with rare exceptions,
they always remained constant, to take the opposite side to the Jews and injure them to the

---

[1] Josephus, Ant. xii. 5. 5.

utmost of their ability. This at last drew down
upon them the vengeance of John Hyrcanus, and
the destruction of their temple about 129 B.C.,
followed by that of Samaria a few years later.
The Samaritans responded by all the means of
annoyance at their command, killing Galilean pilgrims on their way to Jerusalem, and lighting
sham beacon-fires in opposition to those kindled
by the Jews as a signal to their distant brethren
that the Paschal new moon had appeared. On
one occasion it is related how a Samaritan succeeded in polluting the Temple on the eve of the
Passover by scattering human bones over the
pavement[1]. The Gospel narrative shews that in
our Lord's time there was a complete estrange-
ment between the two nations: the very name
of Samaritan had now become a term of abuse[2].
When the independence of Judaea declined and
Palestine passed under the Roman rule, matters
began to look brighter for the Samaritan people.
Pompey freed them from the Jewish yoke; Gabinius rebuilt and fortified Samaria; the national
worship was restored, exiles suffered to return, and
government by a council of elders established: the

[1] See reff. in Neubauer, Géogr. p. 166.
[2] John viii. 48. Cf. also Ecclus. l. 25, 26 (where 'Seir' is
possibly to be read for 'Samaria') and Testamentum XII Patrum,
p. 564: Ἔσται γὰρ ἀπὸ σήμερον Σικὴμ λεγομένη πόλις ἀσυνέτων.

reign of Herod the Great also, one of whose wives was a Samaritan, was marked by the execution of great public works for the embellishment of Samaria.

But the unquiet spirit which had distinguished the old tribe of Ephraim in former times, and is said even now to mark the modern inhabitants of Nablus[1], would not suffer the Samaritans to rest. Their history is a constantly recurring tale of insurrections, massacres, and bloody reprisals taken on them by the conquerors. The severity with which Pilate put down a tumultuous rising occasioned his recall[2]. Under Vespasian a revolt was quelled with the loss of 11,600 persons[3], and Sichem received a garrison and new name from the conqueror. It is uncertain whether they took any part in the Jewish revolt under Trajan[4]: in the terrible insurrection which a few years later burst out with such desperate violence under the

---

[1] Judg. viii. 1-3, xii. 1-6, 2 Sam. xix. 43; cf. Robinson, ii. 301.

[2] Josephus, *Ant.* xviii. 4. 1, 2: a certain man promised to show them the sacred vessels hidden by Moses (or the high-priest Usi, who, according to the Samaritan book of Joshua, chap. 41, hid them 261 years after the entry into Canaan) under Garizim. The legend is borrowed from 2 Macc. ii. 5, where the prophet Jeremy does the same on Nebo.

[3] Josephus, *B. J.* iii. 7. 32.

[4] Juynboll, *Comment. in Hist. Gent. Sam.* p. 129.

leadership of Bar Cochba in the reign of Hadrian the Samaritans apparently at first aided the Jews, but afterwards deserting their allies assisted the Romans in putting an end to the war, being rewarded at the hands of their conqueror by the restoration of their temple on Garizim[1]. With the rest of the empire they benefited from the gentle rule of the Antonines. Under Commodus, Septimius Severus, Constantine and Constantius, their condition was unsatisfactory, but quieter times fell to their lot under Julian, Valentinian, and Valens; their fortunes varied under the later emperors. Laws unfavourably affecting their position were passed by Honorius in 404 and 418; Theodosius II in 426 took from them testamentary rights, and in 439 forbade them to exercise any office which dealt with the affairs of Christians; new synagogues also might not be erected[2].

The hatred with which they had formerly regarded their Jewish rivals began to concentrate itself upon the Christians, now that the new

[1] Juynboll, *Chron. Sam.* cap. 47; Bargès, p. 101; Ewald, vii. (1868), p. 407. Bettar is said to have fallen by Samaritan treachery: as to its position see Neubauer, *Géographie*, p. 103. In *Jer. Kidduschin*, iv. 1, it is said that thirteen places were merged among the Samaritans in the time of 'the destruction,' i.e. under Hadrian: this was done by them in order to avoid the fate of the Jews.

[2] Jost, *Gesch.* i. 76; Juynboll, *Comment.* p. 50.

faith had become that of the empire. In the year
484 while under the rule of Zeno they attacked
the church at Nablus, maimed the bishop, and
murdered many of the worshippers, committing
the like atrocities at Caesarea also. Under Anasta-
sius and Justinian fresh troubles broke out [1]. In
529 a general revolt of the Samaritans took place
against the Christians, whole villages were burnt,
churches destroyed, and the worshippers tortured
to death. The severity with which this was put
down by Justinian, followed by the enactment of
severe laws against them, completely crushed the
Samaritan people [2]. Many fled to Persia, many
became Christians [3]. Henceforth they appear but
little in history. In 636 they fell under Mohammedan rule when the conquest of Palestine was
effected by the Khaliph Omar. After the capture
of Jerusalem in 1099 by Godfrey de Bouillon and
his allies, Nablus and the surrounding country

---

[1] Petermann, in Herzog's *Real-Encyclopädie*, xiii. p. 369.

[2] They were rendered incapable of holding public employ-
ments, or of acquiring property by inheritance or gift among
themselves: their synagogues were to be destroyed and no new
ones erected. Some of these provisions were relaxed a few
years later: some time after again, they were ordered to under-
take civic offices with duties attached to them, without however
acquiring any of the corresponding rights. Their testimony
against Christians could not be received. Jost, i. 78.

[3] Robinson, ii. 294, 295.

came into the power of the Crusaders, and, with
the exception of some temporary occupations
by the Saracens [1], remained Christian till 1244,
when it again became subject to Mohammedan
rule by the complete and utter rout of the
Christian forces at the fatal battle of Gaza.
Brief notices of the Samaritans and their country
appear in the works of Benjamin of Tudela
(twelfth century) and Christian pilgrims and
travellers [2], but little was known of them till
the close of the sixteenth century, when Joseph
Scaliger first opened communications with them,
addressing a letter to the congregations at Nablus
and Cairo [3]. Answers arrived in 1589, but not

---

[1] As, for instance, when Nablus was plundered during a
temporary incursion of the Saracens in 1113, again by Saladin
in 1184 after his repulse from Kerak, and in 1187 after his
victory at Tiberias.

[2] Bargès, pp. 10 sq., 33 sq.; Robinson, ii. 297. Arabian
writers often confound them with the Jews. Ibn Batuta (1326),
while describing Nablus, does not mention them.

[3] A careful description of the correspondence of the Samaritans
with Europeans, from Scaliger to De Sacy, is given by the latter
in *Notices et Extraits des MSS. de la Bibl. du Roi*, vol. xii. (1831),
together with the original texts and a translation of most of the
letters: two (to Ludolf) were published by Cellarius, 1688;
others are to be found in Eichhorn's *Repertorium*, vols. ix.
and xiii. One more has since been published by Heidenheim
in his *Vierteljahresschrift* (vol. i. p. 88), that of Meschalmah ben
Ab Sechuah to the Samaritans of Europe, coming, as is supposed

till after Scaliger's death, and these passing into
other hands the correspondence ceased. But in
1616, Pietro della Valle having in vain endeavoured
at Cairo, Gaza, and Nablus, then centres of Samn-
ritan life, to carry out the injunctions of De Sancy,
then French ambassador at Constantinople, and
procure a Samaritan Pentateuch, succeeded at last
in purchasing one at Damascus, as also a translation of it into the Samaritan dialect. The
publication of these excited great interest and
provoked angry disputes as to their intrinsic
value among the learned of Europe, but no further
communications appear to have been opened with
the Samaritans till 1671, when Huntington, the
learned bishop of Raphoe, whose Oriental MSS.
form part of the treasures of the Bodleian Library,
paid a visit to Nablus, while holding the office
of chaplain to the English factory at Aleppo.
He found there a small community of thirty
families, procured from them a Pentateuch, and
in conjunction with Dr. Marshall, Rector of Lincoln
College, Oxford, carried on a correspondence with

by the editor, between the correspondence of Scaliger and
Huntington. Emendations of the text are suggested by Geiger
in the *Zeitschr. d. D. M. G.* xvi. 725, and by Vilmar, *ibid.*
xvii. 375. The letters are written partly in Arabic, and partly
in Hebrew marked by Samaritanisms and Arabisms; they
display the most complete ignorance of all history and of everything outside the little community of Nablus.

them which lasted with intervals till the latter's
death in 1685. About this time a few letters
also passed between them and the celebrated
Aethiopic scholar Job Ludolf, and then, with the
exception of one letter addressed in 1790 to their
'Samaritan brethren' in France[1], nothing more is
heard of them till 1808, when the bishop and
senator Grégoire set about making enquiries with
regard to them by means of the French consular
agents in Syria. The information thus acquired
and the communications which subsequently ensued between Salameh the high-priest and De
Sacy himself are contained in the memoir drawn
up by the latter. They give the same picture as is
presented by later travellers of a small community
despised and ill-treated by Jew and Muhommedan[2],
from the very fact of their present depressed con-

---

[1] Published by Hamaker in *Archief voor Kerkelijke Geschie-
denis*, v. p. 56. Heidenheim, i. 82.

[2] A touching picture of the miseries undergone by the
Samaritans during the first half of the present century from
the cruelty and avarice of their ever-changing governors is given
in the autobiography of Jacob-eah-Shelaby, London, 1855. He
came at that time to England to collect funds for his impoverished
countrymen and to intercede with the government on their behalf.
A translation of his petition may be seen at p. 50. Another, to
the government of Louis Philippe, is given with a translation in
Barges, p. 65 sq. See also his letter in the *Times* of April 3,
1874. The congregation is now reduced to 135 persons, and
grievously oppressed by the Mohammedans.

dition clinging with all the greater obstinacy to
their lofty traditions of the past and to the hope
of future restoration to the Divine favour; with
little or no education; depending for their history upon legendary mediaeval chronicles drawn
in great measure from Jewish sources; for their
religious knowledge, upon the successive gleanings
of centuries from their Jewish rivals; yet interesting as the possessors of what they assert to be
an independent revision of the Pentateuch, and
as the sole remaining representatives of the people
who have now for more than 2500 years claimed
to be the chosen Israel of God[1].   The correspond-

---

[1] Formerly there were flourishing communities of Samaritans
in other countries besides Palestine.   Alexander the Great is
said to have settled his Samaritan auxiliaries at the siege of
Tyre in Egypt (Josephus, *Ant.* xi. 8. 6): Ptolemy Lagi carried
off considerable numbers with him (ib. xii. 1), other colonists
probably followed during the troublous times of John Hyrcanus:
a dispute between the Alexandrian Jews and Samaritans is said
(ib. xiii. 3. 4) to have taken place before Ptolemy Philometor
(181-146): here the Samaritan-Greek version of the Pentateuch
in all probability and the Arabic of Abu-Said were composed.   A
sect of Dositheans is mentioned there in the sixth century A. D.,
and some remnants of the people lingered on there till the seventeenth.   A colony of Samaritans was found by Edrisi in the
twelfth century in islands in the Red Sea, where they are said
to have taken refuge after the Arab invasion of Egypt in 638.
Meshullam ben Menahem of Volterra (הלמיה or בלמיה, not
מלטה, Malta or Toledo, as Heidenheim supposes, cf. Biscioni,
*Catal. Medic.* p. 128, and Zunz in Asher's *Benjamin of Tudela*

ence is of high value for the light it throws on
the later developements of Samaritan doctrine,

---

(1841), ii. 267) found fifty Samaritan families in Egypt on the
occasion of his visit there in 1480. They hold, he says, partly
to the written Law, but are idolaters ; their writing is different
to that of the Jews, and they have no א, ה, ב, ע, צ, ח (cf. as to
this last statement *Benjamin of Tudela*, i. 67 ; Isaac Helo, A. D.
1344, in Carmoly's *Itinéraires*, p. 152, and Makrizi, in De Sacy,
*Chrest. Arabe*, i. 303) ; they go in pilgrimage thrice each year to
Garizim, where a golden dove may be seen on the altar ; they live
apart from the Jews, having a separate synagogue ; the Sabbath
they observe only to mid-day. See his letter in Heidenheim, iii.
354. He was probably the same that Obadiah of Bertinoro met
on his journey to Jerusalem seven years later, cf. Neubauer's *Zwei
Briefe Obadiah's* in *Jahrb. für d. Gesch. d. Juden*. (1863), iii. 198,
229. The latter (*ibid.* 241, 243) gives much the same account :
he found fifty Samaritan families in Cairo, employed chiefly as
cashiers and agents for the principal officials, occupations in which
they acquired considerable wealth. The anonymous traveller of
1495, whose narration is given *ibid.* p. 271 sq., visited Sichem,
but makes no mention of the Samaritans, his whole mind being
apparently taken up with endeavours to avoid the extortions of
custom-house officials. In the third and following centuries
they seem to have been widely scattered in both East and West,
employing themselves chiefly as merchants and money-changers :
in the time of Theodoric (493–526) they had a synagogue in
Rome. A colony of Samaritans is mentioned as existing in the
fourth century at Babylon (*Gittin*, 45 a). Benjamin of Tudela
in the twelfth century found communities in Caesarea, Nablus,
Askelon, and Damascus : the great number of MSS. written at
the last-named place shews that it must have been an important
centre for them. The chronicle *El-Tholidoth* (see below, p. 126)

and also of interest as shewing the intellectual
condition of this once numerous and powerful but
now nearly extinct religious sect. The later
descriptions of modern travellers, such as Robinson,
Petermann, and others, shew that few changes
have since passed over the little community.

II. In the preceding historical sketch the reader
will no doubt have observed the extreme paucity,
or rather the almost total absence, of any trustworthy information derivable from the Samaritans
themselves as to the circumstances of their origin
and early condition; and for this reason will expect no very exact account of the tenets held by
them in the earlier ages of their national existence.
Even with the fullest details at our disposal,
nothing very definite or distinctive in the way of
religious belief would in all probability have been
found existing among them. For it must be remembered that they were a population consisting
of the poorest Israelites, who had been left behind
by their conquerors as politically too insignificant
to be worth the trouble of removing from their

gives the names of many families settled in Damascus, Palestine,
and Egypt. Cf. Robinson, ii. 293, 300; Basnage, *Hist. des Juifs*
(1716), ii. 140-142, 152; Juynboll, *Comment.* pp. 37-54; in
the last very full references will be found. In a prayer given by
Heidenheim (*Vierteljahrsschr.* i. 418) supplications are offered
for the Samaritan congregations in Damascus, Gaza, Philistia,
Egypt, Aleppo, Hamath, Sefad, and Haserim.

land; they had moreover, after long centuries of
corruption by means of state idolatry and devotion
to the cruel and licentious rites of Baal, Ashtoreth,
and other monstrous deities, afterwards been recruited from time to time by the arrival of fresh
parties of foreign idolaters. The nation had indeed, under the influence of fear, partially abjured
their idolatry and professed the worship of Jehovah, so much so as to be anxious to unite with
the returning Jews in rebuilding the Temple at
Jerusalem, in all probability however their religious views had at this time gained no great
depth or distinctness. But the refusal of the
national party among the Jews to recognise them
as in any way belonging to Israel must have compelled the Samaritans to consider their religious
position, to test the validity of the claims put
forth by them, and to shew both by their faith
and practice that they, and not their rivals of
Jerusalem, were the true disciples of Moses. By
themselves however they were unable, from lack
of the necessary learning, to carry out their purpose, and it will be seen from several instances
which will be brought forward, that the Samaritans, powerless to invent, were compelled to borrow
the doctrines and usages then in vogue at Jerusalem.

No one will be surprised at this who considers
the intimate relations which were from the first

maintained between their leaders and a powerful
section of the Jews. It was in vain that Ezra,
aided by such as had 'separated themselves' from
the heathen of the land, dissolved by force the
marriages which had taken place between the
latter and numberless priests and rulers of Jerusalem. A few years later the mischief had not
abated: Nehemiah complains that his plans were
betrayed by the nobles of Judah, who had allied
themselves with the enemy; his last work
was to purify the Temple from the presence of
Tobiah the Ammonite who had established himself there with the assistance of Eliashib the
high - priest, and to expel the grandson of the
latter for his marriage with Sanballat's daughter.
These temporary checks caused by the zeal of
Ezra and Nehemiah being removed, no doubt
such alliances became frequent as before, and
although the influence of the national party at
Jerusalem was sufficient to prevent a complete
fusion of the two nations, yet a most intimate
connection must have been kept up between
certain members of each, and thus the Law and
the prevailing interpretation of it have readily
passed from Jerusalem into the opposite camp.
More especially after the secession of Manasseh
and his establishment as rival high-priest in the
Temple of Garizim, must all the then existing
Jewish learning have been at the disposal of

the Samaritans. To understand their position
therefore it will be necessary to enquire what
was the state of religious parties and what the
tone of thought which after the return from the
exile prevailed in Jerusalem.

It was not apparently till the pontificate
of John Hyrcanus, about B.C. 130, that the two
rival factions of Pharisees and Sadducees[1] made
their appearance under these names in history.
But they must have existed long before: there
was nothing, as far as we know, in the special
circumstances of the time which could have then
produced them: the principles which actuated
their conduct must have been at work in the
nation in the preceding centuries as well. The
government had all along been in the hands of
the high-priest and the other sacerdotal families
to whom he was related; to these would naturally
ally themselves the other wealthy classes in the
state. In the hands of this, the Sadducee party,
would be all judicial and administrative posts, the
arrangement of the calendar on which all the feasts
of the year depended, the conduct of the services
of the Temple, the authoritative exposition of the

---

[1] Derenbourg (*Palestine*, i. 78, 452) thinks that Pharisee and
Sadducee were nicknames, invented long after the qualities of
*Perishouth* and *Sedaqah* had become the characteristics of the
two parties. See also Grätz, *Gesch.* (1863), iii. 454, sq.

Law. Whatever might be the merits of individual
members of the body, such as Jaddua and Simon
the Just, still the tendency of a privileged and
wealthy class always would be to take life
quietly, to content themselves with following the
requirements of the Law as far as the letter and
ancient tradition required them (in other words to
comply with *Ṣedaqah*), but not to invent rigorous
observances which would interfere with the in-
dulgence of those tastes which their wealth and
position enabled them to enjoy. Their interpretation of the Law was characterised by the same
spirit. Though not always consistent in carrying
out the principle, still as a rule they clung to
the literal meaning, allowing the authority of no
tradition unless some ground was apparent for
it in Scripture[1]. The official sanctity of the
priesthood, as distinguished from the personal
purity of its members, and the maintenance of
its emoluments and privileges were eagerly con-
tended for by them. Their disbelief in the resurrection of the body, which is expressly affirmed
of them by all ancient testimony[2], was due pos-

---

[1] Jost, *Gesch.* i. 214.

[2] Matt. xxii. 23; Mark xii. 18; Luke xx. 27; Acts iv. 2, xxiii.
8; *Bab. Sanhedrin*, 90 b; Josephus, *Ant.* xviii. 1. 4; Origen, *In
Matt.* pp. 467, 811; Epiphanius, *Haeres.* xiv, &c. The celebrated
Antigonus of Socho is said to have taught that 'men should
serve God without any claim for reward;' from this doctrine

sibly to the almost exclusive attention which
their principles led them to give to the Pentateuch (in which this doctrine less clearly stands
forth) in preference to the later books of the
canon, and also to the easy circumstances of life
in which most of this party found themselves.

The Pharisees, or 'Separatists,' were of a different
spirit. They were the descendants and representatives of the national party who at the bidding
of Ezra and Nehemiah had 'separated' themselves
from the heathen of the land, while many of the
priests and rulers had not scrupled to ally themselves with the ancient and deadly foes of Israel.
Though differing in no very important particulars
from the Sadducees either in doctrine or practice,
they found themselves outside the pale of an
official and priestly aristocracy, and were thus
compelled to throw themselves for support and
sympathy upon the middle and lower classes of
the community. Having no official character for
sanctity on which to depend, they laid especial

---

his scholars Sadoq and Boethus developed the further result
that 'no reward is to be expected from God.' and this was
naturally followed by a disbelief in the resurrection and future
judgment. The Boethusians first appear as an offshoot from,
but united with, the Sadducees, about the time of Herod the
Great; the exact points of difference between the parties are
difficult to distinguish. Geiger, *Urschrift*, 105, 149; Jost,
*Gesch.* i. 215.

stress upon personal purity, avoiding contact with
any person or thing which might interfere with
it; by means of brotherhoods[1] and minute regu-
lations endeavouring continually to reach higher
degrees of it, extending their care even to all
vessels used in the Temple service, on the plea
that they might have been defiled by the touch
of an unclean priest[2]. In imitation of the grave
and reverend banquets held by the priests at
which their portion of the sacrifices, the tithes
and offerings were consumed, the Pharisees established brotherhoods for taking solemn meals
together, hallowed by special prayers, especially
on sabbaths and feast-days[3]: in the same spirit

---

[1] Jost, *Gesch.* i. 197.

[2] This circumstance shews that some priests must have belonged to the party of the Pharisees, though these probably
were few as compared with those who joined the Sadducees.
The touching of the Law rendered any one unclean: Derenbourg, i. 133. On one occasion a Sadducee seeing them bathing
the golden candlestick, exclaimed, 'See the Pharisees will at last
purify the sun !' Jost, l. 217. Cf. Mark vii. 4.

[3] The device by which the Pharisees evaded the two prohibi-
tions of not going more than 2000 cubits from home and of
not carrying anything out of their houses on the Sabbath, was
worthy of the legal ingenuity of a more civilised age. By placing
some food on the eve of the Sabbath at a spot 2000 cubits
from their real home, they created there a fictitious domicile,
whence they might move in any direction 2000 cubits more.
Each of the brethren, moreover, at the same time placed some

of rivalry they endeavoured to curtail the emoluments and privileges of the priesthood[1]. Their
interpretation of the Law was marked by a
reverence for tradition and by an absence of the
strict adherence to the letter which distinguished
their rivals[2]. Their method of life was rigorously
simple, spent in carrying out the minute observances of religion: they held the doctrine of
the resurrection and of a future reward and
punishment[3]. This zeal was roused to fury by
witnessing the disgraceful pontificates of Jason
and Menelaus, when the rites of Zeus Olympius
were celebrated in the Temple itself, and a
determined attempt made by these apostates to
trample down obedience to the Law of Moses,
and in its place to introduce the sensuous ritual
of Greece. By an energetic exercise of the influence which they possessed over the people they
must have greatly contributed to the success of
the Maccabees in their war of independence; but
when the victory was once gained, there was but
little place for them in the Court of the Asmo-

---

food in the common hall, thus a sort of community of houses
was imagined, and by joining the ends of the streets with beams
and ropes the whole city was made as it were one house. This
was termed the *Erubh*. Derenbourg, i. 143.

[1] For instances see *ibid.* 135.      [2] *Ibid.* 138.
[3] For Josephus' account of them see *Ant.* xviii. 1. 3; also xiii.
5. 9; xvii. 2. 4; *B. J.* ii. 8. 14; i. 5. 2.

nean princes, filled as it was with warriors and
priestly allies; so they retired to their old and
simple life among the people. The struggle
between the two parties went on till the fall of
Jerusalem, the Pharisees continually gaining more
and more advantages over their rivals: with the
ruin of the Temple and the cessation of its services
the Sadducees disappear from history, all the
teaching and interpretation of the Law falling into
the hands of the Pharisees, or Rabbanites as they
were afterwards termed. Thus matters went on
till A.D. 754, when, at the very moment when the
labours of the two schools of the Geonim appeared
to have established Rabbinism on a firmer basis
than ever, the celebrated Anan ben David raised
his voice against the system then in vogue, utterly
denying the right of tradition either to supplement
or interpret the written word, asserting the sole
authority of the Law, the unchanging character
of its precepts, and the necessity of seeking the
explanation of it in the book itself[1]. Thus after
the lapse of nearly seven centuries was the old
method of interpretation revived, and the obsolete

[1] Jost, li. 294. Here is to be found a very full account of
the literature and dogmas of the Karaites. See also Neubauer,
*Aus der Petersburger Bibliothek*, 88 sqq. They assumed the
name as being skilful 'readers' or interpreters of the 'literal
meaning' of the Law.

teaching of the Sadducees and Samaritans repeated in the Karaite school of Bagdad.

A few instances may be of interest, though the subjects in dispute were not such as modern theology takes much account of. The fruit of a young tree in the fourth year belongs, according to the old interpretation of Lev. xix. 23, 24, to the priest, from whom it must be redeemed by the owner; in this both Samaritans and Karaites agree, while a later explanation directs that the fruit or the value of it be consumed by the owner in person at Jerusalem [1]. According to the ancient interpretation of Lev. xxvii. 30; Deut. xiv. 22; xxvi. 12 and xiv. 28, two tenths of the fruit of trees and fields must every third year be given to the Levites and poor, a third consumed by the owners in Jerusalem; this last direction is not maintained by later doctors, only by Samaritans and Karaites [2]. Samaritans, Sadducees, and Karaites agree in deducing from Lev. iii. 9 that the tail part of sheep belongs to the priest alone, and may be consumed by no one else, whereas the Rabbanites make no such restriction [3]. When in Exod. xl. 31 priestly functions are attributed to Moses, the Samaritans alter the text so as to ascribe them to Aaron alone, and thus heighten the dignity of the latter [4]. For fear of irrever-

---

[1] Geiger, *Urschrift*, 181.　　[2] *Ibid.* 176.

[3] *Ibid.* 467.　　[4] *Ibid.* 381.

ence, the term ha-Shem was in reading substituted by early doctors for the sacred name
Jehovah whenever it occurred; this custom was
afterwards given up, and later again the name
Adonai substituted; the Samaritans still cling to
the old habit, employing the term Shemâ[1]. In
order to avoid anything approaching to an in-
delicacy of expression, the Samaritans interpret
במעלות in Exod. xx. 26 (neither shalt thou go up
'by steps' unto my altar), 'with craft,' as if from
בעל, and this rendering has been revived by the
Karaites[2]. The Samaritans allow the directions
in Deut. xxv. 5 to be carried out only in the case
of a betrothed, not actually married, brother's wife,
and with them agree the Karaites[3]. The decision
as to the exact moment at which the new moon
appeared, on which depended the time of all the
other feasts, was formerly in the hands of the
Sadducees. Gradually the Pharisees wrested this
power from them, and out of spite the Samaritans
and Boethusians endeavoured by false signals and
suborned witnesses to stultify the official intima-
tions of their antagonists. The Samaritans and
Karaites imitate the Boethusians in counting forward to Pentecost in Christian fashion, not from
the Sabbath following the first day of the Passover, but from the day after the Sabbath, in oppo-

---

[1] Geiger, Urschrift, 262.     [2] Ibid. 395.     [3] Ibid. 235.

sition to the Pharisee rule[1]. The same agreement between Samaritans and Karaites in opposition to the Pharisees is to be found in their use of the skin of a properly-killed animal only, not of an unclean one or of carrion[2]; in allowing no fire to burn through the Sabbath[3]; nor any one to move from home on that day[4]; nor any cooking to be done on festivals[5]: they do not permit a dying animal to be killed and eaten, and hold that the unborn young found in a slain animal has a separate existence and so must be properly slaughtered: the high-priest may, according to them, marry only a virgin (not widow) of priestly family[6].

In other and more important points also the

---

[1] Geiger, *Urschrift*, 137.

[2] Geiger, in *Zeitschr. d. D. M. G.* xvi. 718. Petermann, in *Herzog's Real-Encyclop.* xiii. 383, mentions that when they go in procession to Garizim they only use shoes made of leather from lambs killed by themselves; so the famous copy of the Law at Nablus is said to be written on skins of rams which have served as thank-offerings.

[3] *Zeitschr. d. D. M. G.* xx. 532. For their later practice, cf. Eichhorn, *Repertorium*, ix. 32; De Sacy, *Not. et Extr.* xii. 124.

[4] *Zeitschr. d. D. M. G.* xx. 535. As to the Pharisee rule, see above, p. 34.

[5] *Zeitschr. d. D. M. G.* xx. 536.

[6] *Ibid.* 561. Frankel (*Einfluss*, 252) believes that some practices of the Samaritans were borrowed directly from the Karaites.

Samaritans seem to have borrowed Sadducean
theology; for instance, a denial of the resurrection is expressly affirmed of them in the Siphré
and Massekheth Kuthim, a testimony borne out
by the evidence of the Fathers as well[1]. Whence
or at what time they adopted a belief in a coming
Messiah[2] is not clear, possibly from their Jewish
neighbours; as however he was to be a son of
Joseph, not of David, it is more probable that
the idea had its origin among the Samaritans
themselves, and was due to their anxiety to exalt
the tribe of Joseph at the expense of Judah[3].
There was but one point in which they could not
accept the creed of their neighbours, and that was
the choice by God of Judah as the ruling tribe and
Jerusalem as the centre of the national religion[4].
For this reason probably they were compelled to
reject all the later books of the canon, and retain only

---

[1] *Siphré* (on Numb. xv. 31); *Massekheth Kuthim*, see below,
p. 172; Derenbourg, i. 130. Cf. R. Eliezer in *Bab. Sanhedrin*,
90 b; Epiphanius, *Haeres.* ix and xiv; Leontius, *De Sectis*, viii;
Gregorius Magnus, *Moral.* i. 15, &c.

[2] John iv. 25.          [3] See below, p. 69.

[4] They could not admit the assertion of the Psalmist that the
Lord 'refused the tabernacle of Joseph and chose not the tribe
of Ephraim, but chose the tribe of Judah, even the hill of Sion
which He loved: and there He built His Temple on high, and laid
the foundation of it like the ground which He hath made continually. He chose David also His servant .... that he might feed
Jacob His people, and Israel His inheritance.' Ps. lxxviii. 68–72.

the Pentateuch and a mutilated portion of Joshua[1]. In these there was little to wound their susceptibilities: Ephraim was still an honoured and powerful tribe, the place which God would 'choose to put His name there' was still left undetermined[2]: nothing was needed but a few slight alterations which should depress the hated sanctuary of Moriah and establish the glory of its rival of Garizim[3].

From the foregoing sketch therefore it appears

[1] Joel (*Gesch.* i. 53, note) thinks the Samaritans rejected all but the Pentateuch from ignorance of them as being written in a character they did not understand. Loewe (in *Allgem. Zeitung d. Judenthums* for April 18, 1839) asserts that he found the books of Kings and Song of Songs among them. The anonymous commentary described below, p. 134, quotes from the prophets, &c.

[2] But in Deut. xii. 14 they read וחב for יחבר; cf. Ex. xx. 24.

[3] In Gen. xxxiii. 18 the Samaritans read שלים for שלם, 'Jacob came in peace to the city of Shechem,' instead of 'to Salem a city of Shechem,' in order to bar the Jewish interpretation of Jerusalem being here intended. The place is identified by Robinson (ii. 279) with Sâlim near Nablus. In Deut. xxvii. 4 they read 'Garizim' for 'Ebal,' inserting vv. 2-8 and xi. 30 as an additional commandment after Exod. xx. 17 and Deut. v. 21, and adding in xi. 30 the words 'opposite Shechem,' to make certain of its identification, the Jews having asserted that the Garizim and Ebal mentioned in the Pentateuch were not those belonging to the Samaritans: (*Sota*, 33 b; *Jer. Sota*, vii. 3; and *Siphré* on Deut. xi. 30). For other examples of changes made by the Samaritans see Kohn. *De Pent. Sam.* 11 sqq. That 'Ebal' must be the true reading of Deut. xxvii. 4 is well maintained by Friedrich (*De Christologia Samaritanorum*, 57) against Kennicott.

to be abundantly evident that the Samaritans
were in no degree the inventors of any part of
their theology, that they borrowed it wholly from
their neighbours, merely rejecting such parts
as did not square with their prepossessions, and
that they doggedly held on to the old traditional
interpretations, when these had been left by their
rivals centuries behind. They did, it is true,
modify and enlarge their creed, and that in important particulars, at a later period of their
history, but then, as before, by the same process of
absorption; it was in no sense a development of
the religious feeling of the people.

The statements of Jewish writers throw but
little light upon Samaritan theology, nor are they
by any means uniform in their tenour. In some
passages of the Talmud, for instance, the Samaritans are looked upon as Israelites by reason of
their religious observances, and credited with even
greater conscientiousness in carrying them out
than the Jews themselves[1]: on account indeed
of their misinterpretation of Deut. xxv. 5 marriage with them is forbidden, and their slavish
adherence to the letter of Scripture is reprehended,
but their orthodoxy is extolled with regard to
unleavened bread, slaughtering of cattle[2], pollu-

---

[1] *Holin*, 4 a.
[2] *Holin*, 3 a. So in John iv. 8 the disciples do not scruple to
buy food of the Samaritans.

tion from dead bodies or graves, and purifications ; their testimony also is to be admitted in matters of divorce[1]: while in other passages they are excluded altogether from the community of Israel and their very bread forbidden. It is uncertain when this change of feeling took place and to what it was due[2]. No charges of any weight are made against them, merely vague statements such as these ; 'Formerly the Kuthim were plunged in false beliefs, though they observed the Mosaic law ; now they have no idea of it[3].' R. Elieser ben Arakh relates at full length how a curse was pronounced upon them with all solemnity by Ezra, Zerubbabel, the high - priest Joshua, and six hundred of his attendant priests : no Israelite was to eat with them ; to do so would be as if

---

[1] Neubauer, *Géographie*, 165; Frankel, *Vorstudien*, 197; *Einfluss*, 245, where are very full Talmudical references; Winer, *Real-W.-B.* ii. 371, 372.

[2] Frankel (*Einfluss*, 248) attributes it to the influence of R. Simon ben Elieser (*Jer. Yebam.* i. 6), perhaps the same as Elieser ben Simon (*Sota*, vii. 3), who reported to R. Meir, in the second century A. D., the Samaritans' falsification of the Pentateuch, whereupon the latter excommunicated them. R. Simon ben Gamaliel, a contemporary of his, held the Samaritans in great respect, but his son R. Jehuda ha-Nasi considers them as heathen, and is borne out in this by his friend R. Ismael ben Jose. After the time of Diocletian they seem to have been quite excluded from Israel.

[3] R. Simon, in *Jer. Pasahim*, i. 1.

he ate swine's flesh: no Samaritan was to be received as a proselyte: none would have a share in the resurrection of the dead[1]. The ground of this exclusion is variously stated: generally they are charged with the worship of a dove[2], an accusation which originated as early as the second century A.D., is repeated again in a commentary of Rashi[3], revived by Maimonides[4], and reasserted as late as 1808, though repudiated with horror by the Samaritans themselves[5]. Or it is alleged against them that in the time of Diocletian they denied their Jewish origin and offered libations to heathen deities, a charge which must be received with considerable caution[6]. Similar accusations and apparently equally destitute of proof are, that they worshipped one of the idols hidden by Jacob under the oak by Shechem[7], or those

---

[1] *Pirke R. Eliezer*, cap. 38. Cf. Beer, *Gesch. Lehren*, &c., i. 35.

[2] *Holin*, f. 6, et al.

[3] On *Bab.'Aboda Zara*, 26 b; 'The Samaritans circumcise in the name of the image of a dove,' quoted in Drusius, *Observatt.* xiii. 24.

[4] On *Mishna Berakhoth*, viii. 8, in Reland, *De Samaritanis*, iii. So Obadiah de Bertinoro, on *Mishna Berakhoth*, vii. 1. Cf. Friedrich, *op. cit.* pp. 80 sq., and above, p. 27.

[5] De Sacy, *Not. et Extr.* xii. 19, 43, 70, sqq. Cf. Herzfeld, iii. 596. Josephus knows nothing of it. The colonists may have brought the worship of a dove with them from Nineveh; see references in Herzfeld.

[6] Jost, i. 61, from *Jer.'Abada Zara*, v. 4.

[7] *Jer.'Aboda Zara*, v. 4; Gen. xxxv. 4.

of the Samaritan colonists which were buried
under Garizim[1]; or that they circumcised in
honour of Mount Garizim[2], or that they wrote
Ashima for Elohim in Gen. i. 1[3], or that they were
no genuine worshippers of Jehovah, only lion-
converts[4]: charges which the Samaritans were
not slow in retorting, accusing their adversaries
in turn of anthropomorphism and anthropopathism
because they left untouched such passages in the
Pentateuch as seem to ascribe human acts and
feelings to the Deity[5].

The testimony of the Fathers with regard to
the Samaritans' disbelief in the resurrection of
the body has been already quoted; from the
same source we also learn their denial of the
existence of angels, and of the immortality of the

---

[1] Epiphanius, *Haeres.* ix.

[2] R. Jehuda, in *Masekheth Kuthim*; see below, p. 169.

[3] Aben Ezra, in Introduction to *Comment. on Esther*. It was
probably from some Jewish legend that Mohammed relates in
the Koran (*Sura*, 20) how a certain Sameri (Samaritan) made
the golden calf in the wilderness and was punished by Moses with
having to cry *lâ messâsa* (touch me not) to the end of his life.
Masudi and Biruni say the Samaritans still used these words in
their time (tenth and eleventh centuries A.D.); De Sacy, *Chrest.
Arabe*, i. 304, 343; cf. Abulfath, *Ann.* p. 175.

[4] *Bab. Baba Kama*, 38 b.

[5] They themselves were careful to change them; see below,
p. 135.

soul ¹; and also gain some information with regard
to the several sects which made their appearance
among them; these notices are supported by the
statements of Mohammedan writers and of the
Samaritans themselves. It may be as well in this
place to say a few words about them before noticing
the later developements of Samaritan theology.

The most important information on the subject
is derived from St. Epiphanius in the fourth century A.D. He mentions² four different sects, the
Essenes, Sebuæans, Gorthenians, and Dositheans.
With regard to the first of these bodies nothing
further is known, it is however possible that
there may have been separatists known under
the name among the Samaritans. If so, they were
probably an offshoot from the Dositheans, just as
the Jewish Essenes were from the Pharisees; for

---

¹ Origen, *In Matt.* p. 811; Leontius, *De Sectis,* 8; cf. Acts
xxiii. 8, as to the Sadducean disbelief in angels. Makrizi, in
De Sacy, *op. cit.* p. 306, says, 'the Zanâdiqata (i. e. Sadducees)
are of the nation of the Samaritans, sprung from the Sadducees;
they deny angels and the resurrection after death, and all prophets but Moses.'

² *Haeres.* i. p. 18 : he is followed by St. John Damascenus, *De
Haeres.* p. 79, and Nicetas, *Thesaur.* i. 35. For the whole subject see Basnage, livr'. ii. chap. 13; Juynboll, *Chron. Sam.* 112.
Epiphanius strangely asserts (*Haeres.* p. 469) that in his day a
feast was held in the summer at Sebaste in honour of Jephthah's
daughter, to whom divine honours were paid : a statement which
he repeats (p. 1055) with reference to Neapolis.

as the tenets of the latter were a protest against
the literal interpretation[1] and negative teaching
of the Sadducees, so the Dositheans appear to
have had much in common with the Pharisees,
and to have in like manner entered the lists in
opposition to the Sadducean teaching which, as
we have seen before, prevailed in their nation.
Nor is the information with regard to the Sebuaeans[2] more satisfactory: they are said to have

---

[1] Abulpharaj, a Christian writer who died in 1286 (*Hist.
Dyn.* p. 116), makes the Samaritans a Jewish sect who received
the Law alone and interpreted it in its literal sense. Juynboll,
*Chron. Sam.* 111.

[2] The origin of their name has been sought in בוש, who,
according to the *Tanḥuma*, sect. *Wayyeschebh*, and the *Yalquṭ*,
ii. 234, was one of the two Israelite priests sent by the king of
Assyria to instruct the Samaritans at the time of the lion-plague.
Sebuaeans are mentioned in the Chronicle of Abulfath as opponents of Baba Rabba, the Samaritan reformer about 250 A.D.
Sabbaeus was a name in use among the Egyptian Samaritans
(Josephus, *Ant.* xiii. 3, 4). Cf. Herzfeld, iii. 599, for another
explanation and an account of these sects. Herzfeld connects
the name with their peculiar keeping of Pentecost. Ewald,
*Gesch.* (1868), vii. 135, identifies them with the Masbothaei of
Hegesippus, the Basmothaei of *Const. Apost.* vi. 6, 1, the Fasqu-
ṭai of Abulfath. He derives their name from the stress they
laid upon the number 'seven,' as, for instance, in the observance
of that number of feasts. Petermann (in Herzog, *Real-Encycl.*
xiii. 387) could gain no information from the modern Samaritans with regard to any of the foregoing sects. From the
subscription of a MS. dated 1513 it has been supposed that

distinguished themselves by commencing the year
in the early autumn : soon after this they held
the feast of unleavened bread, Pentecost later,
and that of Tabernacles in the spring, when the
Jews were celebrating their Easter : these changes
were made by them out of animosity to Ezra,
and to avoid quarrels with the Jewish pilgrims
who were passing through Samaria on their way
to Jerusalem. Of the Gortheniaus, termed Soro-
thenians by Nicetas, nothing whatever is known [1].
With regard to the last of the four sects and
their leader Dositheus, it is impossible to recon-
cile the discordant testimony of Jewish, Christian, Mohammedan, and Samaritan writers [2].

---

a sect of Músawi existed at Damascus, and that they may have
been connected with Mesawi of Baalbek who lived in the twelfth
century, whose tenets bore some resemblance to those of the
Druses. Cf. Jost, 1. 68. But it is more probable that the name
signified orthodox Samaritans, 'followers of Moses.' Cf. Juynboll, *Chron. Sam.* p. 37 ; *Comment.* p. 60.

[1] Hegesippus (in Eusebius, *Hist.* iv. 22) makes them post-
Christian heretics, deriving their name from a certain Gortheus :
Theodoret (*Haer. Fab.* i. 1) considers them followers of Simon
Magus.

[2] At least three Dosithei, if not more, are mentioned by other
writers besides those cited in the text. (1) Dostai the son of
Jannai, sent to Samaria by Sennacherib, with Sabbai another
Israelite priest, at the time of the lion-plague. *Tanḥuma, l. c. ;*
*Yalqut, l. c.; Pirke Eliezer,* cap. 38. (2) Also a. c. Philas-
trius (*Haeres.* 4) says he was a Jew, the teacher of Ṣadoq. He

St. Epiphanius relates of them that they were
believers in the resurrection, and austere in their

---

held the Law was to be obeyed only according to the flesh,
denied the resurrection, Holy Spirit, angels, and last judgment.
(3) A post-Christian heretic mentioned by Hegesippus (in
Eusebius, *Hist.* iv. 22) and Hippolytus (*ibid.* vi. 22 ; Photius,
*Biblioth.* 121). According to the *Clementine Recognitions*, ii. 8,
*Hom.* ii. 24, he was the teacher of Simon Magus, to whom he
had to resign his claim to be the Messiah. The testimony of the
*Apost. Const.* vi. 8, and Theodoret, *Haeres.* i. 1, is to the same
effect. Eulogius, patriarch of Alexandria in 608, was called
upon to settle a dispute between the Dositheans and other
Samaritans of his day. Photius (*Biblioth.* 230), in describing
this, also makes him coeval with Simon Magus ; he calls him an
insulter of God's prophets, especially of the patriarch Judah.
His followers held him, the other Samaritans held Joshua, to
be the prophet promised by Moses. He denied the resurrection,
corrupted the Mosaic Octateuchus [so], applied the prophecies to
himself, &c. Origen (*Adv. Cels.* i. 57, vi. 11 ; *in Matt.* p. 851,
and *in Joann.* xiii. 27) says Dositheus made himself the
Messiah, the Son of God. His followers, who were almost
extinct in Origen's time, still had his writings, and believed him
to be alive. He ridicules the sect (*De Princip.* iv. 17) for their
excessive strictness in observing the Sabbath. Tertullian (*De
Praescript. Haeret.* 45) says Dositheus was the first who dared
to reject the prophets. St. Jerome (*Adv. Lucif.* p. 197) follows
him ; but whether they are speaking of (2) or (3) is doubtful :
probably of (2), as they make the Sadducees an off-shoot of the
Dositheans.

So much for Jewish and Christian testimony ; that of Mohammedan writers is not more satisfactory. According to Masudi
(who died in 956 A.D.; cf. De Sacy, *Chrestom. Arabe.* i. 305),
there were two sects of Samaritans, Couschan and Rouschan

manner of life, avoiding animal food, some marrying but once, others not at all : as to the
observance of circumcision, the Sabbath, avoiding contact with others, fasting and penance,
they were not distinguishable from the other
Samaritans. Their founder was, he continues, a
Jew who for his learning aspired to be chief
among his party, but being disappointed in his
ambitious schemes, went over to the Samaritans
and founded a sect : later he retired to a cave
and there starved himself to death out of affected

---

(corrected by De Sacy to Cuthâna and Dusâna; but according
to Juynboll, *Chron. Sam.* 112, the former word signifies 'truth-
telling,' not Cuthite) ; one of these held the world for eternal,
i. e. uncreated. Sharastâni (ed. Haarbrücker, Th. i. p. 257), two
centuries later, also divides the Samaritans into Dûsitânija or
Ilfânija ('lying separatists') and Kûsânija ('true people'), the
latter believing in a future life and rewards and punishments,
the former confining them to this world : the two parties differed
in their legal rules and ordinances. Al-Ilfân said he was the
prophet foretold by Moses, the 'Star :' he lived about 100 years
before the Messiah. (The name Ilfân probably signifies that he
was a millenarian ; cf. Vilmar's *Abulfath*, p. lxxii, note : or 'a
strict observer' [ ] of the Law.) To the same effect is the
testimony of Abulfeda, two centuries later, in De Sacy, *op. cit.*
p. 344. He mentions Dostanl or Fani and Cousani, the former
denying future rewards and punishments, the latter admitting
them. The quotation by Abraham Ecchellensis from an Arab-
Samaritan Chronicle in Cardinal Mazarin's library, to be found
In De Sacy, *op. cit.* 337, is probably from Abulfath. Cf. Vilmar's
*Abulfath*, p. xvii.

piety. This account, it will be noticed, mentions
but one Dositheus and one party named after him.
But as the preponderance of evidence is in favour
of there having been at least two heresiarchs of
the name, and two sects taking their title from
them, it will perhaps be best to acquiesce in this
conclusion, more especially as it agrees with the
account transmitted to us by the native Samaritan
chronicler Abulfath. He relates that (apparently
about the time of Antiochus Epiphanes) a sect
appeared calling themselves Dostân or ' the
friends,' who varied in many respects the hitherto received feasts and traditions of their fathers.
Several of their peculiarities are mentioned. They
held for impure a fountain into which a dead
insect had fallen [1]: altered the time for reckoning
the purification of women and commencement
of feasts: forbade the eating of eggs which had
been laid, allowing those only to be eaten which
were found inside a slain bird: considered dead
snakes and cemeteries as unclean, and held any
one whose shadow fell upon a grave as impure
for seven days. They rejected the expression
' blessed be our God for ever [2],' and substituted

[1] It is similarly alleged of all the Samaritans in the *Massekheth Kuthim* (see below, p. 170), that they held oil to be unclean
into which a mouse had fallen.

[2] In *Mishna Berakhoth*, 9, 5, it is stated that the expression
'for ever and ever' was introduced as a protest against the

e 2

52

Elohim for Jehovah[1]: denied that Garizim had
been the first sanctuary of God: upset the Samaritan reckonings for the feasts, giving thirty days
to each month, rejecting the feasts and order of
fasts and depriving the Levites of their portions
of the offerings[2]. They counted the fifty days
to Pentecost from the Sabbath, the day after
the first day of the Passover, like the Jews (i. e.
the Pharisees), not from the Sunday like the other
Samaritans. According to them a priest might,
without becoming impure, enter a house suspected
of infection, as long as he did not speak. When
a pure and impure house stood side by side, and
it was doubtful whether the impurity extended
to the former as well, the question was decided
by watching whether a clean or unclean bird
first settled upon it. On the Sabbath they might
only eat and drink from earthen vessels, which, if
defiled, could not be purified[3]: they might give
no food or water to their cattle; this must be
done on the previous day. Their high-priest was
a certain Zar'a, who had been turned out of his
own community for immorality of life.

---

'sectarians' (םיניִמ) for their disbelief in the resurrection. Dositheus' reason seems to have been the same.

[1] See above, p. 38.

[2] Cf. the account of the Pharisees given above, p. 35.

[3] That they might not be tempted to break the Sabbath by
dipping them in water to cleanse them. Herzfeld, op. cit. iii. 602.

At a later period lived a Jew, a certain Dûsis[1] : being condemned to death for immorality he was respited on the promise of sowing dissension among the Samaritans by founding a new sect. Accordingly he went to Nablus and formed a friendship with a Samaritan distinguished for his learning and piety. Compelled however to fly for his life on account of a false accusation which he had brought against his friend, he took shelter with a widow-woman, in whose house he composed many writings; but finding that a hot pursuit after him was still maintained, he retired to a cave, where he perished of hunger and his body was eaten by dogs. Before his departure, however, he left his books with his hostess, enjoining her to let no one read them unless they first bathed in the tank hard by. Accordingly, when Levi the high-priest's nephew, a pious, able man, arrived with seven others in search of him, they all bathed, one after the other, in the tank, and each, as he emerged from the water, exclaimed, 'I believe in Thee, Jehovah, and in Dûsis, Thy servant, and his

---

[1] He is mentioned just after a certain Germon, whom Juynboll (*Chron. Sam.* p. 347) takes for Germanus, bishop of Nablus in 323, and therefore puts them both at this time: Petermann (*Herzog, R. E.* xiii. 391) in the first or second century A. D. The Chron. *El-Tholidoth* (p. 58), see below, p. 124, appears to place him near the time of Zeno, towards the end of the 5th century A. D.

sons and daughters :' Levi adding, when his turn
came, ' Woe to us, if we deny Dûsis the prophet
of God.' Whereupon they took the writings of
Dûsis and found that he had made many alterations
in the Law, more even than Ezra. But this they
concealed on their return to Nablus, saying only
that Dûsis had disappeared before their arrival,
they knew not whither. At the next Passover
Levi had to read out Exod. xii. 22 in the synagogue, but for 'hyssop' he substituted 'thyme.'
Corrected by the congregation he still persevered,
crying, 'This is right, as God hath said by His
prophet Dûsis, on whom be peace! Ye are all
worthy of death, for denying the prophetic office
of His servant Dûsis, altering the feasts, falsifying
the great name of Jehovah, and persecuting the
second prophet of God whom He hath revealed
from Sinai! Woe unto you that you have rejected
and do not follow him!' Whereupon Levi was
stoned. His friends dipped a palm-leaf in his
blood, and ordained that whoever would read his
writings and see the leaf must first fast seven days
and nights. They cut off their hair, shaved their
beards, and at their funerals performed many
strange ceremonies. On the Sabbath they would
not move from their place, kept their feasts only
on this day, during which they would not remove
their hands from their sleeves. When one of their
friends died, they would gird him with a girdle,

put a stick in his hand and shoes on his feet,
saying, 'if we rise, he will at once get up,'
believing that the dead man, as soon as ever he
was laid in the grave, would arise and go to
Paradise.—Of the later fortunes of the Dositheans
we have no information : they existed however in
Egypt early in the seventh century A.D., when
Eulogius patriarch of Alexandria was called upon
to mediate between them and the rest of the
Samaritan community settled there[1].

This part of the subject would be incomplete
without some mention of the person and teaching
of the celebrated Simon Magus, though a complete
enquiry into his system and an examination of the
sources whence he drew it would far exceed the
limits of the present sketch.   He appears early in
the Apostolic history as practising magic arts in
Samaria, and giving himself out as 'some great
one,' or, as it is otherwise expressed, 'the power of
God which is called great[2],' i.e. the Supreme Deity
himself, as opposed to angelic powers, the creators
of the world.   Converted by the preaching and

---

[1] See above, p. 26, note.   Dr. Beer, in his *Buch der Jubiläen
und sein Verhältniss zu den Midraschim*, considers that it was
compiled in the interests of Dositheanism for the use of Egyptian
Jews ; it is said, on the authority of modern travellers, still to
maintain its influence among the Falascha (Jews) of Abyssinia.
Jost, *Gesch.* i. 66, note.

[2] Οὗτός ἐστιν ἡ δύναμις τοῦ Θεοῦ ἡ καλουμένη μεγάλη.   Acts viii. 10.

miracles of the deacon Philip, he suffered himself
to be baptized, but the unworthy character of his
motives in so acting was soon displayed in his
attempt to bribe the apostles to communicate their
supernatural gifts to him, hoping thus to acquire
greater powers for his own ends.  His answer to
the indignant rebuke of St. Peter betokens rather
apprehension than contrition, and tradition associates
his name with the first entry of Gnostic teaching
into the Christian Church.  The most trustworthy
particulars of his life are given us by his fellow-
countryman Justin Martyr in the middle of the
following century.  According to his account[1],
Simon was born at Gittón, a Samaritan village,
and making his way to Rome in the time of

---

[1] *Apol.* i. 26, 56, ii. 15 ; *Tryph.* 120.  A stone was found on
the island of the Tiber in 1574 with the inscription ' Semoni |
Sanco | Deo Fidio | Sacrum | Sex. Pompeius Sp(urii) F(ilius) |
Col(lina, *sc. tribu*) Mussianus | Quinquennalis | Decur(io) Bi-
dentalis | Donum Dedit' (Orell. 1860, Wilmanns 1300, Gruter
96. 5; the similar one in Orell. 1861, Gruter 96. 6, is suspected
by some critics); and Justin Martyr has been accordingly
charged with having mistaken this for a dedication to Simon
Magus.  The question is discussed in the preface to his works
published in Migne's *Bibl. Patrum*, p. 141.  It is singular that
the deity to whom the inscription refers, the Sabine Semo-
Herculea, is, according to Baur's view (*Christliche Gnosis*, 1835,
p. 308), to be identified with the Tyrian Hercules, and that the
legend of the latter and of Astarte probably gave rise to the
Simon and Helena myth.

Claudius gained so great an influence with both
senate and people by the aid of his magic arts
that they honoured him as god, and erected a
statue to his honour in the island of the Tiber.
As time goes on, more minute and full particulars
of his life are given by ecclesiastical writers. The
author of the Clementines, for instance, knows the
names of his parents, and describes him as having
received instruction in Hellenic literature and
magic at Alexandria[1]. Later in life he, with his
companion Helena, was among the thirty disciples
of John the Baptist, this number having been
chosen by the master as representing the days of
the month, with a woman among them to signify
its incompleteness, as twelve apostles had been
selected by our Lord in correspondence with the
twelve months of the year. On the death of the
Baptist, Dositheus, in the absence of Simon,
succeeded to the headship, but after a while was
compelled to succumb to the superior powers of
his rival. Simon now travelled about in company
with Helena (a dissolute woman whom he had
picked up at Tyre), practising magical arts, and by
their aid making statues to walk, rolling without
hurt in the fire, changing into a snake or kid,
displaying two faces, &c. But St. Peter continually throws himself in his path; at Caesarea

---

[1] *Recogn.* ii. 7; *Epit.* 25.

Stratonis they have a disputation which lasted three days; flying hence he is pursued by his triumphant antagonist to Phoenicia, Antioch, Laodicea, and at last, according to further accounts, is brought to bay at Rome, where, in order to regain his wavering credit with his disciples, he suffers himself to be buried alive, promising to rise again on the third day, but instead miserably perishes. In another version he attempts to fly, but failing in the undertaking owing to the prayers of the Apostle, he falls headlong and loses his life on the spot; or being horribly maimed, he flings himself in shame and anguish from a rock and so perishes [1].

However unsatisfactory many of these details of his history may be, a very complete description of his doctrinal system has descended to us in the works of early ecclesiastical writers, among which are to be found long extracts from the heresiarch's own treatise, the ' Great Apophasis,' or Declaration, in which he unfolds all his wisdom and theories of creation [2]. He explains that there are six original ' roots' or principles whence all things were derived ;

---

[1] The various modifications of the story are well described by Möller in Herzog, *Real-Encycl.* xiv. 392, who also gives a careful account of his system. Cf. also Ewald, *Gesch.* (1868), vii. 124 ; Baur, *op. cit.*; and the art. 'Gnosticismus' in Ersch and Gruber, p. 278.

[2] Hippolytus, *Haeres.* vi. 9, x. 12.

in the intellectual world these are νοῦς and ἐπίνοια, φωνή and ὄνομα [1], λογισμός and ἐνθύμησις; and corresponding to them in the world of sense are heaven and earth, sun and moon, air and water; but as his whole system is based solely upon the relation of the sexes, all of these 'roots' are arranged, as will have been noticed, in pairs, representing the male and female principle of thought, speech, and reflection [2] respectively. These however by themselves are incapable of production: for this they need the help of the seventh, the highest and first principle of all, the unlimited Power (ἀπέραντος δύναμις). This exists indeed in all the six, but only in potentiality, not in realisation (δυνάμει οὐκ ἐνεργείᾳ). For its nature is twofold, it is both hidden and manifest, apparent to the intellect and to the senses (νοητόν and αἰσθητόν): it is described as a supercelestial fire, the treasure-house (θησαυρός) of both αἰσθητά and νοητά, or, to use a Biblical image, it is the tree seen in Nebuchadnezzar's vision whence all flesh was nourished. Now if this fire remain only in potentiality it will vanish, like geometry or grammar from the mind of man, but if it be realised, assume sensible

---

[1] In Theodoret, *Haeret. Fab.* i. 1, *ἔννοια.* I do not venture to translate these terms, being doubtful whether they can be rendered accurately. Ewald gives them as Verstand and Verständlichkeit, Sprachsinn and Sprache, Gedanke and Ueberlegung.

[2] Or, 'understanding.'

shape (ἐξεικονίσθη), take art (τέχνη), then it
becomes the light of all generation (φῶς τῶν γιγνο-
μένων). Again, it may be described as past, present,
and future [1] (ἐστώς, στάς, στησόμενος) : it stands on
high in ungenerated potentiality (ἐν ἀγεννήτῳ δυνάμει),
it stood beneath 'on the face of the waters' in
generated form (ἐν εἰκόνι γεννηθείς) ; it will stand on
high, if it be realised, by the side of the blessed
unlimited Power. The first principle *did* take
form in the person of Simon himself : and by the
aid of him, who is the incarnation of it, all men can
think and speak and reflect rightly ; heaven and
earth, sun and moon, air and water can each
perform their appointed task in union with each
other.

So far possibly the system as taught by Simon
himself extended, but a further development of
it, which may have been due to the imagination
and enthusiasm of his scholars,' has also come
down to us, and in this his companion Helena
plays a conspicuous part [2]. According to this he
is the highest Power, the Father who is above all,
who suffers himself to be called among men by
what name they please, the Supreme Mind ; Helena

---

[1] An idea borrowed from the Jehovah of Exod. iii. 14 ; the
ὁ ὢν καὶ ὁ ἦν καὶ ὁ ἐρχόμενος of Rev. i. 4.

[2] Hippolytus, *op. cit.* vi. 19 ; Irenaeus, *Haeres.* i. 23 ; Theodoret, *loc. cit.* ; Tertullian, *Anim.* 34 ; Epiphanius, *Haeres.* 21.

is the female principle corresponding to him, his Intelligence, the universal Mother, through whom he first conceived the idea of creating angels and archangels. She springing down into the lower regions produced angels and powers who created the world, and afterwards detained her out of envy, wishing to be thought self-produced. Him they ignored entirely, her they subjected to all contumelious usage, making her pass from one woman's body to another that she might not return to the Father. Thus she was once the Helen for whom Greeks and Trojans fought at Ilium, and who after many transmigrations found herself at last in a brothel at Tyre. Then it was that the supreme Power came down from on high to rescue this his 'lost sheep:' he passed through all the angel-spheres, assimilating himself to each, till he appeared as man on earth, among the Samaritans as the Father, among the Jews as Son, where he suffered death in appearance only, among the Gentiles as Holy Ghost[1]. He overcame the powers of the world, each of them ruling unrighteously and striving for the mastery, freed his Intelligence, brought salvation to mankind, and likewise delivered them from the bondage of the spirits who created the world. It was

---

[1] So Jerome on Matt. xxiv. 5. 'Ego sum Sermo Dei, ego sum speciosus, ego Paracletus, ego omnipotens, ego omnia Dei.'

they who inspired the prophets, consequently their
words are not regarded by those who believe on
Simon and Helena; these may act as they please:
they can do no wrong, for nothing is evil in itself,
only by ordinance; certain things have been de-
clared to be so by the creating angels who thought
thus to enslave mankind. The result of such a
doctrine upon the lives of Simon's disciples may
be easily imagined[1].

Greek mythology was also pressed into the
service of Simon in order to illustrate the re-
lationship of him and Helena: their admirers
were fond of representing them under the form
of Zeus and Athena (she according to the legend
having sprung fully formed from the brain of
her sire), and of making offerings before images
and paintings so depicting them. Such was the
strange mixture of Judaism, Christianity, Oriental
legend, and Greek mythology which took such
deep root in Samaria, that, according to the testimony of Justin Martyr, nearly the whole nation in
his days had given in their adherence to it. One
circumstance no doubt powerfully contributed to
this end, that the vanity of the people was flattered
by the idea of possessing a Messiah of their own
whose high pretensions should equal those of the
Christ of Nazareth. The sect however had no

---

[1] Eusebius, *Hist. Eccl.* ii. 13.

great vitality, and had almost ceased to exist in the time of Origen [1].

Roused to emulation by the success of Simon, one of his disciples, Menander of Capparetaia [2], another Samaritan village, endeavoured to improve upon his system. His pretensions were more modest. Unlike his master, he made no claim to be considered as the highest Power, teaching that this is unknown; it had however by means of the divine ἔννοια produced the angels, and by them the world had been created; his own mission was to set man free from the dominion of these powers, and give them immortality; this he promised he would do for all, even in this life, who believed and were baptized in his name. He does not seem to have had any great following among his countrymen, the ground having been too completely occupied by his master: he consequently migrated to Antioch on the Orontes and there founded a school: some of his disciples were still to be found there in Justin Martyr's day.

---

[1] Origen, Cels. i. 57, vi. 11.

[2] Justin Mart. Ap. i. 26, 56. In Theodoret, op. cit. i. 2, his birthplace is called Chabrai. His teaching is described by Irenaeus, loc. cit.; Hippolytus, Haeres. vii. 28; Eusebius, op. cit. iii. 26. In Hippolytus it is said to have resembled that of Saturnilus, but it is not clear how much of the description given of the latter will apply to him.

64

Another disciple, Cleobius, though founding a school of his own, appears to have kept so close to his master's teaching as to have been looked upon as an apostle of his. Nothing is known of him, but that he imitated Simon in his hostility to Christianity, forging and circulating books in the name of Christ and His apostles [1].

To return after this digression to the question of the religious belief of the Samaritans;—it would appear from the foregoing sketch that their original creed was wholly borrowed from their neighbours of Judaea at a time when Sadducean opinions prevailed among them, and that the later Pharisaic views which gradually ousted the former beliefs did not for centuries obtain any hold in Samaria. Thus matters continued till the fall of Jerusalem. This event must have greatly altered the tone of mind with which the Samaritans regarded their old enemies. The sight of the Jews' humiliation and dispersion over the face of the earth must have greatly modified the repugnance with which they would naturally have repelled any acceptance of their rivals' views. Accordingly when next we receive any information

[1] Const. Ap. vi. 16. Ewald identifies his followers with the Εὐτυχται of Clem. Alex. Strom. vii. 17, ascribing the name to the importance ascribed by them to solemn 'supplications:' they are however termed Εὐτυχηται in Theodoret, Haer. i. 1, and distinguished from the Κλεοβαιοι.

with regard to the creed of Samaria, we find it
greatly changed and many of the Pharisaic articles
of faith now forming part of it, to the exclusion of
those Sadducean doctrines which had formerly
prevailed.    Moslem influence also was later
brought to bear upon the Samaritans, when in
636 A.D. they passed under the rule of the
Saracens, and it is no doubt to this, or to the
neighbourhood of the Druses[1],—that strange
eclectic sect which borrowed its principles alike
from the Law, the Gospel, and the Koran,—that
they owe many Koranic expressions and ideas,
for instance, the passionate assertion of the unity
of God, the high and peculiar honour paid to
Moses as the one prophet, and the notion that
the Law was created: ideas all of which find
their counterpart in Mohammedan theology.

Our information with regard to the later developements of Samaritan faith is very full: the
sources from which it may be obtained are the
hymns and other religious documents published

---

[1] The sect was founded by Ḥâkim, the sixth khaliph of the
house of the Fatimites that ruled in Cairo, in opposition to the
Abbasides of Bagdad.   In 1017 A. D. he gave to the inhabitants
of Syria liberty of conscience and leave to rebuild their synagogues.   Hamza his disciple taught that God had manifested
Himself by prophets, last of all by Mohammed and Ḥâkim.   The
latter had, in 1020, disappeared to return later.   Juynboll,
*Chron. Sam.* 116 ; De Sacy, *Exposé de la Religion des Druzes.*

by Gesenius and Heidenheim, the earliest of them
dating possibly from the seventh century, the book
of Joshua and Chronicle of Abulfath, composed in
the thirteenth and fourteenth, the Samaritan correspondence with Scaliger and others from the
sixteenth century downwards, and lastly the very
complete information afforded by modern travellers.

From a combination of these various documents
it would appear that the Samaritans, like the
Mohammedans[1], had five principal articles of
faith[2]: they hold that—

1. God is One, without partner or associate,
without body and passions, the cause of all things,
filling all things; His nature is inscrutable: His
powers were hidden in Him before the creation,
and by it His majesty and magnificence were displayed: He is knowable by reason, by His works
and revelation: from the kindness He formerly
shewed to His own people in continually pro-
tecting them a return of the Divine favour may
be expected: to them alone was His great Name
revealed on mount Garizim.

2. Moses is the one messenger and prophet of
God, for all time: all other prophets are as nothing

---

[1] The five points of the Mohammedan creed are belief in the
unity of God and the mission of Mohammed, prayer, alms, fasting, and the pilgrimage to Mecca. Cf. Weil, *Mohammed*, 288.

[2] Cf. the letter of Meschalmah in Heidenheim, *Vierteljahrsschr.* i. 100.

compared with him : he is the glory of prophecy,
the end of revelation, the friend and familiar
servant of God, the head, the sun, the crown of
the world, above all kings and priests ; none will
arise [1] like him : he is superior even to the Messias :
after ascending into heaven he dwelt in the splen-
dour of God.

3. The Law is perfect and complete, destined
for all time, never to be supplemented or abrogated
by later revelation : it was created in the six days,
before all other creatures; by the study of it men
become partakers of eternal life.

4. Garizim is the one abode of God on earth, the
home of eternal life, the 'mount of blessing[2] :' its
higher eminence is most sacred, it is the 'everlasting hill[3],' the 'house of God[4];' its lower one
is 'Jacob's pillar[4],' the 'stone of Israel[5]:' there
the Tabernacle was placed, there Joshua built the
first altar ; there does God manifest Himself by
His presence : over it is Paradise, thence comes all
rain : they can shew where Adam and Seth raised
their several altars, and the seven steps leading to
that of Noah : they know where Abraham offered

---

[1] The Sam. Targum in Deut. xxxiv. 10 reads םקי for the עב
of the Masoretic text: cf. also the Sam. text in Ex. xviii. 7.

[2] Deut. xi. 29; see above, p. 14, note 6.

[3] Gen. xlix. 26; Deut. xxxiii. 15; where the Sam. Pent.
reads נבעה.

[4] Gen. xxviii. 19.  [5] *Ibid.* xxxv. 14.  [6] *Ibid.* xlix. 24.

up Isaac[1]: there still remain the twelve stones on which is written the Law (Deut. xxvii. 4), the site of the former temple[2]: below it stood the high-priest's house not far from the cave of Makkedah : Garizim was alone spared by the flood when every other mountain was covered[3].

5. There will be a day of retribution, when the pious will rise again; false prophets and their followers will then be cast into the fire and burnt[4].

Other points in their creed may be noticed. The world is twofold, one apparent to the senses, the other spiritual, the abode of angels; it has not always existed, it was created. Man was formed from the dust of Mount Safra, that is Garizim, in the image of the angels, not of God. The Sabbath is to be rigidly observed; great rewards await those who honour it. Angels are the powers

---

[1] Cf. Petermann in Herzog, xiii. 377. The claim of Garizim as the place of sacrifice in opposition to Moriah in Jerusalem is upheld by Dr. Stanley, *Sinai and Palestine* (1866), p. 251, but controverted by Ewald, *Götting. Gel. Anz.* (1863), p. 638, and by Thomson, *Land and Book* (London, 1860), p. 474.

[2] To this the Samaritans always turn in prayer, as the Jews to Jerusalem and Moslems to Mecca.

[3] This is borrowed from the Jewish legend that Palestine was not covered by the flood. *Bereshith Rabba*, 33, and *Zebahim*, 113 b.

[4] See the Sam. Pent. in Ex. xv. 18 and Deut. xxxii. 35. Vilmar (in *Abulfath*, p. xxxvii) thinks that (4) and (5) were later additions to the Samaritan creed.

of the unseen world, and of God: they appeared
at the giving of the Law on Sinai; by one of
them, not in person, God spake to Moses[1].

The belief in a coming Messiah or 'Restorer[2],'
who plays so conspicuous a part in later Samaritan
theology, was probably of home origin, or at all
events, even if borrowed from their neighbours,
adapted to their own ideas and hopes[3]. It is

[1] It is doubtful how the Samaritans regard angels, whether as
attributes of the Deity or uncreated existences. Cf. De Sacy, in
*Not. et Extr.* xii. 26. Their belief on this point and also with
regard to the resurrection is probably somewhat hazy. De Sacy
could extract no satisfactory replies from the priest Salameh.
Petermann was informed by the priest that by the 'Spirit of
God' and 'darkness' of Gen. i. were signified good and bad
angels respectively. He gave him the names of the four greatest
angels, Fanuel (Gen. xxxii. 31), Anusa (Exod. xiv. 25), Cabbala
(Num. iv. 20), and Nasi (Exod. xvii. 15), all founded upon a
misinterpretation of these passages. The devils are Azazel (Lev.
xvi), Belial (Deut. xv. 9), and Jamra (perhaps the 'hornet' of
Exod. xxiii. 28). The descendants of Cain became evil spirits;
the Nephilim (Gen. vi. 4) also are evil angels who fell from
heaven. He varied in his account of the resurrection; at one
time stating that the spirits of good and evil men would receive
their bodies at the last judgment and with them return to Paradise and hell respectively; at another, that they would always
remain in an incorporeal state.

[2] Called also in Arabic El-muhdi, the 'guide.' Robinson, ii.
278.

[3] It is not likely that the idea of a Messiah the son of Joseph
would have its origin anywhere but among the Samaritans, who
were always eager to raise the tribe of Joseph at the expense of

fully explained in the letter addressed by the
Samaritans to their ' brethren in England' in A. H.
1096 ( = A.D. 1684)[1]: 'You have spoken of the
arrival of the great Prophet. This is he who was
announced to our father Abraham, as it is said
there appeared "a smoking furnace and a burning
lamp" (Gen. xv. 17): "to him shall the people
submit themselves" (ib. xlix. 10): of him also it is
said (Num. xxiv. 17), "he shall destroy all the
children of Sheth, and Israel shall do valiantly:"
of him, "the Lord thy God shall raise thee up from
amidst thy brethren a prophet like unto me, unto
him shall ye hearken" (Deut. xviii. 15). Our
teachers have said on this point that this prophet
shall arise, that all people shall submit to him
and believe in him and in the Law and Mount
Garizim : that the religion of Moses son of Amram
will then appear in glory, that the beginning of

---

that of Judah. The summary of Jewish doctrine on the subject is
as follows : Messiah the son of Joseph will come before Messiah
the son of David, will assemble the ten tribes in Galilee and
lead them to Jerusalem, but will at last perish in battle against
Gog and Magog for the sins of Jeroboam. See references in
Gesenius, *De Sam. Theologia*, 43. הַתֵּב or השוב signifies the
'restorer.' *Ibid.* 44 ; Vilmar, p. xlii.

[1] De Sacy, *Not. et Extr.* xii. 209. The Samaritans do not
interpret 'Shiloh' in Gen. xlix. 10 of the Messiah, but of Solomon, the magician, after whose time the sceptre departed from
Judah. Cf. the Samaritan letter to Ludolf in 1691 (Eichhorn,
*Repertorium*, xiii. 281).

## 71

the name of the prophet who will arise will be M [1]; that he will die and be interred near Joseph " the fruitful bough," that the Tabernacle will appear by his ministry and be established on Garizim.' As to the time of his appearance the Samaritans were formerly uncertain ; 'no one knows his coming but Jehovah,' says Ab Zehuta in 1589 [2] : 'it is a great mystery with regard to Hattaheb who is to come and who will manifest his spirit: happy shall we be when he arrives,' writes Salameh in 1811 [3]. But the modern Samaritans are more communicative. 'The appearance of the Messias,' writes Petermann in 1860, 'is to take place 6000 years after the creation [4], and these have just elapsed, consequently he now, though all unconsciously, is going about upon earth. In 1853 the Samaritans expected a great political revolution, but in 1863 the kings of the earth will, according to them, assemble the wisest out of all nations in order by mutual counsel to discover the true faith. From the Israelites, i.e. Samaritans, will one be sent, and he will be the Taheb. He will gain the day,

---

[1] 'The Messiah has not arisen yet, but he will come, and his name will be Hattaheb :' *ibid.* Cf. Vilmar, p. xliv.

[2] In Eichhorn, *Repertorium*, xiii. 266. The Jews, after repeated disappointments, forbade any one to calculate the arrival of the Messiah. Cf. *Bab. Sanhedrin*, f. 97 b.

[3] De Sacy, *Not. et Extr.* xii. 132.

[4] This is borrowed from the Jews ; cf. *Bab. 'Aboda Zara,* 9 a.

lead them to Garizim, where under the twelve
stones they will find the ten commandments (or
the whole Law), and under the stone of Bethel
the Temple utensils[1] and manna. Then will all
believe in the Law, and acknowledge him as their
king and lord of all the earth. He will convert
and equalise all men, live 110 years upon earth,
then die and be buried near Garizim, for upon
that pure and holy mountain can no burial take
place. Afterwards will the earth remain some
hundreds of years more till the 7000 are completed, and then will the last judgment come in[2].'

This part of the subject may be concluded by
a sketch of the religious observances of the Samaritans at the present day. They celebrate seven
feasts in the year, although only one, the Passover,
is observed with its former solemnities; for, the
former obligation to sacrifice having ceased with
the disappearance of the Tabernacle and the cessation of the divine favour, prayers have been substituted for the former rites. For this feast they
prepare themselves some days before by a purification of themselves and their houses: the unleavened cakes[3] are baked of corn specially bought

---

[1] See above, p. 20, note 2.     [2] In Herzog, xiii. 373.

[3] Their number of days for eating unleavened bread seems to
have varied: in the seventeenth century they write to Ludolf
'six' days (cf. Eichhorn, *Repertorium*, xiii. 283); in this century, to De Sacy, 'seven.' *Not. et Extr.* xii. 104, 120.

for the purpose while still in the car, and not
threshed by oxen according to the custom of the
country, but prepared by the women of the congregation: the lambs must have been born in
the previous Tisri (October), and be without
blemish of any sort. On the 14th of Nisan the
congregation ascend to the lower plateau of Garizim and pitch their tents there: at sunset[1] on
the following day the lambs are slain amid the
recitation of prayers, hymns, and passages of the
Law describing the original ceremonial, then
stripped of their wool, cleaned and sprinkled with
salt; next, sticks are run through the leg-sinews
and the animals suspended in a trench lined with
stones which has been well heated by a fire lighted
within; wet earth and turf are then piled over
and trampled down, so that the hole is hermeti-
cally sealed and the lambs thoroughly roasted.
At sunset they are brought forth and eaten in
haste with unleavened bread and bitter herbs,
the men and boys first partaking of them, and
afterwards the women and girls, all with staves
in their hands as if equipped for a journey: the
remainder is consumed with fire. Then follow
the morning prayers, lasting for four hours: the
next day is spent in general rejoicing and the
consumption of fish, rice, eggs, and all sorts of

---

[1] Or after noon, when the Passover falls on a Sabbath.

delicacies (in which however no leaven may be used), in the drinking of wine and brandy, accompanied by the recitation of hymns either extemporary or learnt by heart, suitable passages of Scripture, &c.[1] The 21st of Nisan, or last day of unleavened bread, is also counted as a feast, and is marked by a pilgrimage to Garizim, visiting the various sacred spots there, and recitation of the Law. The third feast is Pentecost, commencing on the Wednesday previous to the day itself: this is also marked by going to Garizim in procession, visiting the holy places, and reading through the whole Law. The fourth is that of Trumpets, on the first day of the first Tisri: on this occasion the oldest synagogue roll is displayed and kissed by the worshippers, as on eight other occasions during the year. The fifth is the Day of Atonement, on which from sunset to sunset[2] no eating, drinking, sleeping, or talking is allowed, but the whole twenty-four hours must be spent in the synagogue in reading the Law from end

---

[1] For a minute and interesting account of the ceremonies of the Passover, as celebrated in 1853, for the first time after an interruption of many years, on Garizim, see Petermann in Herzog, xiii. 378; also Dr. Stanley, *Jewish Church*, i. 513.

[2] Even the children fast (De Sacy, *Not. et Extr.* 177): among the Jews they do not till they are twelve or thirteen years of age. For an account of the ceremonies of this day see Mr. Grove's paper in Galton's *Vacation Tourists* for 1861.

to end and singing hymns.  The first and eighth
days of Tabernacles count for the remaining feast-
days, the intermediate time is spent in huts of
laurel and other fragrant leaves pitched on the
slope of Gurizim, and employed in daily pilgrimage to the top.  The Sabbath moreover is kept
with great strictness : no fire may be lighted on
it [1] : the years of jubilee and release are also still
observed.  The Samaritans have two more days
of assembly, though they do not count them as
feast-days, termed Summoth [2], sixty days before
Passover and Tabernacles respectively : the number
of the congregation is then taken, and in return
each male over twenty years of age presents the
priest with half a shekel (three piastres), in accordance with Exod. xxx. 12–14, receiving from
him a calendar for the coming six months prepared from a table in his possession, originally,
it is said, composed by Adam and committed to
writing in the time of Phinehas [3] : from these
offerings, the tenth of the incomes of the congregation, and other small gifts, the priest gains his
living [4].  He may consecrate any of his family

---

[1] *Not. et Extr.* xii. 124 ; *Repertorium*, ix. 32.

[2] Cf. the chron. *El-Tholidoth* (below, p. 124) in *Journ. Asiat.*
(1869), p. 452.                      [3] See below, p. 125.

[4] The Samaritans allow that their high-priest is only a Levite,
and that the family of Aaron has long died out.  *Not. et Extr.*
xii. 30, 118.

that he pleases to the priesthood, provided the
candidate for the office be twenty-five years of
age and never have suffered his hair to be cut.
Like other Orientals, he never removes his turban,
and so is not easily to be distinguished from the
rest of the congregation; but, in accordance with
Lev. x. 6, he does not 'rend his clothes' by wear-
ing a slit on his sleeve as other Samaritans, and
when the roll of the Law is taken from the ark
he, like his assistants, places a *tallith* or cloth
round his head.  On festal occasions and in the
synagogue the Samaritans wear white turbans;
ordinarily they are compelled, by way of distinction
from Mohammedans, to wear them of a pale red
colour: they may cut their hair or not as they
please, but not their beards, this being forbidden
in Lev. xix. 27; xxi. 5 [1].  Women must let their
hair grow, and may wear no earrings, because of
them the golden calf in the wilderness was made:
for fear of scandalising the Mohammedans, none
but the old ones venture to attend the synagogue.
Great rejoicings are held over the birth of a boy:
his circumcision always takes place on the eighth
day after birth, even though it be a Sabbath [2].
Boys marry as early as fifteen or sixteen, girls at
twelve: the latter receiving as dowry from their

---

[1] The Karaites interpret these passages in the same manner.
[2] Cf. *Repertorium*, xiii. 261.

bridegrooms sums varying from £40 to £60. When a man has a childless wife, he may take a second[1], but if she also be barren, not a third : divorces, though permitted, are uncommon. The dead are prepared for burial by their own friends[2]: the whole body is washed, but especially the hands (thrice), mouth, nose, face, ears both inside and out, (all this in Mohammedan fashion), and lastly the feet : the burial takes place, if possible, before sunset the same day, accompanied with the recitation of hymns and of the whole Law. These readings are continued every day to the next Sabbath, the women of the family watching near the grave : on the Sabbath it is visited by the whole congregation (except the near relations), who eat there together, reciting part of the Law and singing hymns, finishing the recitation later in the day with the relations[3].

III. It will be time to pass on to a review of the

---

[1] This was not always so. In their letter to Scaliger (*Repertorium*, xiii. 261) they say, 'we take but one wife, the Jews many.' In their letter to De Sacy (*Not. et Extr.* xii. 108) they say the same as in the text.

[2] Not by Mohammedans, as reported by M. Pillavoine. See De Sacy, *Not. et Extr.* xii. 34.

[3] Some observances the Samaritans appear to have relinquished : thus in the letters to Scaliger (*Repertorium*, xiii. 260) and Huntington (*Not. et Extr.* xii. 178) they say they use the 'water of separation' (Num. xix. 21), but in 1820 (*ibid.* 127) they did so no more.

literature of the Samaritans when a few remarks
have been made upon the peculiar dialect in which
a great part of it is composed. It is probable that
even before the captivity of the ten tribes the
closer intercourse which had sprung up between
them and neighbouring Aramaean nations had
already had some influence upon the Hebrew of
northern and central Palestine [1]. Doubtless also
the changes which were brought about by the
Assyrian invasion in the removal of the educated
classes into exile and the settlement of a mixed
Aramaean population in their places must have
served still further to corrupt the ancient Hebrew
and give rise to a dialect of the Aramaean which
under some form or other was spoken from Babylonia to the Mediterranean [2]. Other elements also
besides Aramaean are observable in the language.
The non-Semitic settlers left their mark behind in
foreign words which can be traced to no known

---

[1] The existence of a vulgar idiom in the north of Palestine
verging towards Aramaic is possibly discernible even so early as
the song of Deborah. Renan, *Langues Sémitiques* (1864), p. 143;
Ewald, *Grammatik* (1838), sect. 5.

[2] The eastern branch of Aramaean is still spoken by a considerable Christian population on the Upper Tigris, in Koor-
distan, and on the lake of Urmia. The western is entirely lost,
except in Ma'lûlâ and two neighbouring villages in Antilibanus,
and this is not likely to survive long, as the people speak Arabic
as well. Nöldeke in *Zeitschr. d. D. M. G.* xxi. 183.

source [1]. Greek, Latin, Persian, Arabic, and possibly other languages as well, have each contributed something to enrich the vocabulary. The grammar bears all the signs of irregularity which would characterise that of an illiterate people, the orthography is uncertain, there is a profusion of quiescents, and a complete confusion between the several gutturals and cognate letters respectively; the vowels are uncertain, the A sound being most prominent. Such is the dialect which was spoken in Samaria till the Arabian conquest of the country in the seventh century A.D., when the language of the victors was introduced, and by its superior vigour gradually overpowered its rival till, probably by about the eighth or ninth century, it had entirely taken its place. The old language however still continued to be understood and written by the priests, so that like the Jews they had two sacred languages, which however they had not the skill completely to distinguish from each other: the ' Hebrew' consequently which appears in the correspondence of Samaritans with Europeans is largely impregnated with Aramaisms; Arabisms also are not by any means unfrequent.

In the literature of the Samaritans there is little

[1] Kohn, *Sam. Studien*, p. 95. Nöldeke however (in Geiger's *Zeitschr.* vi. 104 sq.) is not disposed to allow this. Kohn recognises Aethiopic, Coptic, and Armenian roots as well.

to be found of much interest or value. For they were a people of neither genius nor originality; as in their creed, so in their literature, all they could for the most part do was to borrow from their neighbours, endeavouring by alteration and loud assertion to hide the fraud which, from the clumsiness with which it was carried out, became apparent on the first searching investigation it underwent [1].

But before passing on to such parts of Samaritan literature as have come down to our times it will be as well to notice the remains, in many cases amounting only to a name, of certain Samaritan Hellenists who appear to have lived during the last two or three centuries B.C. Thus Eusebius has preserved for us considerable extracts made by Alexander Polyhistor, an author living at Rome at the time of Sulla, from the writings of a certain Eupolemus [2]. Many of these have perhaps been

---

[1] In the *Chron. Sam.* chap. xlvii, the Samaritans are stated to have lost the following books in the persecution under Hadrian; the 'book of selections,' consisting perhaps of proverbs and wise sayings; songs and prayers for the various offerings; other hymns; the 'book of the high-priests,' which traced their line up to Phinehas, and lastly their Annals; nothing being left but the Law and a similar book of Annals. In Ahulfath (*Ann.* pp. 120, 121) this loss is ascribed to the time of Commodus.

[2] *Praep. Evang.* ix. Polyhistor himself appears to have been a Samaritan. (Juynboll, *Comment.* p. 49.) The varied character of the fragments attributed to Eupolemus in chaps. 17,

wrongly attributed to his authorship, but there
is one of which the Samaritan origin cannot be
mistaken. It is there related how the Giants
after building the tower of Babel were dispersed
over the earth, how Abraham was the inventor
of astrology and Chaldaean (arts), and after his
removal to Phoenicia taught astronomy to the
inhabitants of that country. After rescuing Lot
from the Armenians he is entertained at Argarizim,
that is, as it is explained, the 'Mountain of the
Most High,' where he receives gifts from the priest
Melchizedek who reigned there. Passing on later
into Egypt, he becomes intimate with the priests,
and instructs them in astrology and other sciences.

In the same book of Eusebius are preserved some
fifty hexameter lines by Theodotus, an Alexandrian
poet, taken apparently from a versified history of

---

26, 30-34, 39, has induced different writers to take the most
opposite view of his opinions, and hold him for a Jew, a Samaritan, and a heathen. The whole question has been fully discussed by Freudenthal in the *Jahresberichs d. Seminars zu Bres-
lau* (1874), pp. 82 sq. He believes chaps. 17 and 18 to be the
work of some unknown Samaritan, and to have been wrongly
ascribed by Polyhistor to Eupolemus. The title περὶ 'Ιουδαίων
also he thinks to be a mistake. The writer, whoever he was,
appears to have known and used the LXX version. The remaining chapters are probably the work of a Jew. Eupolemus is
also mentioned in Clem. Alex. *Strom.* i. 21, as giving 5149
years from Adam to the fifth year of Demetrius Ptolemaeus,
and 2580 from the Exodus to the same time.

82

Sichem, in which the beauties of its situation are described and its sacred character extolled; the history of Jacob also is related in connexion with it from his flight out of Mesopotamia to the destruction of the town by Simeon and Levi[1]. The Cleodemus-Malchas also mentioned by the same historian[2] would appear to be of the same nationality, and a Samaritan hand has been detected in a passage occurring in the eleventh Sibylline book where famine and pestilence are denounced against the Egyptian Jews during the reign of eight of the Ptolemies[3]. Thallus also, possibly the freedman of Tiberius mentioned by Josephus[4], the author of a work on Syria[5], who notices Moses' leadership of the Israelites[6], explains the darkness at the Crucifixion as arising from an eclipse of the sun[7], and, like the pseudo-Eupolemus above mentioned, relates how Belus and the Titans rose in insurrection against Zeus and the confederate gods[8]; he also is supposed to

---

[1] Cap. 22. Cf. Ewald, *Gesch.* (1864), iv. 338; Herzfeld, iii. 520; and Freudenthal, p. 99. No one but a Samaritan would have called Sichem ἱερὰ Σικίμων: the work was probably not περὶ 'Ιουδαίων, but as described in the text.

[2] *Op. cit.* ix. 20; Freudenthal, p. 100.

[3] *Sibyll.* xi. 239–242; Ewald, *ibid.* p. 340.

[4] *Ant.* xviii. 6. 4.      [5] Eusebius, *ibid.* x. 10.

[6] Just. Mart. *Coh.* 9.      [7] Syncellus, *Chronographia*, p. 322.

[8] Theophilus, *ad Autol.* iii. 29.

have been a Samaritan by origin: and another
countryman of his is thought to be designated
by the Σεμπρώνιος ὁ Βαβυλώνιος ὁ Πέρσης of the
Chronicon Paschale[1]. It is remarkable that out
of the nine writings of Hellenists of Israelitic
origin quoted by Alexander Polyhistor and preserved to us by Eusebius, some five or six appear
to have had a decided bias either for or against
the Samaritans; it would seem therefore extremely
probable that a considerable controversial literature
between Jews and Samaritans had sprung up by
the first century B.C., of which only some few
fragments now remain.

Of the Samaritan literature which has come
down to our times, first in importance and order
will be the Pentateuch.

It had been well known to early Jewish and
Christian writers that a recension of the Pentateuch differing in important respects from that in
use among the Jews was in possession of the
Samaritan community. It was regarded however
by these writers in very different lights: the
former treat it with contempt as a forgery. 'You

---

[1] p. 68. The philosopher Marinus, a convert from Samari-
tanism to heathenism, the biographer and successor of the Neo-
Platonist Proclus in the school of Athens in 485, speaks of
Abraham's having 'sacrificed on Argarizim, where is the most
holy temple of the supreme Zeus,' thus betraying his Samaritan
origin. Photius, *Bibl.* p. 345 b.

have falsified your Law,' says R. Elieser ben Simon[1] to the Samaritan scribes about 160 A.D., 'and have done yourselves no good by it,' referring to their insertion of the words 'opposite Shechem' in Deut. xi. 30 to obviate the Jewish objection that it was not the Samaritan Garizim here referred to. 'Who has led you into error,' says another writer of the same period[2], jeering at their ignorance of grammar displayed in the interpretation of the ordinance in Deut. xxv. 5 as to marrying a brother's widow. Early Christian writers on the other hand speak of it with respect, in some cases even preferring its authority to that of the Masoretic text. Origen quotes it under the name of τὸ τῶν Σαμαρειτῶν Ἑβραϊκόν, giving its various readings on the margin of his Hexapla[3].

[1] *Jer. Sota*, vii. 3: the *Siphré* and *Bab. Sota*, 33 b, ascribe the saying to R. Elieser ben Jose. There is much valuable information on the subject of the Samaritan Pentateuch to be found in Frankel's *Vorstudien zur Septuaginta*, pp. 260 sq., but especially in his *Einfluss d. palästin. Exegese auf d. alexandrin. Hermeneutik*, pp. 237 sqq. English readers may also consult the article in Smith's *Bible Dict.* iii. 1106.

[2] R. Simon ben Elieser, *Jer. Jeb.* i. 6. He may however be the same as R. Elieser ben Simon; see Frankel, *Vorstudien*, 197; *Einfluss*, 243. Through ignorance of the use of ה locale they took חוצה to be an epithet of אשה, and translated it the 'outer wife,' i.e. betrothed, who had not yet entered the house of her husband. See above, p. 42.

[3] e.g. on Num. xiii. 1: cf. xxi. 13, and Montfaucon, *Hexapl. Prelim.* i. 8, 9.

Eusebius of Caesarea notices the agreement in the chronology of the LXX and Samaritan text as against the Hebrew, and remarks that it was written in a character confessedly more ancient than that of the latter[1]. Jerome also mentions this fact[2]: in his comment on Gal. iii. 10 he upholds the genuineness of its text over that of the Masoretic one, which he considers to have been purposely altered[3]. Cyril of Alexandria mentions that the Samaritan supplies words wanting in the Hebrew[4]: Procopius of Gaza that portions of Deuteronomy have been inserted in the parallel passages of former books[5]: Georgius Syncellus, the chronologist of the eighth century, is most

[1] *Chron.* i. xvi. 7-11.

[2] *Prolog. to Kings:* 'Samaritani etiam Pentateuchum Moysis totidem literis scriptitant, figuris tamen et apicibus discrepantes.'

[3] St. Paul has, 'Cursed be he that abideth not in *all* that is written,' &c. This word appears in the LXX and Samaritan, but not in the Masoretic text of Deut. xxvii. 26, whence it is quoted, though it does in parallel passages such as xxviii. 15. In his commentary on Gen. iv. 8, St. Jerome speaks more favourably of the Hebrew: 'Subauditur, "ea quae locutus est Dominus." Superfluum ergo est quod in Samaritanorum et nostro volumine est, "Transeamus in campum."'

[4] Παρ' οὐδενὶ τῶν λοιπῶν κεῖται τὰ ῥήματα τοῦ Κάϊν τὰ πρὸς Ἀβέλ, ἀλλ' οὐδὲ παρ' Ἑβραίοις· ἀλλ' ἐν ἀποκρύφῳ φασὶν· παρὰ δὲ ταῖς ο' κεῖται ἔχει δὲ αὐτὰ καὶ τὰ Σαμαρειτικόν: mentioned by Migne in a note on the last quoted passage of St. Jerome as attributed to St. Cyril.

[5] In his commentary on Deut. i. 9.

outspoken in his praise of it, terming it 'the earliest and best even by the testimony of the Jews themselves[1].'

But all recollection of this recension afterwards entirely died out, so that the plain statements of Fathers and other early writers were looked upon as misapprehensions, till in 1616 Pietro della Valle succeeded in procuring a complete copy of it at Damascus, which, after much delay, was published in the Paris Polyglott of 1645[2]. The editor of the part which contained this text, Joannes Morinus, priest of the Oratory, seized the opportunity of the discovery of the long-lost treasure for pressing his own peculiar views as to the value of the Hebrew text of the Old Testament. Ludovicus Cappellus, the learned professor of Saumur, had indeed as early as 1624 attacked the views of the elder Buxtorf and endeavoured to establish the comparatively modern origin of the Hebrew points and accents[3]: and in his

---

[1] *Chronographia*, p. 83. Μέχρι τοίνυν τοῦ κατακλυσμοῦ καθὼς πρόκειται διαφωνοῦσι τὰ Ἑβραικὰ ἀντίγραφα πρὸς τὸ Σαμαρειτὸν ἀρχαιότατον καὶ χαρακτῆρσι διαλλάττον ὃ καὶ ἀληθὲς εἶναι καὶ πρῶτον Ἑβραῖα καθομολογοῦσι.

[2] For the history of this edition see G. W. Meyer, *Gesch. d. Schrifterklärung* (1804), iii. 153 sq.

[3] In his *Arcanum Punctationis Revelatum*; followed by his *Arcani Punctationis Vindiciae* in 1689, in reply to the rejoinder of Buxtorf the younger. In his *Diatriba de Veris et Antiquis*

'Critica Sacra,' which after great delay, caused by the opposition of the Protestants, finally appeared in 1650, he put forth the view that the Hebrew text of the Old Testament has been in numberless places corrupted by the errors of copyists, and that the true reading in such cases is to be found only by comparison of MSS. and ancient translations, and finally by conjecture [1].

But Morinus went to much further lengths. He maintained that the Hebrew original had been so hopelessly depraved by continued blunders and falsifications as to be utterly untrustworthy, and with all a convert's zeal he urged that recourse must under these circumstances be had to the two translations authorised by the Church, the Vulgate, and LXX version [2], and in accordance with these views he naturally took up the cause of the Samaritan text, placing it far above the Hebrew for correctness and importance [3].

The assertion of theories so different to those

---

*Hebraeorum Literis*, 1645, he proved that the Samaritan letters were older than the square characters.

[1] Meyer, *ibid.*, p. 287.

[2] In his *Exercitationes Biblicae*, Part i, 1633. Part ii was published after his death in 1669.

[3] He had first noticed the Samaritan Pentateuch in the preface to his edition of the LXX in 1628, and spoke of it with high praise in his *Exercitationes Ecclesiasticae in utrumque Samaritanorum Pentateuchum*, 1631.

generally accepted called forth doughty champions
on the other side, the most conspicuous among
whom were Simon de Muis, archdeacon of Soissons [1],
and Hottinger, the learned professor of Oriental
languages at Zurich [2]; and the contest was kept up
with great vigour on either side for a considerable
time. But there was too much party spirit infused
into the strife to allow the combatants calmly to
weigh the merits of the questions under debate.
A more moderate position was taken up by Walton,
the editor of the London Polyglott of 1657 [3], and
Richard Simon the Oratorian [4]. They neither,
with the Buxtorfs, upheld the absolute authority
of the Masora on the one hand, nor committed
themselves to the extravagances of Morinus and his
friends on the other as to the excellencies of the
LXX and Samaritan text, but held that the latter,
though on the whole of inferior value, had never-
theless preserved readings which are to be preferred to those of the Hebrew text.

Thus matters rested for a century, when Houbi-

---

[1] He published the *Assertio Veritatis Hebraicae adversus J. Morini Exercitationes* in 1631, and in 1634 *Assertio Altera* in reply to Morinus' *Exercitationes Biblicae;* later again, in 1639, a *Castigatio Animadversionum Morini.*

[2] *Exercitationes Antimorinianae de Pent. Sam.* 1644.

[3] In the Prolegomena to vol. i.

[4] In his *Histoire Critique du Vieux Testament*, published in 1678, but immediately suppressed by the influence of Bossuet.

gant, also a priest of the Oratory, once more
resumed the old weapons of his predecessor
Morinus, contending for the authority of the
Samaritan Pentateuch in preference to that of
the received text[1]: he however found more than
his match in Ravius, Oriental Professor at Utrecht[2],
and the same fate befell the Benedictine father
Poncet at the hands of J. D. Michaelis[3] when he
commenced the discussion once more[4]: since his
time no one has again ventured to put forth the
same extreme views on the subject; though a few
years later the depreciatory estimate of the Samaritan recension put forth by Tychsen, the famous
Orientalist of Rostock[5], was warmly disputed by
Hassencamp of Rinteln, the former holding it for
a mere copy of the Masoretic text, the latter on
the contrary maintaining its importance and contending for the view that from it the Alexandrine
version had been made[6].

---

[1] In his *Biblia Hebraica* of 1753.

[2] *Specimen Observationum ad C. F. Hubigantii Prolegomena*,
1761; afterwards reprinted.

[3] Cf. *Orient. und exeg. Bibliothek*, xxi. 177–189; Meyer,
*op. cit.* v. 363.

[4] In his *Nouveaux éclaircissements sur l'origine et le Pentateuque des Samaritains*, 1760.

[5] *Disputatio historico-philologico-critica*, Bützow, 1765.

[6] *Der entdeckte wahre Ursprung d. alten Bibelübersetzungen*,
Minden, 1775. The dispute was continued into the present century in defence of the Samaritan Pentateuch by Alex. à S. Aqui-

In the course of this protracted discussion, extending over a space of two centuries, the merits and demerits of the Samaritan text had been keenly disputed by the various combatants and many personalities exchanged between them, but till the time of Gesenius no one seems to have attempted the only satisfactory solution of the question. To him the happy idea presented itself of subjecting the recension to a rigid analysis, and arranging its variations under different heads. Later writers who have approached the subject have in some respects modified and amended his conclusions, but no one has succeeded in upsetting the general result at which he arrived, that out of the many hundreds of various readings presented in this text some three or four solitary ones, though of little importance, may be genuine, the rest being due in the first instance to improvements introduced for the sake of avoiding obscurities, and secondly to the Samaritans' ignorance of grammar and exegesis, and to alterations made by them in the interest of their national religion[1].

---

lino, Lobstein, Geddes, Ilgen, and Bertholdt; the opposite side being maintained by Vater, Eichhorn, Bauer, and Jahn.

[1] In his *De Pent. Sam. Origine*, &c. (1815), pp. 26 sqq., he enumerates eight heads of variations:—

(1) Grammatical emendations, such as the insertion of quiescents, ב'- for ב-, ה)- for ה-, &c.; the substitution of commoner for rarer forms of the pronouns, as אתה for את ; of the longer

But with the question of the comparative merits of the two texts, is bound up another which has

---

for the apocopated future, as ויתור for ותנר; of common for archaic forms, as קמן for סבבי (Deut. xxxiii. 16), חית for חיתו (Gen. i. 24); alterations of genders, of common nouns to masculine or feminine, e. g. לחם to masc. (Gen. xlix. 20), ארץ to fem. (ibid. xliii. 6), נער, in the sense of girl, to נערה; the infinitive absolute is changed into a finite verb, וישבו הלך ושוב (Gen. viii. 3) into חלבו ושבו ', or into a participle, as חרדץ נרץ (ibid. xliii. 7) into the meaningless 'ן היחרץ; common forms are substituted for unusual, as עלה תאצה (ibid. ii. 7) for עלי ח', &c.

(2) Glosses received into the text, some being found in the LXX also, others in various versions and Jewish commentaries, most of them therefore the result of exegetical tradition; as זכר ונקבה for איס חיסה (ibid. vii. 2), when spoken of animals; ראהל אברם (ibid. xiii. 18) becomes ' א ילך.

(3) Conjectural emendations of difficulties; as for הלבן מאה שנים ילד (ibid. xvii. 17) אוליד is substituted.

(4) Words corrected or supplied from parallel passages, as לא אדשה (ibid. xviii. 29) becomes לא אשחדת according to ver. 28.

(5) Insertions of long passages derived from the same source; for instances see above, p. 41, note 3.

(6) Alterations to add dignity to the patriarchs, e. g. in the antediluvian chronology of Gen. v, none is allowed to beget his first-born son after the age of 150, consequently years are cut off before the event and added after, as is required. No postdiluvian patriarch, on the other hand (chap. xi), may beget a son before he is 50, nor may in either case a patriarch live longer than his father. Or changes are made for the greater glory of God, as (Gen. ii. 2) 'on the sixth day God ended his work,' instead of seventh, lest He should be thought to have worked on the Sabbath.

(7) Samaritanisms; the substitution of one guttural for

already been incidentally noticed, that of the
relation of the LXX to the Samaritan Pentateuch,

---

another, as הררם for ארדם (Gen. viii, 4) ; of forms of the verb,
especially Samaritan, as צחקתי for צחקת (ibid. xviii. 16) ; אזכרתי
for הזכרתי (Exod. xx. 24).

(8) Alterations in support of Samaritan doctrines ; e.g. in
the interests of monotheism אלהים may never (as in Gen. xx.
13) be joined to a plural, only a singular verb ; or to avoid
anthropomorphisms and anthropopathisms, thus את ידין יהוה
(Deut. xxix. 19) becomes יהר א' 'מ ; ויבא אלחים (Num. xxii. 20)
becomes 'ר' סלאן אל ; ' Take all the heads of the people and hang
them up before the Lord ' becomes ' Order that the men be slain
that were joined unto Baalpeor,' lest God should seem to have
ordered the punishment of the innocent with the guilty, or Moses
to have been directed to act himself as executioner. Other
instances will be found below when the Samaritan commentaries
are discussed. Four readings alone of the Samaritan Pentateuch Gesenius is inclined to prefer to the corresponding ones
of the Masoretic text ; the insertion of נלכה השדה in Gen. iv. 8
as the words of Cain ; איל אחר for אחר 'א, ibid. xxii. 13 (also
found in five fragments of old Jewish MSS. at St. Petersburg.
see Journ. Asiat. 1866, i. 542) ; המר טרם (ibid. xlix. 14) for
'ח טרם, in the same sense ; וידק את חניכיו (ibid. xiv. 14), he
' counted,' for ויך, he ' led forth ;' all of them of very slight importance, which moreover have been rejected by later commen-
tators ; cf. Frankel, Einfluss, 242.

Many of the classes into which Gesenius has divided the variations are evidently cross-divisions : the number has consequently been reduced by Kohn (De Pent. Sam. p. 9) to three :
(1) Samaritan forms of words, (2) corrections and emendations,
(3) glosses and corruptions for religious purposes, and perhaps
(4) blunders in orthography. Kirchheim in his Karme Shomeron
gives them somewhat differently, making thirteen divisions.

for from the time of the first discovery of the latter, its striking resemblance in numerous passages to the Alexandrine version had been noticed by all [1].

The earliest explanation given of this fact was that the LXX had been translated from the Samaritan : this was the view of De Dieu, Selden, and Hottinger, a theory favourably regarded in later times by Hassencamp and Eichhorn, and of late revived again by Kohn. Grounds such as the following have been alleged for it.

The evidence of Origen, supported and amplified by that of St. Jerome, goes to prove that the LXX must have been translated from a Samaritan original, because that in certain MSS. of the LXX existing in their day the word יהוה was retained in the ancient Hebrew (i. e. Samaritan) characters [2],

---

Frankel (*Einfluss*, 238 sq.) notices, in addition to the remarks of Gesenius, the insertion of passages from Onkelos and the LXX, the latter being often mistranslated; the employment of late technical expressions from the Mischna; the improper use of the imperative, as הקריבו for הקרב (Lev. vi. 7); and the approximation in orthography and forms of words to Palestinian Aramaic, but with continual blunderings.

[1] Hassencamp (*op. cit.* p. 215) reckons up some 1900 places in which the LXX agrees with the Samaritan Pentateuch. Gesenius (*op. cit.* p. 10) calculates them at more than 1000, while in as many the Hebrew and LXX agree against the Samaritan.

[2] See below, pp. 100-102.

not in those used at their time, Ezra, according to
tradition, having introduced other letters after the
captivity [1]. It is clear, however, from the statement made by St. Jerome on this point that the
remark of Origen can apply only to the Aramaic
or square characters, not to those in use among the
Samaritans, and consequently the argument based
upon his words must fall to the ground.

Another reason which has been alleged in support of the LXX having been derived from a
Samaritan original is that only on this supposition
can its variations from the Hebrew text be explained ; they must, it is said, have arisen from
a confusion between letters which resemble each
other in the Samaritan, and not in the square
alphabet. On a closer examination, however, it
will be found that although many various readings
are evidently due to such mistakes between similar
letters, yet that these may have occurred quite as
well in the square alphabet, the error being equally
possible in either case.

Or again, the following argument has been used :
—the Samaritans had already brought out for
their own use a Greek translation, that known
under the name of τὸ Σαμαριτικόν ; the translators
of the LXX finding this convenient for their

---

[1] Origen, *Hexapla*, ed. *Montfaucon*, i. 86 ; St. Jerome, *Epi-stola* 136 (ed. Migne, 25), *ad Marcellam*.

purpose with their imperfect knowledge of Hebrew, took it for the basis of their own translation, altering it in parts after the Hebrew original to suit their own ideas[1].

There is however a great objection to this theory, that no one knows of the existence of any such Samaritan Greek Version at so early a period of their history: there is no trace of the translation so called (even if it was a complete one, and not emendations of particular passages) before the third or fourth century A.D.[2] And moreover, if the foregoing sketch of the Samaritan history be trustworthy, it is most unlikely that a people, who had on all other occasions shown themselves powerless to invent, only capable of feeble imitation, should in this one instance have distanced their rivals in the production of so great a literary work

---

[1] Kohn, *De Pent. Sam.* p. 36.

[2] Kohn supposes that the additions of the LXX in Gen. xxxv. 4, καὶ ἀπώλεσεν αὐτὰ ἕως τῆς σήμερον ἡμέρας, were originally inserted in the Samaritan Greek text to stop Jewish cavils at their idolatry, and thence copied inadvertently into the LXX: that they do not appear in the Samaritan Pentateuch because its text was then closed and the difficulty had till now been overlooked; but this gives much too early a date to the Samaritan Greek version: it is quite impossible that the LXX should have had time to copy from it by the third century B.C. The most singular theory was that of Isaac Voss, who held that the Masoretic text was translated from the LXX: he was refuted by Hody.

as a Greek translation of the Pentateuch: it was
only the versatile Jewish spirit, in such a place
as Alexandria, where the union of Eastern and
Western civilisation gave rise to a busy literary
activity, that could have produced such a work.
It is most unlikely moreover that the Jews, with
their intense hatred of the Samaritans, would have
received the LXX translation, manifestly grounded
upon the Samaritan recension, largely departing
from the Hebrew.  Even if the Alexandrian Jews
could have been induced to admit it, would their
Palestinian brethren have received with respect a
text differing widely from that to which they had
been accustomed, one moreover not varying of set
purpose to overcome difficulties, but ignorantly
borrowed from Samaritan interpretations [1]?

This explanation, accordingly, of the similarity
of the two texts must be given up.  The next one
for consideration is the theory of Grotius, Usher,
and others, that the Samaritan Pentateuch was
corrected from the LXX.  This is true to a certain

---

[1] Cf. Geiger in *Zeitschr. d. D. M. G.* xix. 611 sq.  The
Samaritans would have no such scruple in borrowing and then
claiming the text for their own.  Abusaid continually copies
from Saadiah in his Arabic translation of the Pentateuch, all the
while heaping maledictions on him.  The Bab. Talmud (*Megillah*,
f. 9) speaks of the LXX with respect; later the Palestinian
Jews became suspicious of it and unwilling to admit it into
their synagogues.  Frankel, *Vorstudien*, p. 61.

extent; many passages occur in the former which bear all the marks of being interpolations from the Alexandrine version[1]. But still the explanation is inadequate to solve the problem proposed; it gives no reason for the correspondence which exists between the two texts in very many minute instances which cannot be due to alterations made in deference to religious feeling[2]. How moreover, on this supposition, are the equally numerous passages to be accounted for in which the Samaritan Pentateuch differs from the LXX, sometimes in these cases agreeing with the Hebrew, at others departing from it[3]?

---

[1] E.g. Gen. xxiii. 2, בקרית הארבע אל עמק = ἐν πόλει Ἀρβόκ, ἥ ἐστιν ἐν τῷ κοιλώματι: ibid. xxvii. 27, ברח השדה מלא = ὡς ὀσμὴ ἀγροῦ πλήρους: ibid. xliii. 28, ברוך הזה ההוא לאלהים: Exod. v. 13, מארר בחיות החבן נחן לכם: xxxii. 32, אם תשא חטאתם שא: the Hebrew of these examples bears strong trace of a Samaritan origin; see other examples of interpolations in Frankel, Einfluss, 161, 162, 238. On the other hand, portions of the Samaritan Greek version (see below, p. 115) have apparently found their way into the LXX; see Frankel, op. cit. 108, on the insertions in Exod. xxii. 4 (5), and xxiii. 19. This fact raises a doubt whether the insertions from the LXX formed part of the original text of the Samaritan Pentateuch or were later additions.

[2] E.g. the conjunction ו is added about 200 times in the Samaritan Pentateuch and omitted about half as often; in this closely agreeing with the LXX.

[3] Asaria de Rossi (in his Meor 'Enaim, iii. 8, 9) put forth two theories:—(1) 'That the Alexandrian Greeks corrupted the LXX out of hostility to the Jews.' This however must have

h

One theory alone remains, that suggested by
Gesenius, which seems to answer fully all the
requirements of the case. He supposes that both
the LXX and Samaritan Pentateuch were derived
from Jewish MSS. which bore a great resemblance
to each other but contained a text varying from that
preserved in our Hebrew Pentateuch. The origin
of this difference, he thinks, is to be sought for in
the misdirected zeal of revisers and their endeavours
to make the text run smoothly and harmoniously,
and it was in this manner he considers that many
glosses and conjectural emendations found their
way into the text. Add to this the blunders of
successive generations, made especially in the
mistaking of similar letters, and a satisfactory
explanation can be given of the divergence of the
LXX and Samaritan Pentateuch from the older
and more difficult readings which were religiously

been done before the time of Philo, and so the authors of the
corruption must have been heathen: but why should they have
troubled themselves about the matter, or who would have
trusted their work? The variations of the LXX also imply
ignorance more than deliberate falsification. (2) 'That the
LXX was rendered from an Aramaean translation dating from
the time of Ezra, the inaccuracies, paraphrases, and corruptions
of which caused the variations in the Alexandrine text.' No
trace however of such a version exists, and the variations of the
LXX seem to originate partly from a misunderstanding of the
Hebrew and partly from following a different text. Frankel,
*Vorst.* 33 sq.

preserved in the MSS. of Jerusalem. That the
copy which came into the hands of the Samaritans
and that which found its way to Alexandria may
have originally differed from each other is quite
possible, and both may have received subsequent
corrections at the hands of their owners. The
Samaritans, it is evident, set about the work of
revising their Pentateuch without scruple, and the
Alexandrine Jews may not have been entirely
guiltless with regard to their own copies[1]. It is
quite possible also that the two texts were more
alike formerly: that of the LXX had become much
corrupted even in Origen's time, and it is very probable that his exertions have partly contributed to
its still further decay from the reception of many
of his glosses and corrections into the text itself[2].

To the question of the time at which the
Pentateuch first passed into the hands of the
Samaritans, about which so many theories have
been held[3], no satisfactory answer can be given:
if however the view maintained above be correct,

---

[1] In the Prophets and Hagiographa the LXX varies from the
Hebrew still more than in the Pentateuch. *Ibid.* 36.

[2] Gesenius, *op. cit.* p. 14; Montfalcon, *Prælim. in Hexapl.*
cap. iv.

[3] From the ten tribes they succeeded, or from the priest sent
by the king of Assyria during the lion-plague (2 Kings xvii), or
from Manasseh their first high-priest  Smith's *Bible Dict.* iii.
1112; Herzfeld, *op. cit.* iii. 253; Gesenius, *op. cit.* 3.

that Samaritan doctrines were not of home growth
but a late importation from Judaea after Sadducaean
views had had time to develop themselves there,
then it would seem to be highly probable that the
Pentateuch also found its way at a late date into
Samaria. However this may be, it is quite certain
that it cannot have assumed its present form till it
had been subjected to long and continued revisions
by its new possessors.

With regard to the question incidentally alluded
to above, the discontinuance by the Jews of the
old Hebrew, or as it is now called Samaritan,
character for transcribing their Law, the testimony
of the Talmud, Samaritans, and Fathers is unani-
mous in ascribing it to the age of Ezra[1]. It is

[1] *Bab. Sanhedr.* f. 21 and 22. 'At first the Law was given
to Israel in the Hebrew writing and in the holy language: once
more again in the time of Ezra in the Assyrian writing and the
Aramaean language. Israel then chose the Assyrian writing and
the holy language, leaving to the ignorant the Hebrew writing
and the Aramaean language. Who are the ignorant? R. Hasda
says the Samaritans. What is the Hebrew writing? R. Hasda
says that of the Libonai;' i.e. according to Rashi, that of the
inhabitants of Libanus; the character employed in writing
amulets and mezuzoth. (See Luzzat'o in Kirchheim, *op. cit.* 111.)
Again, 'Although the Law was not given through him (Ezra),
yet the writing was changed by him. Why is it called Assyrian?
Because it was brought up with them from Assyria:' Chaldaea
and Babylonia being included under the wider name of Assyria.
Here and in *Jer. Megillah*, i. 11, the 'Hebrew' character is

clear from Neh. viii. 8 that a change in the
language had then taken place[1]. The Hebrew
which till the captivity had been spoken in Jerusalem, the language in which the Law was written,
had during the exile been so much modified by
admixture with cognate Aramaean dialects that
the grandchildren of those who had been carried
captive by Nebuchadnezzar found it hard to understand the ancient language of the Scriptures, and
had thus become dependent for an explanation
of them upon the more learned portion of the
community. With this new Aramaic dialect a
corresponding alphabet also probably had come
into use, and it was in this most likely, not in
the square character of three or four centuries
later, that Ezra according to tradition commenced

termed 'broken.' Other derivations are given of the name
'Assyrian.' R. Jehuda the Holy (*B. Sanh. ibid.*) says it was
so termed as being the 'blessed;' Abr. de Balmis and J. D.
Michaelis as 'upright:' it is also termed the 'square' character.
For Samaritan testimony cf. Eichhorn, *Repertorium*, xiii. 266,
288. Origen (*Hexapl.* i. 86, ed. Montfalcon) says, 'They say
that Ezra used other (letters) after the captivity.' So Jerome,
in his *Prolog. to the Kings*. For the whole subject see Lenormant, *Alphabet Phénicien*, i. 176 sq., 282 sq.; Herzfeld, iii. 76;
and the article on 'Writing' in Smith's *Dict.* iii. 1788.

[1] 'They read in the book, in the Law of God distinctly and
gave the sense, and caused (them) to understand the reading.'
Herzfeld (iii. 58) does not so interpret the passage; he thinks
that Hebrew was still spoken by the Jews on their return
from Babylon, and that Aramaean did not come in till later.

the practice of transcribing copies of the Law[1]. The former character still continued to be used on coins, just as Latin still appears on our present money, long after the general use of it has died out[2]. But the Samaritans could not afford to give it up. With a reputation to acquire as the genuine representatives of ancient Israel they naturally clung to everything which would seem in any way to support their claim; even to the present day they employ a form of it for the transcription of the Law[3].

It may be of interest, before passing on to other

[1] It has been suggested by Phil. Luzzatto as an additional reason for the change of alphabet, besides the fact that the Aramaic may have now been more familiar to the Jews, that it became desirable to be able to distinguish the Jewish copies of the Law from those altered by the Samaritans. Jost, i. 52, note.

[2] They were also likely to be used in neighbouring countries, such as Phoenicia, where an almost identical alphabet was in use; hence it would be convenient to keep the old character. Herzfeld, iii. 89. The old thick shekels, with inscriptions in a character resembling the Samaritan, though with differences, which have been attributed by Cavedoni, Levy, and Madden to Simon Maccabaeus (B.C. 138), are now assigned by Vaux, De Saulcy, and Lenormant to the times of Ezra and Nehemiah. They differ materially in execution from the thin ones struck by the Maccabees. This alphabet was employed on Jewish coins as late as the revolts under Titus and Hadrian.

[3] The Sidonian element also (see Josephus, Ant. xii. 5. 5) in the Samaritan people may have had something to do with the retention of the character so nearly resembling the Phoenician.

subjects, to give some particulars as to the extant
MSS. of the Samaritan Pentateuch. The first
which found its way to Europe was purchased,
as before observed, at Damascus in 1616 by Pietro
della Valle, and a few years later was presented
by Achille Harley de Sancy to the library of the
Oratory at Paris. After appearing in the Paris
Polyglott Bible of 1645, it was twelve years
afterwards reprinted by Walton in the London
Polyglott[1]. Since that time many more copies
have been brought into the West, and most of
the public libraries of Europe now possess some
specimens of this Pentateuch either in fragments
or complete codices[2]. All of these are written on

---

[1] The text of the Pentateuch in the Paris Polyglott was very
indifferently edited by Morinus, being prepared from this MS.
alone, with a Latin translation appended which was intended to
serve for both the Pentateuch and Targum, though in many
places they widely differ. Morinus endeavoured later to supply
some of its deficiencies by the publication of his 'Variae Lec-
tiones,' which appeared among his 'Opuscula' in 1657, derived
from a collation of four other MSS. The Pentateuch text in
the London Polyglott of the same year is almost an exact reprint
of the Paris one, only the most glaring typographical blunders
having been corrected, but a much more complete and exact list
of variations was appended, the Latin version to some extent
amended, and the deviations of the Targum from the Pentateuch
noted.

[2] Kennicott's list of the MSS. of the Samaritan Pentateuch
existing in his time in European libraries, with some additions,
is to be found in Smith's *Dict.* iii. 1113.

separate leaves, none are in the shape of rolls.
At Nablus however, as is well known from the
descriptions of modern travellers, there is still
preserved in the synagogue, and only brought
out with much solemnity on certain festivals, an
ancient parchment roll, purporting by its inscription to have been written by the hand of
the great-grandson of Aaron himself, thirteen years
after the original settlement of the Israelites in
Canaan[1]! It is written on the hair-side of the

---

[1] 'I, Abisha, son of Phinehas, son of Eleazar, son of Aaron
the priest—upon them be the favour of Jehovah—in His honour
I wrote this holy Law at the entrance of the Tabernacle of
Testimony on Mount Garizim, even Bethel, in the thirteenth year
of the taking possession of the land of Canaan and all its boun-
daries about it by the children of Israel.' (Letter of Meschalmah
ben Ab Sechuah in Heidenheim, i. 88; cf. also *Not. et Extr.* xii.
p. 179.) This inscription was not to be found in the time of
Huntington's visit in 1671 (*Epist.* pp. 49, 56). It had been
there, so the Samaritans told him, but had been erased by some
evil-minded person. It has lately been found again, we are told,
by Messrs. Kraus and Levysohn, who saw the famous MS. in
1860 while it was being transferred from its old case to a new
one. They obtained a collation of Deut. xix. 8 sq. from the
priest's nephew, and restored the character, as they best could,
from memory, not being able to procure an exact tracing. Their
description of it and facsimile are given by Dr. Rosen in the
*Zeitschr. d. D. M. G.* xviii. p. 582. It has been thought that it
may have been written for Manasseh's Temple on Garizim, but
it is most improbable that the MS. can be so old. Some guess
as to its age might perhaps be made if a photograph could be

skins of some twenty rams that served as thank-
offerings, so says the priest. They are of unequal
size, some containing five, some six columns of
writing, worn quite thin, torn and in holes,
blackened as if ink has been spilt over it : perhaps
some half of the whole MS. may still be legible.
Other old MSS. are also mentioned as existing
there ; one has the date of A.H. 35 (= A.D. 655)
inscribed on it ; another claims to be the very
identical copy of the Law which figured in the
trial between Zerubbabel and Sanballat in the
presence of the king of Babylon, when the
respective merits of the Jewish and Samaritan
versions were in dispute, as is truthfully set
forth in the 'book of Joshua ;' still bearing on its
worn page the mark where Zerubbabel spat upon
it in order to break the charm, after it had twice
sprung unhurt from the fire into which he had

procured of it which could be compared with other old MSS.
This the Committee of the Palestine Exploration Fund are said
already to have done (see *Journal of Sacred Literature*, x.
p. 240) ; it is however very doubtful whether they have obtained
one from the genuine MS. Mr. Mills, who spent some weeks at
Nablus, says he saw *three* rolls kept in similar cases. Dr. Wilson
was shewn one in *leaves*, and told it was the famous old one !
An endeavour was made to impose on Robinson (ii. 281) also.
The same happened to 'T. L. D.' also, as described by him in
the *Times* of April 6, 1874. He speaks most severely of the
greed, ignorance, and laziness of the Samaritans.

thrown it: the third time it came out again un-
damaged, only the spot was scorched[1]. It is held
in great veneration by the Samaritans; the priest's
blessing in Num. vi. 22 has become black from the
frequent kisses of the worshippers.

Next after an account of the Samaritan Pentateuch itself will come that of the various translations it underwent, into Samaritan, Greek, and
Arabic. Of the date and origin of the first of
these no more satisfactory explanation can be
given than of the Pentateuch itself. It no doubt
must have been submitted to many revisions and
modifications before it reached the form in which
we now possess it, but in its first beginnings it
probably was long anterior to the Christian era.
The Samaritans, it must be remembered, were in
the same condition as the Jews: each nation was

[1] Bosen, l. c. This identical MS. was a few years ago offered
to the Bodleian for the modest sum of £500; but the bid was
not accepted. The same author (D. M. G. xiv. 622) gives a
description of two ancient stone tablets, one containing the Ten
Commandments in an abbreviated form (cf. Heidenheim's Viertel-
jahresschr., lii. 486, for the description of a similar MS.), built
into the wall of a mosque at Nablus; the other is apparently
of later date, found not long ago in a rubbish heap; it contains
the ten commands of Gen. i; it probably belonged to some
former synagogue. Dr. H. thinks them to be anterior to the
time of Justinian, Dr. Blau (D. M. G. xiii. 275) to have belonged
to the Temple on Garizim destroyed by Hyrcanus. For a further
account of the synagogue rolls see below, p. 155.

in the possession of sacred books which were un-
intelligible to the mass of the people. In consequence of this there very early arose among the
Jews, as we know, the custom, instituted according
to Talmudical tradition by Ezra himself[1], of intro-
ducing extemporary translations of certain portions
of the Law into the synagogue services. In process of time a body of well-known and recognised
renderings of Scripture thus came into being,
which were however for many centuries preserved
by oral tradition only, not being committed to
writing for fear they should gain an undue influence and overshadow the authority of the Law
itself. Gradually however this scruple was over-
borne by a feeling of the grave inconvenience
which might ensue from the prevalence of unsatisfactory expositions, and thus the earliest Targum
which we possess, that of Onkelos on the Pentateuch, was first committed to writing, probably
about the third century A.D., in the schools of
Babylon[2].

The same causes were no doubt operating in

---

[1] For references see Smith's *Dict.* iii. 1638. The passage in
Neh. viii. 8 is thus explained : "'they read in the book of the
Law'—this is Mikra (the original reading in the Pentateuch);
'clearly'—this is Targum." *Bab. Meg.* 3 a ; *Bab. Ned.*
37 b.

[2] This however is disputed, many holding the Targum of
Jonathan ben Uzziel on the prophets to be older.

Samaria as well to produce a similar result, and it
is not unreasonable to ascribe the original redaction
of the Samaritan Targum to about the same time
as that of Onkelos, or perhaps a little earlier.
Later it cannot well be, for the Samaritan Greek
version which appears to have been formed on it,
is already quoted by Fathers of the third and
fourth centuries. Samaritan tradition apparently
ascribes it to a certain Nathanael who died about
20 B.C.[1], but to this testimony no importance need
be ascribed. From the many Arabisms which
occur in this version it has been held to be even
subsequent to the Mohammedan invasion of 632[2]:
it is possible however that these may be interpolations, not parts of the original text. It must also
be remembered that the Samaritans were a mixed
race, with Arabs included among them[3], and that
possibly the translator himself may have been
one. Many hands seem to have been employed

[1] Winer, *De vers. Sam. indole*, p. 9; Juynboll, in *Orientalia* (1846), ii. 116.

[2] Frankel (in *Verhandlungen d. ersten Versammlung deutscher und ausl. Orientalisten in Dresden*, 1844) holds that, before the dominion of the Arabs, Arabic expressions seldom occur in Chaldee and Palestinian authors; that the Targums, Midrashim, and Talmud know them not. R. Lewi alone among Midrash authors explains by means of Arabic.

[3] Cf. 'Geshem the Arabian,' Neh. ii. 19 and vi. 1; 'the Arabians,' ibid. iv. 7. Cf. Kohn, *Samaritanische Studien*, p. 60.

upon it before it assumed its present form: the
first thirty chapters of Genesis are apparently
the oldest[1], containing many so-called Samaritan
words which cannot be traced to any known
source: differences in the use of the conjunctions
are observable in the various books: mistakes
which occur in the rendering of one passage do
not repeat themselves in the parallel phrase of
another book. At some period or other the
version has been greatly indebted to that of
Onkelos, so much so that many critics, such as
Hottinger, Eichhorn, and Kirchheim, have held it
to have been copied from it. This however seems
to be rather an overstating of the case: it is true
that ἅπαξ λεγόμενα and words of uncertain meaning
are often rendered by identical or similar expressions in both: moreover when Onkelos borrows
from Jewish tradition, the Samaritan Targum
often follows him. And yet the two are independent; the latter falls into serious blunders from
which the version of Onkelos should have pro-
tected it; it often retains difficulties of the Hebrew
text where the other gives a translation. It
would seem therefore to have been at the outset
an original translation, but in course of time and
during the various manipulations it underwent
to have been interpolated largely from the version

[1] Kohn, ibid. pp. 18 sq.

prevalent among the Jews. It is in general
minutely literal, not however always following the
text of the Samaritan Pentateuch, but sometimes
deserting it for the Hebrew, although in so doing
it displays very little skill or knowledge of the
language, falling occasionally into the most gro-
tesque blunders from a confusion of similar words[1].
The sense of numberless easy passages is per-
verted ; in difficult ones the Hebrew is retained or
rendered by equally ambiguous words, or by such
as refuse to have a certain meaning affixed to
them by a comparison with cognate dialects. In
the style of translation it comes between the pro-
lixity of the Targumists and the slavish literalness
of Aquila: like the Pentateuch, it is careful to
avoid phrases which might seem to impair the
reverence due to the Deity by the imputation of
human feelings or parts, and also to change expressions which might be thought to savour of in-
delicacy into others more suitable to the dignity of

---

[1] e.g. in Deut. l. 44, דברים, 'bees,' is confounded with דברים,
'words,' and translated כליה: to leave you a 'remnant,' שארית,
is rendered חמיץ, 'dough,' as in Lev. xxi. 2 שאר, a 'blood-
relation,' is confounded with שׂאר, 'dough,' and translated עמיר:
אף, 'anger' and 'even,' are confused (Lev. xxvi. 44), and אמש
(Gen. xliii. 11) rendered ארמה: שניהם (Gen. iii. 7) is confounded
with לבושם, and translated עליהן רדפי: בשרים (ibid. xxxi. 27),
with 'songs,' is rendered ברבנים: יער שחותא (ibid. 47) תותב
סערחה: in Num. xix. 6 שני תולע is rendered 'two worms'
instead of 'scarlet wool.'

the subject. For purposes of exegesis the version
is entirely useless: it is simply interesting as
faithfully representing the religious ideas and
literary progress of that strange offshoot and
counterfeit of Israel, the Samaritan people; valuable also for philological purposes as being the
most trustworthy monument of an important
Semitic dialect, though of only a debased one
which has not a literature worthy of the name.
It is to this Targum always that recourse must
principally be had for settling the forms of the
Samaritan language, though it is an unsatisfactory witness to them from the number of Hebraisms it contains and the interpolations it has
undergone; but all the later documents we
possess are still more untrustworthy from the
uncertainty attending their age and the possibility that they may have been written while
the language was no longer spoken[1]. It is of
considerable importance therefore that we should
possess a thoroughly critical edition of the text,
and it is as a contribution to this end that the
present fragment has been edited.

The oldest MSS. hitherto known to exist are
both at Rome, the Barberini triglott and the
Vatican. The former was bought by Peiresc at
Damascus in 1631, and bequeathed by him to

---

[1] Cf. Nöldeke in Geiger's *Zeitschr.* vi. 204 sq.

Cardinal Barberini, in whose library it still remains.
It is written on parchment, with the Hebrew-
Samaritan text of the Pentateuch, the Arabic
version of Abusaid, and the Samaritan Targum
in three parallel columns. It is imperfect: the
oldest parts were written in A.D. 1226, and the
end of Deuteronomy was supplied by a later hand
in 1482. It has never been published: only a
single page of it, with some of the variations of
its Targum and Pentateuch, and a specimen of
the Arabic version, have as yet appeared[1].

The Vatican MS. was bought by Pietro della
Valle at Damascus in 1616: it is much later
than the one just described, on paper, dated 1514
A.D., with considerable lacunae of words and even
verses[2]. This is the only text that has ever been

---

[1] It is described by De Sacy in *Mém. de l'Acad. des Inscr.*
l. 49, p. 3; by J. B. de Rossi at the end of his *Specimen Varr.
Lect.* (1783); by Adler in his *Bibl. Krit. Reise* (1783), p. 139.
A triple page was transcribed by Blanchini in his *Evangeliarium*
(1749), ii. 604. See also Hwiid, *Specimen ined. vers. Arab.
Sam. Pent.* (1780). It seems to have been lost at the end of
the last century, but has since reappeared. Some of the variations of its Pentateuch and Targum may be found in Castellus'
*Animadv. Samar.* in vol. vi. of the London Polyglott of 1657,
and also in Morinus' *Opuscula Hebr. Sam.* (1657), pp. 103-196,
cf. also p. 96. The text has lately been collated by Heidenheim
with a view to its publication.

[2] It is fully described in Assemani, *Bibl. Vatican. Catal.* i. 1.
p. 464.

published: it appeared in the Paris Polyglott of
1645, and was thence copied, without however a
fresh collation of the MS., into the London Polyglott of 1657. The most glaring blunders were,
it is true, corrected by conjecture in the process of
revision by the editor Castellus, but the results are
eminently unsatisfactory[1]. The Latin translation
also, being intended to serve as a version both of
the Hebrew-Samaritan text of the Pentateuch and
also of the Samaritan Targum, is not to be depended
upon. It is hoped therefore that the publication
of the present very ancient fragment may prove of
some assistance for a future critical edition of the
Targum[2].

The MS. is undated, but from the character of
the writing and condition of the parchment it is
in all probability considerably older than the
Barberini triglott. From the circumstance that
no Arabic translation, as in the case of the MS.
just mentioned, appears by the side of the Samaritan text, it may be conjectured that it was
copied at a time when the language was still

---

[1] See Kohn, op. cit. p. 22 sq.

[2] Prof. Petermann of Berlin is publishing an edition from
MSS. collated by him at Nablus; they are on parchment,
I understand, and of the seventeenth century. Genesis only has
as yet been published. Dr. A. Brüll also is reprinting at Frank-
fort-am-Main Walton's text in Hebrew characters; Genesis,
Exodus, and Leviticus have already appeared.

i

understood, and had not as yet been superseded
by Arabic. In the character of the writing it
resembles the ancient MSS. still existing at
Nublus described by Dr. Rosen [1]. The text varies
very considerably from that of the Vatican MS.,
and also from the printed specimens of the Barberini fragment. It has unfortunately suffered many
corrections from a later hand, most frequently in
grammatical forms, sometimes in whole words [2];
but as they have not been carried out with con-
sistency it has generally been possible by comparison with other parts of the MS. to restore
the original form with certainty. In all such
parts of the MS. as are in good preservation the
corrections are easily to be detected, and these
are distinguished in the printed text by round
brackets: additions made by the editor from conjecture are enclosed in square brackets: as this
has been done with the greatest care, the present
text may be relied upon as a faithful reproduction
of the original. The punctuation of the MS. may
be seen from the photograph appended. I find no

---

[1] See above, p. 104, note 1. The facsimile on the frontispiece
is the exact size of the original. The MS. is numbered Opp.
Add. 8vo. 29. When it first came into the possession of the
Bodleian it had but thirty-nine leaves, another has lately been
added by the liberality of the Earl of Crawford and Balcarres, in
whose collection it was found.

[2] See the notes appended to the text passim, especially p. 25.

traces of any such elaborate system as is described
by the Abbé Bargès in his notice of some fragments of a Samaritan Pentateuch in his possession, nor are the vowels marked [1]. Occasionally
however, not always, the masculine and feminine possessive pronouns are distinguished from
each other, the former by a dot, the latter by a
line, over the ה. The marginal notes are of the
same age as the body of the MS., but they have
in many cases become illegible, and the sense
of those which can be deciphered is often very
obscure [2].

The second translation in order of time which
the Pentateuch underwent at the hands of the
Samaritans was that into Greek: whether, like
the LXX in the case of the Jews, for the benefit
of the flourishing community of Alexandria [3] is
uncertain. By many writers its existence has

[1] *Notice sur deux fragments d'un Pentateuque Hébreu-Sama-
ritain* (1865), p. 15. Ewald (*Götting. Nachrichten*, 1867, p.
221) thinks many of the signs noticed by Bargès to be identical,
and the whole question doubtful. The Samaritan use of diacritic
points is described by Geiger, *Zeitschr. d. D. M. G.* xxi. 172.

[2] I had hoped to have added to this edition another fragment
belonging to Trinity College, Cambridge, of which a notice
appeared in the *Journ. Asiat.* (1870), p. 525; it is to be found
in the Catalogue of Hebrew and Samaritan MSS. of Trinity
College, p. 234. Not however having succeeded in procuring
the loan of the MS. I have been obliged to bring out the present
one by itself.            [3] See above, p. 26.

been denied[1], and the quotations[2] of Fathers of
the third and fourth centuries from τὸ Σαμαρειτικόν
have been understood to refer to the version of
Symmachus, or the Samaritan Targum, or the
Pentateuch, or the LXX[3]. It is doubtful whether
it was a complete version or only consisted of
emendations of particular passages; possibly the
latter, and if so, it may have related to difficulties
in the Samaritan Targum[4].

The third translation was into Arabic. At first
the Samaritans did not scruple to use the translation of Saadiah, who died in A.D. 942, but in the
succeeding century[5] Abusaid set about preparing

---

[1] e. g. Isaac Vossius. His theory is ably discussed by R. Simon
in his *Hist. Critique du V. T.* (1680), p. 261.

[2] They are to be found collected in Hottinger, *Exercit. Anti-
morin.* p. 29; see also Eichhorn's *Einleitung*, i. p. 388; Walton,
*Prolegg. to London Polyglott*, xi. 22.

[3] Winer, *De vers. Sam. indole*, p. 7. Nöldeke, in the *Götting.
Gel. Anzeig.* (1865), p. 1311, considers the Σαμαρειτικόν to be the
Hebrew text as received from the Samaritans. De Wette,
*Einleitung ins A. T.* (1852), 89, doubts whether it was an independent translation, or extracts from the Samaritan Targum,
or corrections of the LXX. Epiphanius (*De Mens. et Pond.*
p. 172) mentions that Symmachus, in the time of Severus, made
his version after the Samaritan [? Greek] translation, but this
seems doubtful. Origen takes no notice of it, though mentioning the Hebrew-Samaritan text. Eichhorn, i. p. 387.

[4] Kohn, *De Pent. Sam.* p. 68; Winer, *De vers. Sam.* p. 7.

[5] Probably about 1070. Saadiah was an Egyptian Jew;
Abusaid was also in all probability of the same country. Cf.

one which should be more in accordance with the
tastes of his Samaritan countrymen. He appears
to have employed the Hebrew-Samaritan text, the
Targum, and also Saadiah (when the latter does
not differ from the Samaritan), though he never
quotes him without abusing him. Like his
countrymen generally, he is careful to alter phrases
which seem to impute human qualities or parts
to the Deity, or in any sort to offend against
delicacy : like them, he loses no opportunity of
exalting the position of Moses, nor depressing the
dignity of Judah. He occasionally substitutes
later geographical names for those of the text :
his style is marked by many vulgarisms, and
many Hebrew and Samaritan expressions are to be
found in it. About the year 1208 his translation
underwent a revision at the hands of Abu-l-barakat,
in Syria as is generally supposed, receiving both
corrections and annotations from him : the two
versions became intermixed, and are now not to
be distinguished from each other.

Next in importance to the Pentateuch and its
translations will come the historical literature of
the Samaritans comprised in various chronicles

---

Juynboll, in *Orientalia*, ii. 116. The three first books of the
Pentateuch according to Abusaïd's rendering have been edited
by Kuenen. It is described by De Sacy in *Mém. de l'Acad. des
Inser.* vol. xlix, and by Van Vloten in his *Specimen Philologicum*,
1803.

which have come down to us. In them however
it will be a mistake to look for any sober narrative
of facts: nothing was further from the mind of a
Samaritan chronicler than to give an exact relation
of past events. His object was rather to stir up
the minds of his degenerate countrymen to an
emulation of the mythical past glories of their
race and the heroic deeds of their ancestors, to
console them in their present troubles by the hope
that, when like their forefathers they returned to
the earnest study of the Law and practice of its
requirements, the same Divine favour would be
shewn them as had attended the nation in the
happy and glorious days of old. He has no idea
of a continuous narrative, but selects passages of
past history which will best suit the purpose of
his tale. These he chooses from any source which
may be open to him, chiefly from the Bible and
Jewish legend, distorting, amplifying, and omitting
till the result proves satisfactory to his taste. In
accordance with Oriental fashion he endeavours to
enliven his narration by the introduction of hymns
and proverbs, and for the same purpose he puts
long speeches into the mouths of his heroes. His
efforts, however well meant, prove highly unsatisfactory ; he only succeeds in producing a dull,
wordy parody of a chronicle, full of the most
astounding historical blunders.

All these characteristics are found exemplified

in the 'Samaritan Chronicle,' or 'Book of Joshua'
as it is termed, composed in all probability in
Egypt at the close of the thirteenth century[1]:
so termed because its greater part is occupied with
narrating the glories of Joshua, the successor of
the one great prophet of Israel, himself born of
the tribe of Ephraim and therefore unconnected
with the hated Judah, in whose time Shechem
and Garizim derived new honours from the solemn
rites and ceremonies there performed by him.
After a short preface, the book relates Joshua's
assumption of office, the history of Balaam, and
the slaughter of the Midianites, in the main following the Biblical account, though with many
amplifications, such as the falling down of the
wall of Midian at the blast of the trumpet, Balaam
being found within the temple speechless from
terror, and his slaughter by the soldiers against
the desire of Joshua. Next comes an account
of the last words of Moses, Joshua's lamentation
over him, the renewal of the covenant between
God and Israel, the ordering of the army, the

---

[1] Published by Juynboll (Leyden, 1848) from an Arabic MS.
written in Samaritan character, the earlier part of which is
dated A. D. 1362, the latter 1513 (there is another copy in the
British Museum, dated 1502). The author appears to have
woven into his book one Samaritan and three other Arabic
chronicles, besides employing commentaries on the Pentateuch
and annals of the priests.

sending out of the spies (who endeavour to scare
the Canaanites to flight by tales of what Israel
had done to Sihon and Og, Midian and Moab),
the passage of the Jordan, the taking of Jericho,
the theft of Achan, who steals 2250 lbs. weight
of gold (though no mention is made of Ai), the
craft of the Gibeonites, the slaughter of the
Canaanites, and the division of the land between
the several tribes. This part of the narration ends
with the appointment of Nabih as king of the
tribes east of Jordan, and for the next twenty years
Israel enjoys a profound peace, all wending their
way thrice in each year with joy and gladness
to the 'Mount of Blessing.' This calm is broken
by a formidable confederacy of the king of Persia,
the greater Armenia, the lesser Rumia (Asia
Minor), and others against Israel; they send
a challenge to Joshua, who is greatly alarmed at
the missive, but puts on a bold face before the
messenger and sends back a defiant reply : in an
hour's time he mounts 300,000 men, the half of
Israel, and seeks his foes, but is by magic sur-
rounded by seven walls of iron. Nabih however,
the king of Israel on the other side of Jordan,
informed of his danger by a letter brought to him
by a dove, soon comes to the rescue, slays Shaubak
the king of Persia by throwing a dart up into
the air which in its fall transfixes man and horse,
and piercing the ground causes a fountain to burst

forth. The walls raised by magic art collapse at the first blast of the priests' trumpets, at Joshua's bidding the light stays, the winds aid him, the enemies' swords turn against them, and a mighty slaughter ensues so that the horses wade in blood to their nostrils, and the enemy are utterly destroyed. During the happy reign of Joshua, which with that of his nine successors lasted for 260 years, Israel observed the Law, kept the Sabbaths and Feasts, observed the sabbatical year and the payment of tithes, all crime was immediately detected, the sacrifices were duly offered on Garizim. But after the reign of Samson, the handsomest and strongest of all the kings, Israel falls into sin, the divine glory disappears from the Temple, 'Ozi the high-priest hides the sacred vessels in a cave on Garizim, Eli the apostate priest builds an opposition temple at Shiloh, and, after instructing his pupil Samuel in all the magical arts in which he himself excelled, perishes at receiving the news of the death of his impious sons in battle and the loss of the ark. The chronicle now makes a leap of some hundreds of years to the time of Bokhtonâsor (Nebuchadnezzar) king of Persia, who reigned at Mausul. He carries away, not Judah, but Israel into captivity; but on the complaint of the new colonists that a blight rested upon the produce of the land, suffers Israel, to the number of 300,000, to return,

the colonists making way for them. The Jews wish
to build a temple at Jerusalem, the rest of Israel
on Garizim, and on an appeal to the King the
famous trial of the merits of Sanballat's and
Zerubbabel's copies of the Law is made in his
presence, when the latter is at once burnt on
being cast into the flames, the former jumps out
thrice unhurt[1]; Judah repents, and all Israel
worships on Garizim. Then comes another break
in the narrative till the time of Alexander, the
whole of whose history as it appears in the
chronicle is borrowed from Jewish history. Thus
the Samaritans, and not the Jews, refuse to
break their league with Persia and give aid
to Alexander[2]: he marches against Shechem,
not Jerusalem, but spares it, overawed by the
dignity of the Samaritan, not the Jewish high-
priest, whose figure had appeared to him in
dreams and promised him victory. The tale of
Alexander's three days' journey to the land of
darkness, the dust of which was rubies and
pearls[3]; of his ascending to the clouds in a car

---

[1] See above, p. 106.

[2] Josephus, *Ant.* xi. 8. 3. There it is told how the Jewish
high-priest Jaddua refuses to break his league with Darius,
which Sanballat (*ibid.* 4) at once does. Alexander marches
against Jerusalem, but at the sight of Jaddua prostrates himself
before him (*ibid.* 4, 5).

[3] To be found with variations in *Tamid.* 32 a, and Josephus
ben Gorion, ii. 16.

drawn by eagles who rose or fell according as
the lumps of flesh which they endeavoured to
catch were held above or below them[1]; the
device by which the priests evaded tho king's
injunction of erecting statues to him by calling
all new-born sons by his name[2],—all these can
be traced to Jewish sources, whence they have
been drawn by the Samaritan chronicler for his
own purposes. Next follows a narrative of the
great revolt under Hadrian, during which Jerusalem falls into his hands by means of two
Samaritans; a confusion probably with the capture of Bettar, as the latter is said to have been
betrayed by Samaritan intrigue[3]. The whole
concludes with a short account of the high-priest
'Aqbun, his son Nathanael, and grandson Baba
Rabba, the last of whom was born in grievous
times, when the Roman hand lay heavy upon the
Samaritans, when circumcision was forbidden, and
no worshipper might approach the holy mountain,
a miraculous bird being set there to warn the
Roman guards when a Samaritan approached, who
thereupon would issue forth and kill him. Baba
Rabba endeavours to alleviate his country's sorrows,

---

[1] *Jer. 'Aboda Zara*, iii. 1. This was a common mediæval
legend; it is related of Nimrod by the Moslems; cf. Weil, *Bibl.
Legend*, p. 77.

[2] Also to be found in Josephus ben Gorion, ii. 7.

[3] Ewald, *Gesch.* vii. (1868), p. 418.

and sends his nephew Levi to Constantinople, there
to acquire all the learning of the enemy, that, con-
cealing his birth and faith, he might rise to
honour, and returning to Nablus, destroy the fatal
bird, and thus enable his countrymen to ascend
the mountain and obtain by their prayers deliverance from the enemy. In this he completely
succeeds, and the narrative breaks off abruptly
at the point when, after thirteen years' absence,
he pays a visit as Archbishop to Nablus. The
above sketch will show how much genuine light
we may expect to have shed upon Samaritan
history by the truthfulness and historical skill
of native chroniclers.

The next chronicle to be noticed, El-Tholidoth[1],
or The (book of) Generations, is of a more modest
character. In the first instance it professes to
have been written by Eleazar ben Amram in (A.H.
544 =) 1149 A.D., copied and continued by Jacob
ben Ismael 200 years later, and carried down by
other hands to 1859, when the present MS. was
written by Jacob ben Aaron the high-priest[2]. At

---

[1] Called also by Abulfath التلاتی or the 'catena.'

[2] Published by Neubauer in the *Journal Asiatique* for 1869,
pp. 385 sq. He gives the Samaritan, or rather Hebrew, text
with notes and translation, citing the Arabic translation when
the sense is not clear. His text is that of the Bodleian MS.
numbered *Bodl. Or.* 651, collated in some passages with one
belonging to a private owner.

its commencement it relates how Adam received
from God through the mediation of angels the
method of calculating the months and years for
the proper arrangement of the calendar of festivals.
This passed by tradition through the patriarchs to
the time of Phinehas the grandson of Aaron, in
whose days it was committed to writing by his
son Abisham, and according to this record, which
is still in the hands of the Samaritan high-priest,
is the sacred calendar still every six months compiled[1]. Each period of seven years ends with a
*shemittah* (year of release) ; seven of these form
a *jubilee :* the first *shemittah* counts from the entry
of Israel into Canaan. Three books are mentioned
as having been given to the Fathers from the time
of Adam to Moses, the book of 'Wars,' that of
'Astronomy,' and that of 'Signs[2].' Next are given
the ages of the patriarchs from Adam to the death
of Moses, and then a list of high-priests down to
the present times : interwoven with this latter are
a few scattered notices of important events, such
as the Babylonian captivity, the return from it,
the death of our Lord[3], &c. ; but as these have all

---

[1] See above, p. 75 ; Petermann, in Herzog, xlii. 376, note.

[2] See below, p. 132.

[3] 'In the time of Jehonathan was put to death Jesus the son
of Miriam, the son of Joseph the carpenter, Ben Hanahpheth,
at cursed Salem (בן הנימה באירי שלם), under the reign of
Tiberius king of Rome, by Palitah his governor.' pp. 402, 438.

been inserted in the chronicle of Abulfath which
will next be noticed, they need not be further
here described. The chronicle is of interest to
geographers as, while mentioning the various
Samaritan families settled in Damascus, Palestine,
and Egypt, it incidentally introduces the names
of a considerable number of places inhabited by
them [1].

The third chronicle to be noticed is that of
Abulfath, composed by him at the request of the
high-priest in A.D. 1355, and continued by other
hands to later times [2]. Its literary and historical
merit is no greater than that of the two just
described, considerable portions of which were
copied into the present work by its author [3]. The
same distortion of facts in the interest of national
vanity, the same confusion between different
periods, the same omission of important events,

[1] The importance of this chronicle for comparison with the
'Book of Jubilees' is shewn by Rönsch in his *Buch der Jubiläen*
(1874), p. 361.

[2] Published from four MSS. by Ed. Vilmar, Gotha, 1865. It is
written in Arabic containing many vulgar grammatical forms.

[3] Besides these two, Abulfath also appears to have had at his
disposal several other books, viz. one entitled the قصص البلدان,
probably an account of the division of the land among the
twelve tribes, other chronicles bound up in one volume with the
book of Joshua, three more in Hebrew obtained from Damascus,
a book termed the كراس or 'quires,' and a chronicle of Sadaqa;
the last however he does not appear to have used.

the same unacknowledged borrowing from Jewish sources, is observable. It commences at the Creation, which is placed at 4350 B.C.; from this point to the settlement of Israel in Canaan, which, together with the 250 ensuing years of peace under the rule of Joshua and his successors to Samson, makes altogether a period of 3050 years, was the Ridván or time of the Divine Favour. Then the royal and pontifical dignities were both preserved, then the 'king' with the aid of his seventy elders and twelve princes of the tribes guided the state in accordance with the Divine will, the high-priest in company with the priests and Levites rightly performing the services of the Temple, while the rest of the people each in his proper station fulfilled the requirements of the Law. Then the Divine Presence manifested itself in the shrine on Garizim, whence the fire of the Lord came forth and each day consumed the sacrifices offered upon the two altars of the holy Mount. With Eli's schism commenced the period of Fanúta, or 'disappearance' of the Divine Favour and of its visible sign: Israel fell into idolatry: Saul, the schismatical monarch set up by the apostate prophet Samuel, persecuted the true people of God and prohibited their approach to Garizim; many therefore fled their country to avoid his tyranny, and thus commenced 1000 years of migrations and exiles to the time of Alexander, which is placed at 250 B.C. David proceeds to yet greater lengths, usurps the priestly offices of benediction and sacrifice, appoints Jerusalem as the Qiblah whither Israel should turn in prayer, and there establishes the schismatical ark of Shiloh, though formerly he too had offered on Garizim. Solomon's wisdom and glory are beyond denial: he is the 'Shiloh' after whose days the sceptre departed from Judah[1]. Rehoboam was the last king who reigned with any show of right, having been elected at Shechem[2] in an assembly of the tribes. Jeroboam, corrupted by his residence in Egypt, introduced the worship of the calves at Sebaste[3] and Dan: Elijah and Elisha are also deserving of the deepest reprobation for the part they took in seducing Israel from their true allegiance. Divine vengeance comes at last in the shape of Nebuchadnezzar's invasion, who destroys Jerusalem and Sebaste: 'Aqbia the high-priest buries the sacred vessels in Garizim, and with his countrymen departs to exile in Harran and Edessa, carrying with him a copy of the Law; the Jews with their king 'Jumaqim' proceed to Babylon. Seventy years later, 3790 years after the Creation, Israel returns from captivity, but

---

[1] Gen. xlix. 10.       [2] 1 Kings xii. 1.
[3] Not at Bethel (or Luz), for that is the higher summit of Garizim. See above, p. 67.

a second exile ensues 120 years later, which lasts
for fifty-five years; the subsequent return from
this, by permission of King Surdi, took place not
long before that of the Jews from Babylon [1]. Then
ensues the famous contest between Zerubbabel
and Sanballat as to whether Jerusalem or Garizim
should be the Qibloh of Israel, ending in the
defeat of the Jews and the re-establishment of
sacrifice on Garizim. Kesra, the next king of
Persia, suffers the Jews to return and build Jerusalem : his successors were Zaradushti, Ahash-
varush, Artahast, Darius. This last king favours
the Jews, and subjects Samaria to them, which
accordingly is cruelly oppressed : a revolt ensues
in which Jerusalem is destroyed, but the rising
is quelled, the Samaritans severely punished, and
the exercise of their religion interdicted : many
thereupon fly to Kutha, and from this circumstance
the name of Kuthim was maliciously fixed upon
them by the Jews in order to rob them of their
true designation of Israelites. Alexander died
A.M. 4100, about 1000 years before the era of
Mohammed. It is false that the Jews only translated their Pentateuch into Greek: King Ptolemy

---

[1] In No. xxvii, p. 290, *Codd. Or. Bibl. Acad. Reg. Scient.
Lugd. Bat.*, is an excerpt from a historical work, relating how at
this time 'Abdeel the high-priest gave his son in marriage to
the daughter of Sanballat, telling Sanballat at the same time to
instruct him in the Law.' Cf. De Jong's *Catal.* p. 62.

k

sent for Samaritan translators as well, and after
hearing the arguments on both sides as to the
merits of the respective copies of the Jewish and
Samaritan Law, pronounced in favour of the latter
and offered sacrifice on Garizim[1]. In A.M. 4350
Christ was born, and crucified by the procurator
of Tiberius: John the Baptist had before this
suffered at Sebaste by the order of Herod. Vespasian's reign is passed over in silence: the events
occurring in those of Hadrian and Commodus are
apparently confused[2]. In the days of Alexander
(Severus) Baba Rabba restored the independence
of Samaria and the study of the Law, though in
many of his enactments he departed from the
polity established under the Ridvân. He ended
his days in captivity at Constantinople, having
been allured there by the promises of the Emperor
Philip. Notices occur of the reign of Marcian,
when the possession of the tombs of the patriarchs
was decided by single combat between a Christian
and Samaritan in favour of the latter, and of the
persecution of Zeno, &c. to the time of Mohammed,
whose flight is fixed at 700 A.D., and with this

---

[1] The legend of the three days' darkness which came over the
world at the translation of the Law (Abulfath, *Annal.* p. 95) is
to be found in the *Hilkoth Gedolath Ta'anith*, ed. Ven. f. 39 b:
cf. Grätz, *Gesch.* iii. 430.

[2] The destruction of Samaritan books is attributed to Commodus, which in the book of Joshua, chap. xlvii, is ascribed to
Hadrian. Vilmar's *Abulfath*, p. lxv.

the original chronicle of Abulfaṭḥ appears to have
terminated, though later events have been added
by other hands, together with a list of high-priests
down to the present time.

From the foregoing sketch it will be seen how
little trustworthy a source of information is in
this chronicle presented to us, in consequence of
the large gaps and historical blunders occurring
in it. For instance, the Assyrian invasion is
ignored, not a single fact related which occurred
between the reigns of Tiberius and Hadrian, nor
for the hundred and more years which elapsed
between Zeno and Mohammed; Zerubbabel and
Ezra are made contemporaries, Hadrian builds a
Christian church on Garizim; the Arab Philip
rules at Constantinople, Gordian incites the Jews
to rebuild Jerusalem. Amid this general confusion it would be unwise to accept anything as
genuine which comes to us recommended only
by Samaritan authority.

Hardly to be distinguished from the class of
literature just described is one which may be
classed under that of 'Agadah.' A specimen
of this may be found in the 'Legends ascribed
to Moses,' a commentary on which is preserved
in the British Museum [1]. It borrows largely from

---

[1] *Add. MS.* 19656, fol. 1-29. The title is مجموع شرح
الاساطير. It has been translated by Dr. Leitner in Heidenheim,

k 2

Jewish sources. Adam and Eve, we are told,
spent eight days in Paradise: the former instructs
Lamech in the 'Book of Truth' for 180 years;
after leaving Paradise he dwells in Safra, that is
Nablus, and is afterwards buried at Hebron: Noah
collects three writings called the 'Books of the
Covenant,' viz., the 'Book of Adam,' or of
'Wonders,' that of 'Nagmuth,' or Astronomy,
and the Book of 'Wars'.' Enoch dies and is
buried opposite Garizim in Navus on Mount Ebal,
lamented by Adam. Jared founds Salem Rabtha
or Nablus, in which God foretold that Melchizedek should hereafter reign: there also is
Noah buried. Great honour is given to Abraham:
he is cast by the tyrant Nimrod into the fire, but
escapes unhurt, and Haran is killed by it: 6000
years are to intervene between the Creation and
the 'day of vengeance.'

Of a similar type is the 'Jewelled necklace in
praise of the Lord of the human race,' composed
in (A.H. 944 =) A.D. 1537 by Ismaʿīl Ibn Badr Ibn

---

iv. 184. Identical with, or similar to this, must be the chronicle
on sixteen leaves written by Muser, extending from the creation
to the end of the world, still preserved by the high-priest at
Nablus. The Samaritans have also a similar one in Arabic by
Jacob Besini, who lived before Mohammed. Petermann in
Herzog, xiii. 376.

' See above, p. 125.

Abu-l-'Izz Ibn Rumaiḥ [1], in honour of Moses; it
sets forth his divine nature, and extols the glories
of his birth and miracles.

With this may be classed a 'tract' in which is
contained a 'complete explanation of the chapters
on Balak' by Ghazâl Ibn ad-Duwnik [2], with re-
flections on the same for the edification of the
reader; and another small tract by the famous
Abû Sa'îd explaining the cause of the fear felt by
Jacob on his way to Egypt (Gen. xlvi. 1, 3) and
by Abraham after the conquest of the five Kings
(*ibid.* xv. 1)[3], with a third by an unknown author,

---

[1] *Brit. Mus. Add. MS.* 19031. العقد الجوهري في مديح سيد البشر. (The same author also
wrote a book termed اسماعيل بن بدر بن ابو العز بن رميح. by
شرح الاثنتين وسبعين لوروت or 'an expla-
nation of the 72 laws.' Geiger, in *Zeitschr. d. D. M. G.* xxii.
531.) Another copy of this MS. is described by Neubauer in
*Journal Asiatique* (1869), p. 467. This and the other MSS. there
mentioned as belonging to Dr. Pusey now form part of the collection of the Earl of Crawford and Balcarres, which also contains, besides the works mentioned in the text, a Pentateuch
containing Gen. i. 12 to Deut. xxix, and fragments to xxxi. 13,
dated A.D. 1211; another with Arabic version in Samaritan
characters (not that of Abusaid, as I understand from Dr. A.
Löwy), dated A.D. 1328; another, apparently a copy of the last,
containing most of Genesis and Exodus; nine liturgical volumes,
written A.D. 1722–1794; some astronomical treatises, fragments
of Pentateuchs, &c.

[2] *MS. xxvii*, غزال ابن الدويك by مقالة في ملخص شرح سور بلق
*Bibl. Acad. Reg. Scient. Amst.* pp. 265–289.

[3] *Ibid.* pp. 292, 293.

in which the fifteen occasions are quoted from
Exodus and Numbers when the Israelites by
their complaints and abuse of Moses and Aaron
tempted God, and the times mentioned at which
the divine glory appeared[1].

Of great importance for ascertaining the doctrinal views of the Samaritans, especially as
showing the tenacity with which they clung to
ancient traditional interpretations, are their commentaries on the Pentateuch. Probably one of
the oldest now extant is in the Bodleian Library:
it was composed (A.H. 445 =) A.D. 1053 by an unknown Samaritan for the benefit of a certain Abû
Sa'ïd Levi, possibly the well-known translator[2];
certainly it was written before his translation of
the Pentateuch was made, as this is never quoted
in it. Like others of his countrymen who will be
afterwards quoted, the author was well acquainted
with the works of Arabian grammarians, but the
triliteral system for the formation of verbs discovered by Ḥayug was unknown to him. He is
singular in quoting not only from the Pentateuch,
but also from the former and later prophets,
Nehemiah, the Mishnah, &c., but strangely enough

[1] MS. xxvii. Bibl. Acad. Reg. Scient. Amst. pp. 294-296.

[2] Opp. Add. MS. 4°. 99. At its commencement it has two
short Samaritan liturgies. It has been described at length by
Neubauer in the Journ. Asiat. (1873), pp. 341 sq. It is written
in Arabic, and dated (A. H. 749=) A. D. 1348.

does not mention the Samaritan Targum. Like a
genuine Samaritan he shuns anthropomorphisms,
attributing to angels actions ascribed in the original to God Himself, but he is singularly peaceful,
sometimes even agreeing with Rabbanite interpretations, but never taking occasion to attack them.

Another interesting and important one is that
of 'Ibrahim from the family of Jacob,' now preserved at Berlin[1]. He thoroughly represents the
national feeling as exhibited in opposition to the
Rabbanite school of thought among the Jews.
For instance, he points out the error of the latter
in interpreting the 'I am come down' of Exod.
iii. 8, as of actual change of place on the part of
God, rather than of the direction of His Omni-
potence to a certain point: so he renders 'I will
stretch out My hand' (ver. 20) as 'power,' imputing
a literal interpretation' of the expression to the
Jews: the Lord 'repented' of the evil (xxxii. 14)
must signify 'turned from,' 'wiped away.' This
extreme anxiety to avoid anything approaching
anthropomorphism has been often pointed out
before. His desire to glorify Sichem and its sur-
roundings may be seen by his remark on Gen.
iii. 23, that Adam, on being driven out from
Paradise, was sent back to Garizim, for from thence

[1] Large extracts are given from this by Geiger in the Zeitschr.
d. D. M. G. xvii. 723 sq., xx. 147 sq., xxii. 532 sq.

had he been taken. Jered (*ib.* v. 18) he tells us
built Salem Rabtha, the city of Melchizedek, but
Achidan built Zion, with regard to which the Jews
have a tradition that 'the Law of Truth shall
go forth from Zion and abrogate the Law of
Moses,' but rather perish the Law of Ezra! Like
a true Samaritan he places Abraham's sacrifice,
Jacob's dream, &c., at Nablus. Very character-
istic also is his anxiety to uphold the fame of
Joseph against the charge of having married a
daughter of Potiphar or Dinah, and to rescue
the great prophet Moses from the imputation of
having postponed the circumcision of his son; the
means by which he effects this last point is a
miracle of exegetic ingenuity. So all connected
with Moses must likewise have no shadow of
suspicion resting upon them: Jethro is no idola-
trous priest, Zipporah is no 'Ethiopian' (Numb.
xii. 1), but 'beautiful:'—these instances are sufficient to give a just idea of the style of his
commentary.

Of just the same type is an anonymous com-
mentary on Genesis preserved in the Bodleian
Library, brought from the East by the learned
Bishop Huntington[1]. The great reverence of the
Samaritans for all belonging to the priesthood

---

[1] *Hunt. MS.* 301. The forty-ninth chapter was published
by Schnurrer in Eichhorn's *Repertorium*, xvi. 154.

has been already noticed, they felt it therefor·
necessary at all hazards to explain away the
severe judgment of Jacob upon his son Levi for
his slaughter of the Shechemites in conjunction
with Simeon. Consequently the words 'O my
soul, come thou not into their secret' &c. (xlix. 6)
are thus explained, 'they had no occasion to take
counsel of me, for they knew that their counsel
was right, seeing that their zeal was righteous.'
So in the next verse, 'Cursed (ארור) be their
anger' &c. is paraphrased, 'Most excellent (אדיר)
is their anger,' or, 'exceeding is their generosity
and fortitude:' 'I will divide them in Jacob,' he
prays that their strenuousness may remain and be
distributed in Jacob. On 'thy father's children
shall bow down before thee' (ver. 8) he remarks,
'Some weak people interpret it, "they will bow
towards thee because the Qiblah is in thy domain,"
but this is false, for the Qiblah is in the territory
of Ephraim.' He paraphrases ver. 10 thus, 'knowledge of the Law and obedience towards God shall
not fail, or a lawgiver from between his feet till
Shiloh (Solomon) shall arise, who shall change the
Law, and many shall follow him, since they love
license and are prone to it.'

In this class must also be included an agadic
commentary on the Pentateuch containing Genesis
and Exodus, termed the 'dissipater of darkness
from the secrets of revelation,' written in 1753-4

by Ghazâl Ibn Abu-s-Surûr aṣ-Ṣafawî al-Yûsufî al-Mûṣawî al-Ghazzî[1]; and another containing fragments of a commentary on Genesis, Exodus, and Leviticus, often quoted by Castellus in his notes on the Samaritan Pentateuch[2]. Other writers seem to have devoted their energies to the same subject, but nothing now remains to us but their names and the titles of their books. For instance, Mangâ Ibn ash-Shâ'ar is mentioned as the author of three commentaries on the Pentateuch[3]: Abû Sa'îd of scholia on the Decalogue[4]; Amîn ad-Dîn Abu-l-Barakât of a commentary on the same[5]: commentaries on the Pentateuch are said to have been composed by the celebrated poet, philosopher, and physician, Ṣadaqa Ben Mangâ Ben Ṣadaqa[6], who, after living high in the favour of al-Malik al-'Âdil the Ayyûbid prince ruling at Damascus, died near it in A.D. 1223; by Muhadhdhib ad-Dîn Yûsuf Ben Abû Sa'îd Ben Khalaf,

---

[1] *Brit. Mus. Add. MS.* 19657; title كاشف الغياهب عن اسرار الغزّي, or, غزال بن ابو السرور الصفوي اليوسـي الموسوي الغزي by المواهب as his name is otherwise written, غزال بن ابو السرور ابن غزال ابن ابو السرور ابن صلي الصفوي المطري.

[2] *Brit. Mus. Harl. MS.* 5495.

[3] *Amst. MS. xxvii,* p. 309 منبا ابن الشاعر.

[4] *Ibid.* p. 315.      [5] *Ibid.* p. 314.

[6] صدق بن منبا (not صحبا or بخـتا, cf. Juynboll, *Comm.* p. 56) بن صدق. He wrote a commentary on the aphorisms of Hippocrates.

pupil of the famous Ibrahim Shams al-Hukamâï, and vizier to al-Malik al-Amgad Magd ad-Din Bahrâm Shâh, sultan of Baalbek ; he died in 1227[1].

Under the head of miscellaneous theology must be classed a number of works many of which are closely connected with those just described. To this will belong a work of Abu-l-Ḥasan of Tyre, of which the title probably should be the 'book of cookery,' i.e. relating to lawful and forbidden meats, or 'of force[2].' In it the peculiar dogmas of the Samaritans as differing from those of the Jews are set forth and. supported by arguments

---

[1] Wüstenfeld, *Gesch. d. Arab. Aerzte*, p. 121 ; Jaynboll, *Comment.* p. 56. Yûsuf's nephew Abu-l-Ḥasan Ben Ghazâl Ben Abû Sa'id was noted for his acquirements in medicine, natural history, and astronomy, composing many books on these subjects. Embracing Islamism, he entered the service of his uncle's patron, and later into that of al-Malik aṣ-Ṣâliḥ Isma'il Ben al-Malik al-'Âdil, sultan of Damascus, who made him his vizier. His library is said to have consisted of 10,000 volumes. Another celebrated Samaritan physician, Muwaffaq ad-Din (موفّق الدين) lived in (ابو يوسف يعقوب ابن ابي اسحى غنائم الدمشقي السامري) the same century: he wrote a commentary on the canon of Avicenna (*Bodl. MS. Marsh.* 464), on logic and theology ; cf. Wüstenfeld, *op. cit.* p. 141 ; Ḥaji Khalfa, v. 160, 472. For other notices of commentaries see below, p. 158.

[2] *Bodl. MS. Hunt.* 24; title كتاب الطباع by ابو للسن الصوري ; see notice of a similar MS. in *Journ. Asiat.* (1869), p. 468. He appears to have lived some time in the eleventh century ; before Abû Sa'id, who translated the Pentateuch about 1070 A.D. Cf. Jaynboll in *Orientalia*, ii. 117.

drawn from the Pentateuch : it treats, e.g. of the
dignity and perpetual succession of the high-
priests ; of animals which may be eaten ; of the
sabbath ; that believers must have a Qiblah
whither they may turn in prayer, i.e. Garizim ;
of the differences between Karaites and Rabbanites
as to the fixing of the new moon ; of angels ; that
there is no distinction of Persons in the Deity,
nor conjunction of the human nature with the
divine, &c. Closely resembling this is a work
entitled 'a book sufficing to those who satisfy
the knowledge of the book of God,' by Muhadhdhib
ad-Din Yûsuf Ibn Salâmah Ibn Yûsuf al-'Askarî,
commenced in A.D. 1041 ; it treats of the office
of the priest, of purifications, of tithes, usury, &c.,
thus corresponding to the Mishneh Thorah of
Maimonides[1].

Another work by the same Abu-l-Hasan has
come down to us, containing long and somewhat
uninteresting disquisitions in proof of a future life,
with arguments drawn from the Pentateuch[2].

In the same class must be included an 'abridg-

---

[1] *Brit. Mus. Add. MS.* 19656. (2); title كتاب الكافي لمن كان
مهذب الدين يوسف بن سلامة بن by بالمعرفة لكتاب الله موالي
يوسف العسكري. The commentator Ibrahim mentioned above
quotes him in proof of the reason why for a stolen ox fivefold,
for a lamb fourfold should be restored. *Zeitschr. d. D. M. G.*
11, 569.

[2] *Bodl. MS. Hunt.* 350. (1); title كتاب المعاد.

ment of the Mosaic Law according to the Samaritans,' by Abu-l-Farag Ibn Isḥaq Ibn Kuthâr [1], a
work occupied in scholastic questions of the Kalâm ;
everything according to it is to be decided by
means of logic applied to the Law. The author
knows the 613 precepts, 248 of which, equalling
the limbs in number, are positive in their character,
while the 365 corresponding to the days of the
solar year are prohibitory ; like the Rabbanites
he distinguishes between local and temporary commands and such as are of universal application.

By one of the same family, in all probability,
is the 'book of penitence,' a work in which are
collected together such passages of the Pentateuch
as relate to repentance and a reformation of morals,
with observations thereupon by the author himself

---

[1] *Paris, Bibl. Nat. ancien fonds,* 5, *Peiresc.* His name is
نفيس الدين ابو الفرج ابن أُسَعى ابن كثار (not كثار, see *Zeitschr.*
*d. D. M. G.* xxii. 532–538, where will be found a quotation from
this or a similar work given by Ibrahim the commentator on
the meanings of מום and פו, אסא and כבד ; his view is also mentioned as to the increase of the Israelites in Egypt and with
reference to Moses' staff. It is probable that he wrote a commentary also). The كلام ('word,' 'discourse,') was a dogmatic
or scholastic philosophy which originated among Mohammedans
in the second century of the Higra : so called either because it
first was occupied with questions with regard to the divine
'word' addressed to the prophets, or because it is equivalent to
*mantiq* or logic. Cf. Munk, *Mélanges de Philosophie Juive et
Arabe,* p. 311; *Guide des égarés,* i. 335, note 2.

and others of his countrymen[1]. In the same MS.
are other works of miscellaneous character: one
treating of the nature of God and man and the
worship due to the former by arguments drawn
from the Pentateuch, its authorship is ascribed to
the Sadaqa Ben Mangâ Ben Sadaqa mentioned
above[2]: questions and answers, with interpretations of the Pentateuch[3]: and in the same work
allusion is made to the 'special enactments of the
holy Law' by Muwaffaq ad-Din al-Gahbadh[4]: the
list may be closed by the mention of a treatise
on the second exile by Ghazâl Ibn ad-Duwaik,
followed by two homilies by Sâliḥ Ibn al-Marḥûm
Surûr Ibn Sadaqa and by Abû Sa'ïd[5].

The liturgical remains of the Samaritans are
very extensive. They consist of prayers and
hymns arranged in twelve parts for use on
sabbaths and festivals throughout the year, and

---

[1] *Amst. MS.* xxvii. p. 304: ابو للحسن ابن by كتاب التورية
. غنائم بن للحكيم النفيس ابن كثار

[2] He is here named موفّق الدين صدقة : Ibn Abī Oṣaibi'a as-
signs two works to him, the كتاب الاعتقاد, or 'book of faith,'
which may possibly be the present MS. (*Amst.* xxvii. p. 223),
and a مقالة في التوحيد وسمها يكتاب الكنزلي الفوز, or 'treatise
on religion,' surnamed 'the treasure which concerns deliverance.'

[3] *Ibid.* p. 297.

[4] *Ibid.* p. 310: موفّق الدين للهبذ : not the same as the Muwaffaq
ad-Dîn mentioned above, p. 139: Juynboll, *Comment.* p. 60.

[5] *Journ. Asiat.* (1869), p. 458: المقالة الثانية تبون الدولة
.الثانية تاليف الشيخ غزال بن الدريلة

also for special occasions, such as circumcisions,
marriages, and funerals. Several of the former
have been published by Heidenheim from the
rich stores of the British Museum : the following,
occurring at the end of the 'Litany of Marqah,'
may serve as a specimen. 'Lord, for the sake of
the three perfect ones, of Joseph the interpreter
of dreams, of Moses chief of the prophets, of the
priests, the masters of the priests, of the Thorah,
most sacred of books, of Mount Garizim, the
everlasting hill, of the hosts of angels—destroy
the enemy and foe, graciously receive our prayers,
O Everlasting, grant us relief from these troubles,
open to us the treasure of heaven[1].'

The hymns of the Samaritans, their sole poetical
inheritance, are of little devotional or literary merit,
nor does there seem good reason for ascribing any
very great antiquity to them, however august and
remote may be the parentage assigned to them.
The earliest pieces, so we are informed, were sung
by the angels on the occasion of the completion
of the tabernacle and the death of Aaron, others

[1] Heidenheim, ii. 487. The British Museum possesses nineteen
volumes of prayers and hymns, besides the fragments of liturgies
from Damascus published by Gesenius in his 'Carmina Samaritana,' and edited again by Kirchheim in the 'Karme Shomeron:'
three 'prayers of Moses and Joshua' and five 'prayers of the
angels' (from the 'Defter') are printed in Petermann's *Gram-
matica Samaritana* (1873), p. 18 sq.

are ascribed to Marqah and Amram Dari who lived some time B.C., others again to Abisha in the thirteenth century. The present Samaritans have two collections, which they call Durrân ('string of pearls') and Defter ('book'), the latter comprising the former, the arrangement of which they ascribe to the above-mentioned Amram Dari[1]. The language in which they are written varies; some are in almost classical Hebrew, others in a dialect resembling that of the Targum but with peculiarities, containing an admixture of Arabisms and Hebraisms: to some a translation in Arabic tinged with Hebrew, Aramaean, and Samaritan is appended. The metre also differs considerably; some stanzas are arranged in distichs, others in tristichs, others again in tetrastichs; some poems are alphabetical, in others the verses rhyme; the rhythm also varies, that in use among both Arabs and Syrians being employed. From the general style of their composition and the fact that many of the authors bear Arabic names it is most probable that they were mostly written at a time subsequent to the Mohammedan invasion, in some cases long after it[2].

---

[1] Petermann in Herzog, xiii. 376.

[2] For instance, the metre employed in Marqah's Paschal hymn (Heidenheim, iii. 96) does not seem to have been known before the ninth century A.D.: see Geiger in *Zeitschr. d. D. M. G.* xxii. 534. Some of the titles of the pieces published by Heiden-

The Samaritans, following the example of the ancient Jews, calculate their year by the lunar months, and, in order to bring it into harmony with the solar year and the revolution of the seasons upon which their feasts depend, are accustomed each year to intercalate a thirteenth lunar month. The arrangement of this, and also the authoritative fixing of the exact moment at which the new moon may be considered to have appeared, upon which depended the festival at the beginning of each month, were among the Jews

---

heim may be of interest : e. g. (i. 279, 408) titles of the prayers to be used throughout the year : one festival with two supplicatory hymns (i. 421) : drama of the priest Abiscba (ii. 80), who sees Moses on mount Garizim and is taken by him to visit heaven and Eden : the prayer of Ab Gelogah (ii. 213) : passover hymns of Phineas and Eleazar (iii. 94) : a passover hymn (iii. 474) containing an invocation of the Holy Spirit : a prayer of Marqah (iv. 237), and of Amram (ibid. 243) : three prayers of Amram (iv. 390), one ending with the Mohammedan sentence 'there is only one God :' a prayer (ibid. 545) in which are described the order and ministry of the angels and the motions of the twelve planets, these being likened to the twelve tribes of Israel. There is a volume of prayers and hymns in the Paris Bibl. Nat., numbered ancien fonds, 4, Peiresc, apparently of the fifteenth century, and a liturgical MS. numbered Add. MS. 334, in the Univ. Library, Cambridge, of which the title has been kindly communicated to me by Mr. Bensly the Sub-Librarian. It is שׁיִיה, הַחֵלֶק, הָרְבִיעִי. | אֲמֹוּת יְדֵי. הַשֻּׁבְעֹות. | קַ. מִיסֵר. It is רַבְעִגִים. | הַקַּקִים. לָכֶם. | רַצֵן. יְחֹת, | וְסַלַּיחְתֹו | אָמֵן | אָמֵן | dated A. H. 1185 = A. D. 1771.

1

left in the hands of the high-priest for the time
being, and formed, as we have seen before, a
fruitful source of dispute between the rival factions
of Pharisees and Sadducees[1]. Till long after the
captivity of Babylon it is probable that actual
observation and not calculation of the appearance
of the new moon was practised by the Jews[2].
The Samaritans, as has been already remarked[3],
claim to possess astronomical tables drawn up by
the great-grandson of Aaron himself, and every
six months the high-priest draws up a calendar
for the use of the congregation. Scaliger published two such, and De Sacy has also edited one
with a translation[4]: several more MSS. of the kind
have found their way to Europe, one written (A.H.
1164=) A.D. 1750, another commencing with 574
of the Jezdegird era (=A.D. 1204), written (A.H.
1101=) A.D. 1689; a third, which calculates also
according to the Jezdegird era, dated (A.H. 1137=)
A.D. 1724[5]: St. Petersburg also possesses several
specimens[6].

In grammar and lexicography the Samaritans
have nothing of much value to shew. Possessed
of little learning themselves and living secluded

[1] See above, p. 38.
[2] De Sacy, *Not. et Extr.* xii. p. 34.
[3] See above, p. 125.    [4] *Op. cit.* pp. 135, 153.
[5] See *Journ. Asiat.* (1869), pp. 467, 468.
[6] See below, *App.* I. 7.

from their neighbours, enclosed in their limited
circle of ideas, they did not imitate the Jews in
taking advantage of any opportunity of self-
improvement which offered itself to them. The
latter, as soon as ever the system of vowel points
had been introduced among the Syrians and Arabs,
eagerly took it up and for centuries patiently toiled
at the work of improving and adapting it to
Hebrew; then, dissatisfied with the results of
their labour in the Assyrian punctuation, threw
it over and took up the one now in use, the
Palestinian, in its place. Whatever fault may
be found with minute details of the system,
still the warmest thanks of scholars are due to
those who elaborated it with so much patience
and skill for having thus rendered Hebrew grammar possible. The Samaritans attempted nothing
of the kind, but trusted entirely to tradition for
the pronunciation of their Hebrew Scriptures; it
consequently must have deteriorated and become
more uncertain from age to age under the influence
of the living Aramaean and Arabic with which it
had to cope. Thus matters went on till the
tenth or eleventh century, when the literary
activity of the Arabs communicated itself at last
even to the sluggish spirit of the Samaritans,
and they set about enquiring into and settling
the laws of Hebrew grammar. But it was then
too late: the fatal bar of a corrupt and uncertain

pronunciation met them at the outset and rendered all their efforts fruitless [1].

The truth of these remarks will be seen by an examination of three grammatical treatises of Samaritan authorship which have been published from a MS. at Amsterdam [2]. The first of the three [3] is an extract made by the high-priest Eleazar, the son of Phinehas the son of Joseph, probably about 1400 A.D., from the second, a grammar [4] by Abû Ishaq Ibrahîm Ben Farag Ben Mârûth, surnamed Shams al-Hukamâî, whose name has already occurred above in connection with his celebrated pupil Muhadhdhib ad-Din; the third is a tract by Abû Saîd, probably the famous commentator of that name, intended to correct the faults of pronunciation prevalent in his time [5]. They are built entirely on the philological views of Arabic grammarians, some sections, such as those on transitive and intransitive verbs, being copied word for word from their works, but the writers have not proved themselves such apt scholars as their Jewish brethren. From their want of a system of punctuation, their varying orthography,

---

[1] Cf. Geiger in *Zeitschr. d. D. M. G.* xvii. 718.

[2] By Nöldeke in *Gotting. Nachrichten* (1862), pp. 337, 385.

[3] المقدّمة في كتاب التوطئة: they are from the *Amst. MS.* xxvii. mentioned above, pp. 1—220.

[4] Title كتاب التوطئة في نحو اللغة العبرانيّة.

[5] Title قوانين المقرا.

and the complete or partial disappearance from
their language of sounds still written in Hebrew,
they are especially uncertain in the parts of
grammar concerned with these particulars; the
arrangement also of the second of these tracts is
very unskilful, needlessly full in some parts, defec-
tive in others [1]. Old Samaritan blunders, which
had before been pointed out by Jewish opponents,
recur again in Abû Sa'îd, as for instance the
mistaking of ה local for a post-positive article;
he also misunderstands the ה of the Hiphil, taking
it for a strengthening particle. Transcriptions of
Hebrew words into Arabic, shewing the Samaritan
pronunciation of the eleventh century, will be found
in the anonymous commentary quoted above [2].
The commentator Ibrahim, who has been quoted
above, does not appear to have made any advance
beyond the views held by his countrymen, as far
as one may judge from the grammatical views
expressed in his work [3].

---

[1] E. g. on account of the irregularities of לקה a separate
chapter is devoted to verbs פ״ל: in some cases the vowels are
expressed by letters as הבומיר, but generally by the three
Arabic vowels which are naturally unsuited to express the
niceties of punctuation: a distinction is sometimes made between great (֖ and ֜) and little (-) fatḥa, that between long and
short vowels is generally overlooked, as also between full and
half-vowels. [2] See above, p. 134.
[3] See the extracts by Geiger in *Zeitschr. d. D. M. G.* xvii.
723-725.

So much for the grammatical acquirements of the Samaritans seven or eight centuries ago. Their present system of pronunciation has been made the subject of an elaborate enquiry by Professor Petermann, who has transcribed the whole book of Genesis after the manner in which it is now read in the synagogue of Nablus, together with a Hebrew grammar embodying the views of the present Samaritans on the subject[1]. It is possible that in some points the system now in vogue among them may be an improvement upon that invented by the Masoretes[2], but at this period of time it is naturally more difficult (or rather impossible) to decide even than in the days of Abû Sa'îd how much of the system is due to genuine tradition and how much to Syrian and Arabian influence; the enquiry is consequently not of much practical value[3].

In the matter of lexicography there is little information to give. Of dictionaries proper none have as yet come to light: at Paris there is a concordance of forms occurring in the Scriptures with the corresponding Arabic and Samaritan word in parallel columns, and a similar one is

---

[1] Published in *Abhandl. für d. Kunde d. Morgenlandes herausg. von d. D. M. G.* (1868), Bd. v. Th. 1.

[2] Cf. Nöldeke in *Götting. Nachrichten* (1868), p. 485 sq.

[3] Cf. Derenbourg in Cahen's *Archives Israel.* xvi. 53.

preserved at Cambridge, in which however the
Samaritan equivalent is omitted [1].

With this account of the literature of the Samaritans my task is concluded. In the notes ac-
companying the foregoing sketch reference has
been made to all the important works I have met
with bearing on the subjects discussed, but I have
not thought it either necessary or desirable to
swell the volume by the mention of such literature
as has now been superseded by better works, which

---

[1] *Bibl. Nat., ancien fonds, 6, Peirax*, it is dated A.D. 1476;
the Bodleian MS., numbered *Bodl. Or.* 466, is a copy of it : the
Cambridge MS. is in the library of Christ's College : it, is dated
(A.H. 1188=) A.D. 1774, its title is كتاب الترجمان and it was
arranged by the priest Phinehas. It is an independent com-
pilation, but nearly corresponds with the Paris MS.: e. g. in the
former are found זרים פאסדין, זרים מאלבן, זרים זאנין; in the
latter זרה פסיד, זרים מאלף, זנה ואזיה. See also below, *App.* L v.

There is a very vague notice of the MSS. still preserved at
Nablus given by Löwe in the *Allg. Zeit. d. Judenthums*, 1839,
No. 47 (see above, p. 41). In Mills' *Nablus*, p. 317, is to be
found a rough list drawn up by the priest Amram. He there
mentions, in addition to the works described in the text, (1)
commentaries (شرح) on the Law, in Hebrew with Arabic translations, by Marqah (termed ' El-Amir,' الأمير, אלאמיר), Ibrahim
el Kaisi, Ghazāl ibn ad-Duwaik, Musalem el Murjam (المرحوم),
Ghazāl al Matri, El Hhabr (الحبر) Ya'qûb; (2) various 'orders'
(ترتيب) of prayers in Hebrew for the various festivals; (3)
miscellaneous works, including one on marriage (المسائل في النكاح),
and another on inheritance (كتاب الميراث) by Abū-l-Barakāt; an
explanation of the feasts entitled رسالة اخبار اسرائيل by the

were moreover written at a time when fuller information was obtainable than by preceding
authors; references however to the earlier literature will be discovered by any one interested in
the subject by turning to the books quoted by me[1].
In the two appendices that follow will be found,
i. an interesting description of the Firkowitsch
Collection of Samaritan MSS., recently added to
the Imperial Library of St. Petersburg, with which
I have been kindly supplied by Dr. Harkavy; and
ii. a translation of the Massekheth Kuthim, an
important Talmudical tract written probably in
the second century A.D.

---

priest Eleazar, and a book of 'direction' for the same, called
الرشاد الاهداء, by Ibrahim el Ahi; an anonymous history of the
Samaritans (تاريخ); and, lastly, a treatise on the astronomical
work الحساب, חשבון, which is described above (p. 115) as
attributed to Adam.

[1] See also the list in Zenker, *Bibl. Orient.* (1861), ii. 149, 150.

# APPENDIX I.

## The Collection of Samaritan MSS. at St. Petersburg.

IN the year 1870 the Russian Minister of Public Worship purchased from the well-known Karaite traveller and archaeologist Abraham Firkowitsch his collection of Samaritan MSS. for the Imperial Library of St. Petersburg. It consists almost exclusively of fragments, this circumstance arising from the fact that the collector during his stay in Nablus and Egypt completely ransacked the Samaritan Genizoth[1] (that is to say, the garrets and cellars of the synagogues whither their worn-out books were conveyed), thus acquiring several fragments of Samaritan Pentateuch rolls—none of which have before this, to

---

[1] The word גניזה in Hebrew is equivalent to the Samaritan מסמרה, as seems to be proved by an epigraph quoted by Rosen (Zeitsch. d. D. M. G. 1864, p. 588); as however he has misunderstood it, I give it here with a new translation: הזה התורה הקדושה שנה תשט מאות ושמנה ותשעים שנה למסלכות בני ישראל היתה לנו מסמרה לט ארון ומסמרה אוקרת את אחמצית מן את וסלקת אלי אלא מן מסמרה מן אש על יומי רבנא בבא חטן חנדול ונסיא אברחם, that is to say, 'This Holy Law was A.H. 598 in the Mafamra, in a chest: the Mafamra caught fire, but the Law was preserved from fire by passing out of it through the window; (אלף accordingly must not, with Rosen, be translated 'oak,' but be taken for אלה, a various reading for the same word in Gen. viii. 6): this happened in the days of our lord Baba the high-priest and prince of Abraham.'

the writer's knowledge, ever reached Europe—about 6000 parchment and paper leaves from various Pentateuch MSS. written in the shape of books, several fragments of commentaries on the Bible, liturgical, grammatical, and lexicographical works, and lastly a number of marriage-contracts. The writer of the present notice received directions from the Minister to make a complete catalogue of the collection, and the first portion of it is already in print; the MSS. shall now be briefly described in general terms.

A collection such as the present could on account of its fragmentary character hardly have claimed any particular attention on the part of the learned world had it contained another and better known literature. It is different however when the literary remains of a people are concerned whose existence, though an unimportant one, extends over a historical past comprising thousands of years, and who now are threatened with extinction; a people moreover whose inner life and intellectual activity, though they were early developed, have hitherto remained almost unknown. Every fragment accordingly, however slight it may be, which belongs to the literature of such a people has a value of its own, as being capable of giving information on many points which interest the learned world, especially too at a time when so great activity is being displayed in the field of Semitic studies, and an attempt made to follow the example of Aryan scholars by enquiring more closely into separate peoples and stems, and thus gradually to gain an idea of the whole Semitic race.

In describing the collection, the existing divisions have been preserved; the first accordingly will consist of—

i. Fragments belonging to twenty-seven parchment Pentateuch rolls. None of this kind, as has been already remarked, have hitherto been discovered in any European library, all the existing ones being in the shape of books; the reason of this appears to be that the Samaritans hold such rolls as especially sacred from their being intended for use in the synagogue, and so will part with them for no sum, however large, to those of another faith. Accordingly in 1811 the high-priest Salameh ben Tobiah made answer as follows to the request received in a letter from the well-known senator Abbé Grégoire, that he would sell him two Pentateuchs; 'As to your request that we would send you the holy book of the Law, we could only do so if ye were Samaritans like us, and had like us observed the ordinances prescribed to you [1].' As however the Samaritans had already frequently sold MSS. of the Pentateuch (for instance, to Pietro della Valle and Huntington in the seventeenth century), this 'non possumus' of the high-priest must refer to rolls used in the synagogue.

Be this as it may, these fragments have been till now the only ones known in Europe, and so they are of considerable importance to us for explaining to us how the Samaritans write their sacred Law for use in Divine worship. Unfortunately, as might have been guessed from the place where they were found, they are for the most part in very bad condition; and as Samaritan palaeography is not yet in a condition to decide with certainty upon the age of an undated MS., it is only such as contain dated epigraphs whose age can be without doubt ascertained. Only six of the fragments contain such notices, and only three of this number have their dates perfect; one (no. 4) was written (A.H. 599=) 1202-3, another (no. 10) in (A.H. 605=)

---

[1] De Sacy, *Not. et Extr.* xii. 25, 105, 121. So Robinson, *Palestine* (1867), iii. 130.

1208-9, the third (no. 15) in (A.H. 808=) 1405: it is however quite certain that several other fragments in the collection belong to a much earlier age.

It is interesting to notice the way in which the Samaritans insert these epigraphs in their Pentateuchs. For this purpose the column of text in the roll or page of the book is divided down the middle by two perpendicular lines, the interval between the lines being left vacant, except for the insertion of such letters from the text as serve the writer to compose the epigraph. For instance, the first word in general will be אני, or אנה, signifying 'I:' the writer will wait till an א presents itself in or near the middle of a line of text, he sets this in the space intervening between the two lines and goes on with his writing till he reaches a נ in the middle of a line, this he sets in the same space, doing the like with י or ה, and so on to the end of the epigraph, which is thus made to extend over several columns or pages without a single letter being added to the text of the Pentateuch, which thus itself, so to speak, supplies the materials for a memorial both of the writer and of the person who ordered the MS. to be written.    *    *    *    *    *    *

Among the fragments of about 300 Pentateuch MSS. written on parchment or paper are to be found the oldest Samaritan MSS. known in Europe, viz. of A.H. 571 and 577, corresponding to 1176-7 and 1181-2; the dated ones however are not by any means the oldest, and it may without exaggeration be asserted, if one may judge from the writing and appearance of the MSS., that some go back to the eleventh or tenth century, if not even further. The collection offers the richest spoil for Samaritan palaeography which is to be met with, not in Europe only, but throughout the world, Firkowitsch having completely stripped the only archives belonging to the people, the above-mentioned Genizoth[1].

ii. The collection contains also many fragments of the Samaritan-Arabic translation, as well as of the Samaritan

[1] The only palæographical note known to me in Samaritan literature is an epigraph at the end of a Bodleian MS. (*Hunt.* 14), which reads thus, هذا حروف العبراني بالخط المجلس القديم اثني وعشرين حرف ا'ب': &c.: then follows the usual alphabet, called by Gesenius (*Mon. Phoen.* tab. 3) 'letters of the MSS.;' by Juynboll (*Book of Joshua*) 'larger letters.' خط المجلس must be taken in the sense of 'official,' or 'settled,' 'abiding,' so 'square' writing. وهذا ايضا حروب العبراني بالخط الطرش اثني وعشرين حرب ا'ب'ج'د, &c.: (here follow the characters called by Gesenius the 'Gotha' letters, by Juynboll 'ordinary.' خط الطرش I take in the sense of טרש as used in the *Bab. Baba Kama*, f. 98, and explained in the *Aruch*, 'erased,' 'unclear' writing: according to Arabic lexicons طرس signifies to renovate faint writing). There is also an allusion to Samaritan writing in an epigraph inserted at the beginning of Deuteronomy in the Bodl. MS. *Pocock*, 5: אנה אב עזי בן אב קיתי בר מביה בן רשח כתבתי הדה ארהותה קרישתה לארבעתה וקיחה תבתבה חיטבחה ומטעניה אב עזי בר מטניה עבר יהוה בר אב חזסה ברשטה מדיטה ובללתי אתה ביזח החנה שנח א' וכ' ח' פ' לישמעל היא מלוי ג' ארח כתבת אורה את יהוה על כן אחטללח יסלחה מאלטה לבנים תני בנים אמן אמן. The words ברשטה מדיטה may mean 'tasteful,' 'beautiful' writing, or may signify a particular style. I have fully explained the expression ארח . ג מלוי ויא and the like in my catalogue, pp. 49, 50. I forgot to mention in the text that our Pentateuch fragments are also of great value for the Samaritan text, as, quite by chance and without searching for them, I have discovered a great number of variations from the Samaritan text of the Polyglotts which are also unmarked by Kennicott. Many of these I mention in my catalogue, the rest I keep for a special work.

Targum, with the restoration of which the learned are now
so much occupied; for instance, Petermann and Geiger in
Berlin, Kohn in Pesth, Brüll in Frankfurt-am-Main, &c.[1]

iii. Another division contains smaller or greater portions
of several commentaries on the Pentateuch. These are

---

[1] I add in this place a collation of some passages in the
Targum edited by Mr. Nutt with a fragment to which I have
not yet given a number, and which I accordingly designate by
the provisional number put on it by Firkowitsch, ii. 29.

| | Nutt. | | F. ii. 29. |
|---|---|---|---|
| Num. xxviii. 9. | למנח בסיס | : | מנחא בדמא |
| | ונסכיז | : | ונסכה |
| 10. | שבת משבה | : | [שב]תא בשבתא |
| | תסכידן | : | תסוכיהן |
| 11. | וכראשי | : | ובריש |
| | אמרין | : | אמרין |
| 12. (twice) | בסיס | : | בסימא |
| | לפר חד | : | לפרח אחדה |
| | לדכר חר | : | לדכרא אחדה |
| 13. | כסיס | : | בסימא |
| | לאמדי חד | : | לרכרא אחדה |
| 14. | ונסכיהן | ı | ונסכידן |
| | איתא | : | ויתה |
| | לפר חר | : | לפרח אחדה |
| | איתא לדכר ותבתותה | : | ויתא לרכרח דבכתא |
| | איתה לאמחר חד | : | ויתא לאמרח אחדה |
| | בחרחותה | : | בחרחתה |
| 15. | עפ | : | על |
| | תסכיהן | : | תסוכיהן |
| 16. | בארבעה עפר | : | בארבעסר |
| 17. | הך | ı | הרגן |
| | Here is a lacuna. | | |
| 24. | רתוה | : | רעוח |

of the greatest importance for a knowledge of the religious and moral views of the Samaritans, their relations with those of another creed, and their theory of the universe; these also possess especial value in the general dearth of their literature as frequently citing fragments of ancient theological, philosophical, poetical, and other works [1].

| | | |
|---|---|---|
| Num. xxviii. 24. תסכידן | : | ונסוכידן |
| 25. פלסן | : | פלחן |
| 26. פלסן | : | פלחן |
| 27. רהזח | : | רעוח |
| אסהדין | : | אמרין |
| 28. לפר חד | : | לפחה אחדה |
| לדכר חד | : | לדכרה אחדה |
| 29. לאמהר חד | : | לאמרה אחדה |
| אמהריה | : | אמריה |
| 31. ונסביהן | : | תסוכידן |
| xxix. r. פלסן | : | פלחן |
| xxxi. 51. סובד | : | דעוובר |
| 52. דהל | : | [ד מהק]אין |
| 54. ואיתו | : | האעל |
| xxxii. 1. וקנין סני | : | וקניאן סוי |
| קין | : | קניאן |
| 2. לנסיד | : | ולנסאי |
| 3. ובען | : | ובתן |
| 4. קין | : | קניאן |
| 5. אט(תקט)(נג) | : | אסחכזגה |
| חובדתן | : | תעברנו |
| 6. אחיבן ייסלק | : | רא אחיבן יישלק |
| 7. עבר | : | רמעבר |
| 8. א]כן[ | : | ברתן |
| 9. תבאלה | : | אבלח |

[1] Especially interesting are the quotations from earlier writings or poetical productions in the Aramaic dialect. I

iv. To the same class belong fragments of Samaritan law-books; these are very rarely to be found in Europe [1].

---

quote some passages from MS. F. iii. 2, a fragment of a Midrash-like commentary on the Pentateuch:

(١) وبيد ذلك القول المنسوب الي مرقه او ولده ننح رضي الله
عنهما اذ بقول بيّن مسعفن مهو وبهو بريح رسّم אלהים אמנה
חלק מנח בריאן מליח הוה משלח לנו מי תתו ובהו אנך מעחרן
מעינך בראך. Marqa and his son Nana were, as is well known,
the earliest writers of hymns among the Samaritans. The first
word בּין is doubtful, can it be for כּאנך ? The remainder is
plain enough.

(٢) ما يدل علي ذلك قول (يعني قول مرقه) הות מלחת נפקה
מסמך קרישה כפסח רמלכה חיח וקעישה תחחח לנו חללת עלאה
ונחחת לנו חלמה רסיח וברקיח רקיח חלה לנו אבחה וכסקה מנו
חשכה תקחה לנו מן חללת הלכתל. A person might say he had
a bit of the Sohar before him. The phrase חלמה רסיח is important for the interpretation of בחלימ in the Samaritan Targum (Gen. xli. 2), as it shews that the latter word is no mere
copy of the Hebrew בְּאֵמ as many people supposed. Moreover
Petermann in his edition has not the word in question.

(٣) ومما يويد ذلك ما ينسوب [sic] الى مرقه او غيره من السلف
الشريف رضوان الله عليهم في قول اهنو כתבה רבה اذ بقول رضي
الله عنه سمח ואלהותה כתבה על רישה סם מסח כתבה בעקובה
אלהים ברא וכסה קעם על ים נקם • • • • • • • I have also collected fragments of philosophical works written in the Samaritan
dialect, the publication of which I reserve for myself.

[1] Among the law-books are some fragments written in Arabic,
but in Samaritan characters, e. g. F. iv. 18; here is a specimen:

‏• באב אלחמהיד חלחח ומא יחעלק בהמא •

אלמהארה מענמחא אחאלח אלננם הי ענרנא בקסמן באלמא ואלנור
מנהא מא יחחץ באחזהמא פטלני אן אלסיאה אלתי יגי אלחמהיד
ברא כתה מא אלסמא ומא אלבחר ומא אלנחד ומא אלחלג ומא
אלביד ומא אלעקן ואלמסיה עלי אר[נ]זה אקסאם מאצר וסמחד עיד

v. The fifth division contains fragments of grammatical
works and of Hebrew-Arabic dictionaries, or Tardescheman's (Interpreters), as they are termed by Samaritans
and Arabs. These last are of so much greater importance,
because in the only example of such a dictionary hitherto
known to exist[1], that preserved in Paris[2], three letters
at the commencement (א, ב, and half ג) are missing,
and now fortunately may be supplied from the present
fragments[3].  *  *  *  *  *  *

---

סכיחה הו אלמא אלסמלק והאהר מסהר הו אלמראו [?] אליסיר
אלסמם וסאהר עיר מסהר הו אלמא אלסתתכסל ואלמחעיר במא
חאלסה מן אלאהיא אלסאהרה וסא נגם הו אלרי הלה מיה נואסא
הו אלרי יסכם עלי אלנואסכה בקלתה נסחגיר האקסאם אלסאהרה
חלאהה רחיח הביסה ומבילה מסן אלסמאואת מא ילם חמהיה:
באלחלאהה הסהא מא ילם באתנתאן וסהא מא ילם באאחרה פכם:
מאלרי ילם באאחרה מחל סרי לילה וכבבח ועע רחיח חאלרי באתנתאן
מחל חערעח חוב אלרי באלתלאהה מחל סבוא מח &c.

[1] [But see above, p. 151.  J. W. N.]
[2] [See above, p. 151.  J. W. N.]
[3] These dictionaries are termed in Samaritan מלץ, in Arabic
ترجمان: there are six fragments in the collection; viz.

(1) F. v. 7; 21 leaves, from אביך to בלי.
(2) F. v. 7; 9 leaves, from ארבו to אלהים.
(3) F. v. 8; 46 leaves, from אב to עסב.
(4) F. v. 9; 33 leaves, from אביסע to רסח.
(5) F. v. 10; 1 leaf, from אביך to אדני.
(6) F. v. 10; 9 leaves, from נפש to עלה.

The only copy which has the beginning perfect has the following inscription on the title-page: بسم الله الرحمن الرحيم
هذا [sic] كتاب ملص من تاليف سيدنا مكهن حرب فينحس
رعوا بهمو عليم امن بعمل مشد هناس امن ودلك تعريب للدي [؟] الي
جميع الناس [؟] طالب والله مرالموفق لجميع ما فيه صواب وحسبي
الله ونعم الوكيل ولا حول ولا قوا الا بالله العلي العظيم ٢.

vi. In this class are works containing historical matter, not only the already edited Book of Joshua and Annals of Abulfath, but such as have never yet appeared ; for instance, fabulous tales of the birth and death of Moses[1].

vii. To this division belong several astronomical works, some entire, some imperfect. These are unique of their kind, for as far as the present writer knows, no public library in Europe has any such to shew[2]; from them alone however can we discover how the Samaritans reckon their time, arrange their feast-days, &c. Two eras are employed by them, one dating from the entry of the Israelites into Canaan, and the other from the Persian king Jezdegird: two more are also used, most frequently the Mohammedan, and, much less often in epigraphs, the Creation of the World; as for instance in the epigraph of the Pentateuch numbered *Add. MS.* 22369 in the British

---

At the end of נם is the following epigraph :

كان التمام من نسخ نصف دلله الترجمان العبراني لي عمريت
نهار الاربعا المبارك م شهر صفر لخير سنت (مد) كمانية وخمسون
ومايه والف على يد افقر العباد العبير للفقر المسكين الراجى
غفران لخطيا والذنوب الولد سوق غزال ابن المرحوم اسماق ابن
المرحوم ابراهيم ابن اسعق ابن سدنة ابن غزال مكهن هلوى
بشكم غفر اللذ تعالى لة ولوالدية ثم لمن علمه واحسن عليه لم
لجميع قهل بشرال حجوديم لهرهريزيم بيت ال امن امن.

From the first epigraph we see that the author of the Meliz was called Phinehas, but this gives us no information as to the date of its composition, as there have been very many Samaritan high-priests of this name. I reserve to myself the supplying of full information with regard to these fragments and the Paris MS.

[1] [See above, p. 132. J. W. N.]
[2] [For similar works, see above, p. 146. J. W. N.]

Museum. Calendars also for a single year, giving the portions which are to be read each Sabbath from the books of
Moses, are to be found in the collection [1].

viii. This part consists of very varied fragments which
have not yet been carefully examined, but it may be
mentioned that it contains a good deal relating to medi-

---

[1] [See above, p. 75. J. W. N.] The epigraph in *Brit. Mus.
Add. MS.* 22369 is written in after the manner described above
in p. 156. As this is almost the only instance, as far as I know,
in which the three eras are put together, I give the passage. It
commences at Deut. xv, and runs thus: אני אברהם בד אבי
מען בר אבי אסקר בן אב חסדה בן אבי עלוה חנדי חבתב כתבתי
זאת התורה הקדושה לנפשי והי שמי תורה כתב הבללת סנת אמר
וסדים וסבע מאות סנה לממלכות יסמאל היא סנת שלסת אלפים
חמסה וסלסים סנה לצאת בני יסראל ממצרים היא סנת ח: אלפים
10 .וסבע מאות וסגים וסמנים סנה לבריאת עלם אודי את דוה.
the astronomical tables the eras mentioned are סני העקר למיסב
שני העקר לידורד lmd בני יסראל ארץ בגע. The tables themselves
are called in the epigraph הסדיסב העברי.(as at the beginning of
Neubauer's chronicle): single technical expressions are סנ'לים;
סבביס; סנזח ,סנים; רסח ,רקים; סבידוח; רמח; רחים;
הלכח (תך הלכח or); מסם ומצרף, מסם הצדק, מסם צדיקות; כנוח
הלסח סנלוח; סנלוח היוח בקבוח הנגסות (חנמדות or) והחרסים;
הלבח ראס התגן בקבוח מנגסות החרסים; היח ביסם וחסעות
דמן זוהה לסהסה כל יוח זמן אזור; הלכח ראס התגן ביסים והסעות
סרוח וחסבנה דסהסה סן; והקדיום מחוסא ד: חלקים סן ס: חלק
סרוח וחסבנה; חוין חסרי וכל סמנה תרסיים סנה מעזר מסרי סן ריס
סרנבם; חזריח סן סיכח וכל חסע עסר סנח מעזר מסרי סן ריס
רקי נלנל תנינה צדר כמח רקי נלנל זריח ומח אגן ואקרסן לעו תרן
וסד אצמסד לוא רקי נלנל תנינה יסתבה בארית רבן; ומלן תעסד
דמה בתוך חבמה ברא. The names of the twelve signs of the
zodiac are עקרב; סיח; סבלה; אדיה; סרסן; נוא; סוד; כסב;
קסח; גד; רלו; חגן; partly, it will be observed, Hebrew, and
partly Arabic.

m 2

cine, though it is doubtful whether all belongs to Samaritan authors. Some fragments of historical works have also found their way by mistake into this division.

ix. In this are contained, according to a rough list made of them, fragments of 276 MSS. of a liturgical character, written on 6300 leaves, partly composed in Arabic also. The knowledge of Aramaic idioms in general, and of the Samaritan dialect in particular, gained from the small collection of hymns published by Gesenius and Heidenheim, makes one long to see the whole cycle of Samaritan hymns and prayers in print, at all events such as are composed in Aramaean; then only, when this is done, will it be possible to bring out a Samaritan dictionary worthy of the name. The said cycle consists of at least twelve quarto volumes, of which the twelfth is contained in *Add. MS.* 19019 belonging to the British Museum ; should the various parts which are now dispersed among all the libraries of Europe—Rome, Paris, London, Oxford, Berlin, Gotha—ever be united, still it will never be possible from them to make up (auftreiben) a perfect copy. By means however of the vast number of fragments belonging to the St. Petersburg collection one may hope to fill up these lacunae, and so make an edition of the whole cycle possible ; though this cannot be decided with certainty till these fragments have been more carefully examined and collated with those of other European libraries [1].

---

[1] A very imperfect idea will be gained of the liturgical hymnology of the Samaritans from a study only of the specimens published by Gesenius, Heidenheim, and quite lately by Petermann. Some that have never been edited are far from heavy, and not without a certain poetical vigour. The following is from *Cod. Firkowitsch*, iii. 3:

x. The last section contains twenty-two documents in
Arabic relating to civil matters, and ranging from the
seventeenth century to the nineteenth century, about seventy contracts of marriage, and six amulets. As regards the contracts, none had hitherto been discovered older than the
seventeenth century, and Firkowitsch in a memorandum

אה מולית | לי הרסד | בכשה | מן עתי | הקסה | ורום נפשי | אה
עשה | וקימני | בשמי | בכקרישך | סקרסי | בארשי | אותן | הכסיח

These are a few lines from the eighth part of the Samaritan
liturgy (*Berlin, Coll. Petermann*, No. 7):

על כריו כל מסלל נדי : לצעוין ריתוri
בחמרו לן ימדי : את חלקת השרה
אתיקרו ואמתהו ענה : וסאעו מימר מסכרתה
ולכו ברמטוה העדנה : על חלקת השרה
חלקת השרה תוסר במפה : סובחי הסדור וכמא
תרא בי הכסא : אחן יש לאל ידי
חלקת הסדח תוסר אנה : יעקב זכאה לי בנח
לקח יתי דינה : אחן יש לאל ידי
חלקת הסדה תוסר : אצי חיום בחסר
הרשעים בני הגר : אחן יש לאל ידי

חלקת הסדה תוסר בסלו : הרשעים מני בסלו
התושבחן הזלו : אחן יש לאל ידי
חלקת הסדה תוסר לא תבסי : הדין קרא על ראס
ואתרחק מני כם מסה : אחן יש לאל ידי
חלקת הסורה תוסר על נמיבה : נרול עתי מנסא
אתרחיק מני התורה הקדושה : ואחן יש לאל ידי
חלקת הסדה תשא הקל : סובחי חיום במול
ליח בו כחן נדול : אחן יש לאל ידי
חלקת הסדה תבכי : ותוסר אבכי
כל מן יראני יבכי : אחן יש לאל ידי

I hope very soon to publish a good deal of similar matter in
a separate work.

attached to the collection asserted that the Samaritans had
none till this time, when they learnt from a Karaite
traveller how to compose them. This is however a
mistake, as the present writer not long ago published
one dated (A.H. 916=) 1510–11, which was found by
him among the fragments of a Pentateuch belonging to
the collection [1]. Before this nothing had been brought
out but two badly copied specimens by Wilson [2]. The
whole number should however be edited, first because
each begins with a solemn hymn specially composed for
the occasion, which accordingly offers a new Samaritan text;
and secondly, because the names of persons and families
are of special interest, and present rich materials for a
Semitic Onomasticon [3].

---

[1] In *Hamelia*, 1873, no. 8, pp. 62, 63.

[2] *The Lands of the Bible* (1847), ii. 689–695.

[3] I here communicate some personal names from contracts of
marriage. The appended numbers betoken the years (A.H.) when
the documents were written. Of women's names the following are
of interest: אלטרח (1068, 1103, 1134, 1181), אלצרח (1209, probably identical with the foregoing), אצובתא (1132), חרבה (1148,
1158, 1191, 1202, 1216), הצביה (? with the article, 1181), חרח
('moon,' 1181), חנתה (1170), חנתיח (1142), כספח (1134), במתריה
(1149), כתובה (1118, 1148, 1218), מתבח (1177), מיטרה (1180),
סלך (1084), מחא (114.), פרה (1242), צדיקח (1161, 1164, 1175,
1194), רץ (1220, 1268), ציּרח (1198, probably the same as the
foregoing), צמר (1158), רבתח (1118), רצח ותּשמיר (' very beautiful,' 1118), רבתח (916, 1101, 1154), רחח (1101), שׂארח (1203,
1134), שרח (1165, both probably identical with שרח), שלח
(1211), שלחח (1244), שלחה (1124, 1143, 1146, &c.), שלמח
(1146, 1209), שמֹח (1191), חמח (1223), תחימה (1244), תנומה
(1149, 1168), תנופח (1211, probably the same).

Of men's names I will mention—זחרח (1149, 1168, also a

The collection contains also the following objects: (1) a case for a Pentateuch-roll made of brass plates and adorned with a variety of figures, Samaritan and Arabic proverbs; (2) the capital of a column found on Garizim, taken possibly from the old Samaritan temple there; (3) the stone tablet from the Samaritan synagogue at Nablus, on which are inscribed several verses of the Pentateuch for liturgical purposes, as described by Dr. Rosen and Prof. Rödiger[1].

DR. A. HARKAVY.

---

woman's name), ישמעאל הישמף (1180), עבר יהח (1103, 1116, 1191, &c., probably in imitation of the Arabic عبد الله), עבר חנתה (המהנה), probably the same as עבר חסם (1101, 1209, עבר רמחה (1191, 1248), עבר העטיד (1142, 1190, &c.), עבר רמחה (1168, 1244), סדח (1273), שלח (1209, 1211, &c., also a woman's name).

The family names most frequently occurring are רתמתה (also written רתמתה), מבסה (also ערסתה) or חרמחה (not the patriarch), מבר, מרהיג, עפר: once occur צמרה (1158), ארמתאי (1118), רחסיח (1244), &c. The expression רם בהי תאבן is twice (1068, 1084) used; can it mean 'priests of the altar'? Compare also the family names mentioned in Neubauer's chronicle. There is a specimen of a letter of divorce to be found in *Brit. Mus. Add. MS.* 19956, f. 96.

[In the Cambridge dictionary described above, p. 151, is a marriage contract, dated A.H. 1186, between سرور ابن غزال ابن يوسف ابن المطري dwelling at Joppa, and the daughter of يعقوب ابن سرور المطري of Nablus.

In a later account Dr. Harkavy draws attention to some more peculiarities of Samaritan Pentateuchs. In Exodus ii, where the birth of Moses is related, the following epigraph is inserted: מברי עלסח וסה אתילד לבה 'Hail to the '*Almah* (Jungfrau) and to her offspring!' Exodus xiv or xv generally has the title יהה נצוחי קרביה 'The Lord is Victor in fights.' J. W. N.]

[1] *Zeitschr. d. D. M. G.* xiv. 622-634.

# APPENDIX II.

*The Massekheth Kuthim, or Tract on the Samaritans*[1].

i. As to the usages of the Kuthim, in some they resemble heathens, in some Israelites, but in most of them Israelites. We do not accept from man or woman among them who has been afflicted with an issue or from their women after childbirth offerings of doves or pigeons[2], nor sin-offering, nor trespass-offering, but we receive from them vows and free-will offerings : we do not suffer them to acquire immovable property[3], nor do we sell them sheep for shearing[4], nor crops to cut, nor timber still standing[5], but we let them have cattle for killing. We do not sell them large cattle though wounded, nor foals, nor calves[6], but we let them have cattle that are wounded

---

[1] I have mostly followed the text of the Massekheth Kuthim as amended by Kirchheim, but many important variations are to be found in the Mishnah, Tosifta, and the two Talmuds, for which the reader is referred to Kirchheim's elaborate notes.

[2] Lev. xv. 14, 29.

[3] Because they might sell it to heathens : לֹא תְחָנֵּם (Deut. vii. 2, 'Thou shalt not shew mercy upon them') was read by the Rabbis תַּחֲנֵם 'Thou shalt not settle them :' *Bab. 'Aboda Zara*, 20 a.

[4] They might sell it to heathens, and so the first of the fleece (Deut. xviii. 4) might not be given to the priests; so with regard to crops also.

[5] Lest they might have a claim upon the ground ; *Bab. 'Aboda Zara*, 20 b.

[6] As they might sell or lend them to heathens, and the provisions of Exod. xxii. 9 sq. not be observed.

beyond the possibility of a cure. We sell them no weapons nor anything which could damage persons: we neither give nor take wives from them, but we give and borrow on usury with them: we let them have the gleanings, and that which is forgotten, and the corners of our fields [1]; and they too have the same custom with regard to that which is forgotten and the corners of their fields, and are to be relied upon to carry out all these practices in their proper time and the tithe for the poor in its year [2]; the fruit of their trees is held for untithed, as that of heathens, and their instrumentality in the ' Erubh ' is as if done by heathens [3]. A daughter of Israel may not deliver a Samaritan woman nor suckle her son [4], but a Samaritan woman may perform these offices for a daughter of Israel in her (the Israelite's) house; an Israelite may circumcise a Samaritan, and a Samaritan an Israelite, though R. Jehuda says a Samaritan should not do so, for he circumcises in honour of mount Garizim. We may stand a beast in the stable of a Samaritan or hire a Samaritan to follow and tend our cattle [5], or give a son in the charge of a Samaritan to teach him a trade: we associate and converse with them everywhere, as is not the case with heathens. A Samaritan suffers the halitzah from his sister-in-law [6], and gives a letter of divorce to his wife: he may be trusted to bring such from beyond the sea to an Israelite. The following are things we do not sell to them,—that which has died of itself, what has been torn, abominations, reptiles, the abortion of an animal,

---

[1] Lev. xxiii. 22 ; Deut. xxiv. 19.

[2] Every third year; Deut. xxvi. 12.

[3] See above, p. 34, note 3.

[4] As she might be rearing the child for idolatry.

[5] Exod. xxii. 19.          [6] Deut. xxv. 9.

oil into which a mouse has fallen, an animal that is
mortally ill, and a fœtus, (though these last two are eaten
by Israelites,) because in so doing we should be leading
into error. And as we do not sell such things to them,
so neither do we buy them from them, as it is written,
'For thou art a holy people to the Lord thy God[1];' inasmuch as thou art holy, thou shalt not make another
people more holy than thyself. A Samaritan may be
trusted to say whether there is or is not a sepulchre [in
a field], or of an animal whether it is first-born or not,
of a tree whether it is four years old or still impure, and
also is credible with regard to grave-stones, but not with
regard to spreading trees[2] nor stones projecting from walls,
nor with regard to the land of the Gentiles[3], nor to a
field in which a sepulchre has been ploughed up, inasmuch
as in these things their belief is open to suspicion. In
fine, they are not to be trusted in a matter in which their
belief is open to suspicion.

ii. We do not buy meat from a Samaritan butcher except
such as he himself eats, nor strings of birds unless he has
first put them into his mouth; it is not enough that he
offer them to an Israelite, as before now they have been

---

[1] Deut. xiv. 21.

[2] They can be trusted with regard to grave-stones, as these
are distinctly marked: not with regard to a spreading tree or
a stone projecting from a wall, under which a dead body might
have been buried; these would be considered by the Rabbis as
a tent, and cause pollution to any one sitting below. The Samaritans are not of this opinion, and so their testimony would not
be received, as they would naturally be careless in the matter.

[3] Probably because the Jews would hold it for unclean, which
the Samaritans would not do.

suspected of giving us to eat what had died of itself. A
Samaritan and Israelite are on the same footing with
regard to all damages mentioned in the Law: an Israelite
who kills a Samaritan, or a Samaritan who kills an Israelite,
goes into exile[1] if he have done it unwittingly; if of set
purpose, he suffers death: if the ox of an Israelite gores
the ox of a Samaritan the master escapes free, but if the ox
of a Samaritan gores one belonging to an Israelite, should
it be the first offence, half the damage is paid; should
warning before have been given, the whole[2]: R. Meir says
that if the ox of a Samaritan gores one belonging to an
Israelite, whether for the first time or not, the whole
damage must be paid, and as if the animal had been of
the best. The cheese of Samaritans is allowed: R. Simeon
Ben Eleazar says that of householders only, while that
of dealers is forbidden: their pots and presses are forbidden, because they make wine and vinegar with them.
The priests of Israel may share with the Samaritan priests
in Samaria, inasmuch as they are, as it were, thus rescuing
their property from their hand, but not in the land of
Israel, in order not to establish their claim to the priesthood: a Samaritan priest while unclean may give what he
is eating to an Israelite, but not if he be clean[3]. We buy
no bread from a Samaritan baker at the end of the Passover until after three bakings, nor from householders till
three Sabbaths are past, nor from villagers till it has been
made three times[4]. When is this to be observed? When

---

[1] To the city of refuge; Numb. xxxv. 25 sq.   [2] Exod. xxi. 36.
[3] Because what he eats when unclean must be a common, not
a holy thing.
[4] See Kirchheim's note. Leavened bread baked during the
Passover was forbidden.

www.ingramcontent.com/pod-product-compliance
Lightning Source LLC
Chambersburg PA
CBHW030357270326
41926CB00009B/1146

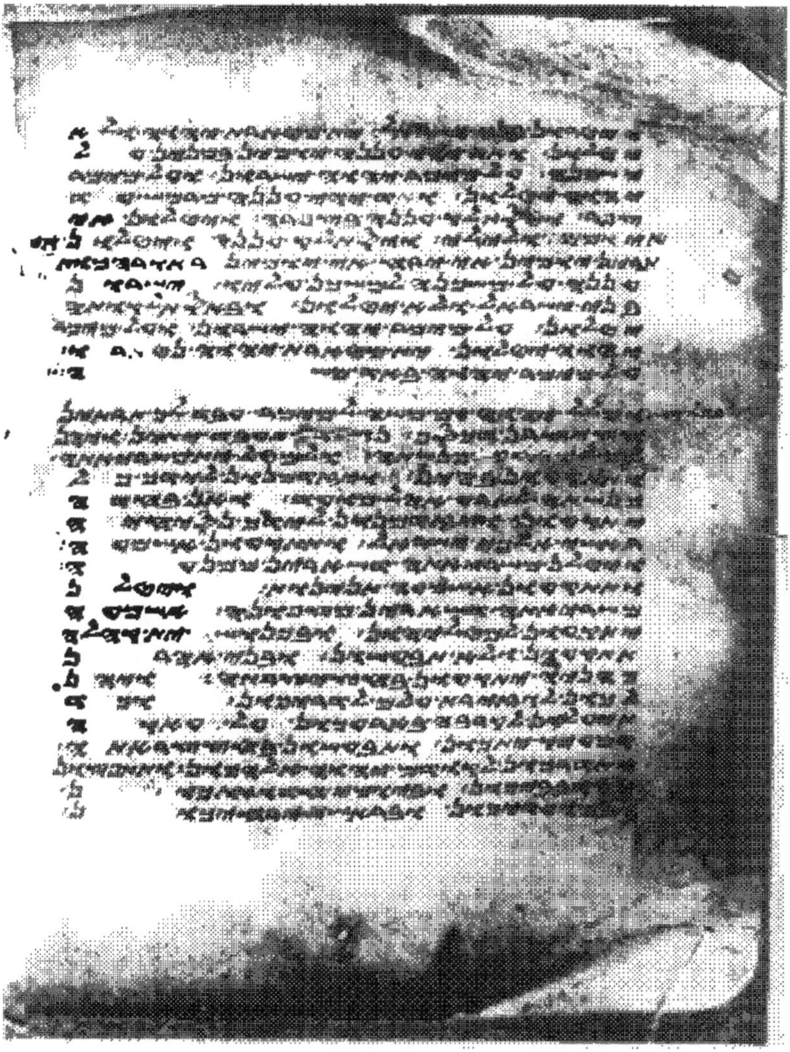

MS. fol. 14. b. Text, p. 28.

# LEVITICUS.

xxv. 26 ואנש הן לא יהי לה פרוק וחמ[טי אדה] וישכע
27 כלקובל אפחקתה : ויחשב [ירח שני] זבונה ויעזר
28 ירח דיאתר לגברה [חוב:] לה ויעזר לסחנתה: ואן
לא אשכ[עת] אדה לקובל לכעזרה לה ויהי זבונה
ב[אד] רזבן יתרה עד שנת יובילה ויפ[ק] ביזבלה
ויעזר לסחנת[ה]ה :

29 ואנש אן יזאבן בי כדור קריח שור' ותהי אפרקותה
30 עד דתשלם שנת זבונה יומין תהי אפרקותה: ואן
לא יתפרק עד דתשלם לדה שנה שלמה ויקום
ביתרה, דבקרחתה דלה שור לעלוטין לדזבן יתרה
31 לדריו לא יפק ביזבלה: ובתי כפרניה דלית להון
שור סהר עם חקלת ארעא יתחשבון אפרקה תהי
32 לה ובזבלה יפק : וקורי ליואי בתי קורי סחנתון
33 אפרקורת עלם תהי לליואי : ודיתפרק [כ][ן] ליואי
ויפק כזבן בי וקורי' סחנתה ביזבלה הלו בתי קורי
34 ליואי היא סחנתון בגו בני ישראל : וחקל מרבח
קריתון לא יזבנון הלו סחנת עלם היא להון :

¹ After שור on marg. an illegible gloss beg. with ו.
² The first ו is written over.

B

ואן יכך אחוך וחמוט ארדה עמך ותתקף' בה      ₃₅

גיור ותותב ויחי אחוך עמך : אל תסב כלואתה      ₃₆

כפל ורבי וחדחל מן אלהך ויחי אחוך עמך : ירת      ₃₇

כספך לא תתן לה בכפל וברבי לא תתן סיכלך :

אני יהוה אלהכון דאפקרת יתכון מן ארע מצרים      ₃₈

למתן לכון ירת ארע כנען למהי לכון לאלהים:

*[ואן יסך] אחוך עמך ויזדבן לך לא תש[חמש בה      ₃₉

תשמיש] עבד : כאגיר כתותב יהי עמך [עד      ₄₀

שנת] יובלה יעבד עמך : ויפק מן עמך [הוא] ובניו      ₄₁

עמה ויעזר לכרנה ולסחנת [אבה]תה יעור : הלא      ₄₂

עבדי אנון דאפקרת [ית]ון מן ארע מצרים לא

יזדבנון [ז]בון עבד : לא תפלח בה בקשי ותדחל      ₄₃

מן אלהך : ועבדיך ואמהתך ויהון לך מלואת בואיה      ₄₄

דסחרתכון סנהון תזבנון עבד ואמה : ואף כבני      ₄₅

גיוריה דמתותבין עסכן סנהון תזבנון וככרניזתן

דעמכון דאתילדו בארעכון ויהון לכון לסחנה      

: ותחסנון יתון לבניכון בתרכון לסירת סחנה לעלם      ₄₆

בהון תשתמשון ובאחיכון בני ישראל גבר באחיו

לא תפלח בה בקשי :

*ואן תסטי אד גיור ותותב עמך ויסך אחוך עמה      ₄₇

ויזדבן לגיור ותותב עמך אי לעקר כרן גיור : באתר      ₄₈

דאזדבן אפראקה תהי לה חד מן אחיו יפרקנה :

אי עביבה אי בר עביבה יפרקנה אי סן עסיר בסרה      ₄₉

סכרנה יפרקנה אי סטארת אדה ויתפרק : ויחשב      ₅₀

עם זבנה משתה דאזדבן לה עד שנת יבולה ויהי

כסף זבינה במנין שנין כיומי אגיר יהי עמה: אן ‏‎51
עוד סוגי בשניה (לפם דאנון) יעזר אפרקותה מכסף
זבנה: ואן זעור אתשר בשניה עד שנת יובלא ‏‎52
ויחשב לה כלקובל שניו יעזר ית אפרקותה:
כאגיר שנה בשנה יהי עמה לא יפלחנה בקשי ‏‎53
לעיניך: ואן לא יפרק באלין יופק בשנת יובלא ‏‎54
הוא ובנוי עמה: הלא לי בני ישראל עבדין עבדי ‏‎55
[אנון] דאפקרת יתהון מן ארע מצרים אני יה[וה]
אלהכן: לא תעבדון לכון אלילין [ופסל] וקאמה ‏‎xxvI. 1
לא תקימון לכון ואבן מסכ[ית] לא תתנון בארעכון
למסגד עליה ה[לא] אני יהוה אלהכון: ית שובתי ‏‎2
תטרו[ן] ובמקדשי תדחלון אני יהוה:

אן בגזירתי תהכון וית פקדי תטרון' ותעבדון ‏‎3
יתהון: ואתן מטריכון בזבנון ותתן ארעה עללתה ‏‎4
ואילן ברה יתן פיריו: ויכטי לכון דרכה ית (קטפ)ה ‏‎5
ו(קטפ)ה' יכטי ית זרעה, ותיכלון לחמכון לסבע
ותדרון לרעוצן בארעכון: ואתן שלם בארעה ‏‎6
ותדמכון ולית' רינעט ואבסל חיה בישחתה כן
ארעה' וחרב לא תעבר בארענכן: ותרדפון ית ‏‎7
דבביכון ויפלון לקודמיכון לחרב: וירדפון מנכון ‏‎8
חמשה מערה ומערה מנכון רבואן ירדפון ויפלון
דבביכון לקודמיכון לחרב: ואתרעי לכון ואפרי ‏‎9
יתכון ואסגי יתכון ואקים ית קיאמי עמכן: ותיכלון ‏‎10
עתיק דעתק ועותקה מקדם עדתה תפקון: ואתן ‏‎11
משכני בגבכון תלא (תגלעט נפשי) יתכון: ואתהלך ‏‎12

---

' After תטרון on marg. אים.

' Between lines ending with רינעט and חרב on marg. ם.

בגבכון ואי' לכון לאלהים ואתון תהון לי לעם:

13 אני יהוה אלהכון דאפקרת יתכון מן ארע מצרים
מדמהי להון עבדין תברת עטרי ניריכון ואיתירת
יתכון סקוכמין:

14 ואן לא תשמעון לי ולא תעבדון ית כל' פקדיה

15 האלין: אן בנזירתי תציקון י[ואן ית] דיני תגעל
נפשכון דלא למעבד [ית כל] פקדי לבטולכון ירת

16 קיאמי: ראבז [אני] אעבד הדה לכון ואכסר עליכון
[ית ח]ילו ירת שהפתה ירת (קדע)חדא כסמיאן
[עינ]יה ומדביאן נפשה וחזרעון לריקה [זר]עכון

17 ויכלונה דבביכון: ואתן [רב]חי בכון ותתברון
לקדם דבביכון וישלטון בכון סניכון ותערקון לית
דרדף יתכן:

18 ואן' עד אלין לא תשמעון לי ואוסף לטרדי יתכון

19 שבע על חוביכון: ואתבר ית חיולי תקפיכון
ואתן ית שופיכון כפוחלה ירת ארעכון כנחשה:

20 וישלם לריק עמלכון ולא תתן ארעכון ית עללתה

21 ואילן ברה לא יתן פיריו: ואן תהכון עמי מר
ולא תתרעון למשמע לי ואאחף עליכון סעה שבע

22 כחוביכון: ואשלח בכון ירת חירת ברה ותתכל
יתכון ותעקר ירת בהמתכון ותזער יתכון וישמן
אורעתכון:

23 ואן' באלין לא תדרון לי ותהכון עמי מרי:

24 ואהך אף אנה עמכון במרי ואמעי יתכון אף אנה

---

1 Perhaps originally וֹאתי; a letter has been erased after וֹאת,
the י of which may be by a later hand.

2 After כל on marg. שרע. 3 Before ואן on marg. עברין.[ן]

4 Before מן on marg. קטר ...

שבוע על חוביכון: ואיתי עליכון חרב גבי (פריע 25
קיאמ)ה ותתכנשון לגו [קריתכון] ואשלח מותנא
בגווכון ותתיהבון באד דבבה: בהברי לכון עטר 26
לחמה ויאפין עסר נשין לחמכון בתנור חד ויתעזר
לחמכון במתקל ותיכלון ולא תסבעון:

ואן' בהדה' לא תשמעון לי ותהכון עמי מר': 27
ואהך עמכון בחמרה פרי' יואדי' יתכון אף אנה 28
שבוע על חוביכ[ון] : ותיכלון בסר בניכון ובסר 29
בנתכון [תיכלון] : ואשיצי ית (רמואתכו)ן ואעקר 30
ית חומ[ניכון] ואתן ית פגריכון על פגרי גלוליכו[ן]
ותרגעל (נפש)י יתכון: ואתן ית ק(רי'חבנ[ון] חרבן 31
ואשם ית דאקדשכון ולא אר[ח] בריח 'רחוחכון:
ואשהם אנה ית ארע[ה] וישאמון עליה דבביכון 32
דראריז בה: ויתכון אדהרי ב(גוא)יה ואפלם בתרכון 33
חרב ותהי ארעכון שאמה וקריחכון יהן חרבן: אד 34
דתרעי ארעא ית שוביה כל יומי שממה ואתן
בארע דבביכון אד דתשבת ארעה ותרעי ית
שביה: כל יומי שממה תשבת ית דלא שבתת 35
בשביכון במדרכך עליה:

חדמשחירין בכון ועאל מרוכה בלבון' בארעת 36
דבביהון וירדף יתון קל עלי דנתר ויערקון מערוקית
חרב ויפלון ולית רדף : ויתקלון אנש באחו כמקדם 37
חרב ורדף לית ליח ולא תהי לכון תקומה לקדם
דבביכון: ותיבדון ב(גוא)יה ותס(יף) יתכון ארע 38
דבביכון:

<hr>

[1] Before ואן סח דין...

[2] The MS. has a line over ית in ותתכן.

[3] After בלבון on marg. וחלח לבה.

‏39 וּדמשׁתּארין בכון 'ישתנקון בעוביהון' בארעת
‏40 דבביהה ואף בעובי אבהתח (יה)ין ישתנקון: ויתודון
‏ ית עוביהון ית עוֹבֵי אבהתון בשקריהון דשקרו בי
‏41 ואף דהכו עמי מרי: אף אנה אהך עמהון בקרי
‏ ועאל יתון בארע דבביהון אי אד יכנע לבהון ערלה
‏ ואד ירעון ית חוביהון:

‏42 •[ודכ]רת ית קיאמי יעקב ואף ית קיאמי [יצ]חק
‏ ואף ית קיאמי אברהם אדכר בארע [ארכ]ר :

‏43 וארעה תשבק מנון ותרעי [ית] שוביה בשככה כנהון
‏ ואנון [יר]עון מן חוביהון גזו בבזו בדיני [א]ציקו ית

‏44 בזירחי בלעטח נפשהון: ואף 'בדה בהודון בארעת
‏ דבביהון לא אציקתון ולא בלעטתון למסכתתון
‏ לכבסלה: קיאמי דעמהון הלה אני יהוה אלהון:

‏45 ואדכר להון קיאם קדמאין דאפקרת יתה מן ארע
‏ מצרים לעיני גואיה למהי להון לאלהים אני יהה:

‏46 אלין בזיריה חדיניה ותורואתרה דיהב יהוה בינה
‏ ובין בני ישראל בטור סיני באד משה:

‏1 'ומלל יהוה עם משה למיכר: כלל עם בני
‏2 ישראל ותימר להון גבר אן יפרש נדר בשיאם(ה)
‏3 נפשן ליהוה: ויהי שיאם דכרה כבר עשרין שנין
‏ ועד בר שתין שנין ויהי שיאם(ה)' חמשין (כתקלין)

---

‏¹ This ' appears to have two dots over it.
‏² After קט בעוביהן .. on marg. בעת קט.
‏³ Apparently corrected from בהרה.
‏⁴ Before וכלל on marg. [1] תן ישרח ....
‏⁵ In this chapter the suffix of the second person, as in the Hebrew text, often appears to have been altered into that of the third, as in the Chaldee.

4 כסף במתקל קדשה : ואן נקבה היא ויהי שיאב(ה)

5 תלתין סתקלין : ואן כבר חמש שנין ועד בר עסרין

שנין ויהי שיאב(ה) דכרה עסרין סתקלין ולנקבתה

6 עסרה סתקלין : ואן כבר ירח ועד בר חמש שנין

ויהי שיאמך דכרה חמשה סתקלין דכסף ולנקבתה

7 שיאב(ה) תלתה סתקלין דכסף : ואן כבר שתין

שנין ולעל אן דכר יהי שיאב(ה) חמשה עסר[1]

כתקלין ולנקב[זה] עסרה סתקלין : ואן פעת הוא כן 8

שיאמך ויקימנה לקדם כהנא וי[שום] יתה כהנה

על מימר דתתבטי א[ר] נאדרה ישובכנה כהנ[ה] :

9 ואן בהמה ד(יח)קרב סנה קרבן ליהוה כל דיתן[2]

10 סנה ליהוה יהי קדש : לא יחלפנה ולא יפרך יתה

סב בביש אי ביש בסב ואן (פר)וך יפרך בהמה

בבהמה ויהי הוא ופריגיתה יהי קדש :

11 ואן כל בהמה מסבה (דלא ית)קרב סנה קרבן[3]

12 ליהוה ויקים ויקים ית בהמתה לקדם כהנה : וישום

כהנה יתה בין טב ובין ביש כשאם כהנה כן יהי :

13 ואן אפראקה יפרקנה ויוסף חמשה על שיאמך :

14 ואניש (אן) יקדש ית ביתה קדש ליהוה[4] וישובנה

כהנה בין סב ובין ביש כמה דישום יתה כהנה

15 כן יקום : ואן דמקדש יפרק ית ביתה ויוסף חכוש

כסף שיאב(ה) עליו ויהי לח :

16 ואן מן עקל סחנתה יקדש אנש ליהוה ויהי

---

1 י is written over the line, after עסר.

2 After מנה on marg. רב.

3 After ליהוה on marg. ו.ד...

4 After ליהוה on marg. נסב.

שיאבך לפם זרעה זרע חזמר ס(ע)רין בחכסין

17 מתקל[י]ן כסף : ואן משנת יובלה יקדש עקלה

18 כשיאמ(רה) יקום : ואן בתר יבולה יקדש חקלה
ויחשב לה כהנה ית כספה על מיסר שניה
דאתותרי עד שנת יבולה וידבצר מן שיאמ(ה) :

19 *[ואן] אפראק יפרק ית עקלה דמקדש יתה [ויו]סף
חמוש כסף שיאבך עליו ויקום [לה] : ואן לא יפרק

20 ית חקלה ואן זבן ית [חקל]ה לגבר עורן לא יפרק

21 עוד : ויהי [חק]לרה במפקה ביובלה קדש ליהוה
כחקל [ח]רכה לכהנה תהי סחנתה :

22 ואן ית חקלה ׳ זובנה דלא מן עקל סחנתה יקדש

23 אנש ליהוה : ויחשב לה כהנה ית סכום שיאמ(ה)
עד שנת יבולה וית; ית שיאמ(ה) ביום הרוא קדש

24 ליהוה : בשנת יבולה יעור חקלה לרובגה מן עכה

25 לדו לה סחנת ארע : וכל שיאמ(ר) יהי במתקל
קרשה עסרין [גי]רה מתקלה :

26 ברן כל בכור דידבכר ליהוה בבהמה לא יקדש

27 אנש יתה אן תור אן נקי ליהוה הוא : ואן בבהמה
ססבה ויתפרק בשיאמ(ר) ויוסף חמושה עליו ואן לא
יתפרק ויזדבן בשיאכ(ה) :

28 ברן ²כל חרם דיחרם אנש ליהוה סכל דלה
מן אנש ובהמה ומן חקל סחנתה לא יזדבן ולא

29 יתפרק כל חרם קדש קרשין הוא ליהוה : כל חרם
יתחרם מן אנשה לא יפרק קטל יתקטל :

30 וכל מעסר ארעה מזרע ארעה ומפרי אילנה

ליהוה הוא קדש ליהוה: ואן אפרקה יפרק אנש יג
כמעסרה וחמשת יוסף עליו:

יוכל מעסר תור(ן) ועאן כל דיעבר תחו[ת] לג
שורבטה עסיראה יהי קדש ליהוה: לא ירער בין לג
טב לביש ולא יבח[רנה] ואן בחור יבחרנה ויהי
הו[א] ובתורה יהי קדש לא יחפר[ק]:

אלין פקדיה דפקד יהוה ית משה לבני ישראל לד
בטור סיני:

# NUMBERS.

[ומלל] יהוה עם משה במדבר סיני באהל [מוע]ד   א א,ב
בחד לירחא תנינה בשתה תנינתא [למפ]יקיהון
מן ארע מצרים למימר: סבו [ירת] סכום כנסת   ב
בני ישראל לכרניהן [לב]ירת אבהתון במנין שמהן
כל דכר [לג]ולגלתון: מבר עשרין שנין ולעל כל   ג
[נ]פק חיל בישראל תמני יתהן לחיליהון אתה
ואהרן: ועמכון יהון גבר גבר לשבטה גבר ריש   ד
לבירת אבהתה הוא: ואלין שמהת גבריה דיקמון   ה
עמכון

| | | | |
|---|---|---|---|
| ל ראובן | אליצור | בר | שדיאור : |
| ל שמעון | שלמיאל | בר | צורישדה : |
| ל יהדה | נחשון | בר | עמינדב : |
| ל ישששכר | נתנאל | בר | צוער : |
| ל זבלן | אליאב | בר | חילן : | לבני יוסף |
| ל אפרים | אלישמע | בר | עמיהוד |
| ל מנשה | גמליאל | בר | פדהצור : |
| ל בנימים | אבידן | בר | גדעוני : |
| ל דן | אחיעזר | בר | עמישדה : |

| | | | | |
|---|---|---|---|---|
| ל אשר | פגעיאל | בר | עכרן: | 13 |
| ל גד | אליסף | בר | דעואל: | 14 |
| ל נפתלי | אחירע | בר | חילן: | 15 |

אלין זמיני כנשתה נסיאי שבטי אבהתון ראשי 16
אלפי ישראל אנן: ונסב משה ואהרן ית גבריה 17
האלין דכריזו בשכהן: ית כל כנשתה כנשו בחד 18
ליחרה תנינה ואסתדרו' על כרניהון לבית אבהתון
במנין שכהן כבר עסרין שנין ולעל לבלגלותהון:
כבה דפקד יהוה ית כישה וכנאתון במדבר סיני: 19
והוו בני ראובם בכור ישראל תילדתון לכרניהון 20
לבית אבהתון בכנין שכהן יכל דכר לבלגלותהון
כבר עסרין שנין] ולעל כל נאפק חיל': בניניהון 21
לשב[ט] ראובן שתה וארבעין אלף וחמש מאה[ן]:
לבני שכעון תולדתון לכרניהון לבי[ת] אבהתון 22
מאסוראתון במנין שכהן לגלגולאתהון כל דכר סבר
עסרין 'שנ(ה) ולעל כל נפק חיל' בניהניהון' לשבט 23
שבעון תשעה וחכשין אלף וחלת כאון:
לבני גד תולדתון לכרניהון לבית אבהתון במנין 24
שמהן כבר עסרין שנ(ה) ולעל כל נאפק חיל:
כניניהון לשבט גד חמשח וארבעין אלף ושת סאון 25
וחכשין:
לבני יחודה תולדתתן לכרניהון לבית' אבהתון 26
בכנין שכהן כבר עסרין שנ(ה) ולעל כל נאפק

----

¹ So MS.     ² The ח of אסתדרו is written over.

³ A letter has been erased in this and the following verses
after חיל.

⁴ Formerly סנין, as in following verses.

⁵ So MS.     ⁶ After לבית on marg. ... .קודם.

כז חיל : מניניהון לשבט יהודה ארבעה ושבעין אלף
ושת מאון :

כח לבני יששכר תולדתון לכרניהון לבית אבהתון
במנין שמהן סבר עסרין שנ(רה) ולעל כל נאפק

כט חיל : כנין שמהן לשבט יששכר ארבעה וחמשין
אלף וארבע מאון :

ל לבני זבלון תולדתון לכרניהון לבית אבהתון
במנין שמהן כבר עסרין שנ(רה) ולעל כל נאפק

לא חיל : מניניהון לשבט זבלון שבעה וחמשין אלף
וארבע מאון :

לב לבני יוסף לבני אפרים תולדתון לכרניהון לבית
אבהתון במנין שמהן י-[כבר] עסרין שנין ולעל כל

לג נאפק חיל : [מנ]יניהון לשבט אפרים ארבעין אלף
וחמש [מא]ין :

לד [לב]ני מנשה תולדתון לכרניהון לבית [א]בהתון
במנין שמהן סבר. עסרין שנין [ו]לעל כל נאפק

לה חיל : מניניהון לשבט מנשה תרין. ותלתין אלף
ומאתן :

לו לבני בנימים תולדתון לכרניהון לבית אבהתון
במנין שמהן כבר עסרין שנין ולעל כל נאפק חיל :

לז מניניהון לשבט בנימים חמשה ותלתין אלף וארבע
מאון :

לח לבני׳ דן תולדתון לכרניהון לבית אבהתון במנין
שמהן כבר עסרין שנין ולעל כל נאפק חיל :

לט מניניהון לשבט דן תרין ושתין אלף ושבע מאון :

מ לבני אשר תולדתון לכרניהון לבית אבהתון

¹ Before לבני on marg. מבתר דינה.

בכנין שבטהן כבר עסרין שנין ולעל כל נאפק חיל :

41 סניניהון לשבט אשר חד וארבעין אלף וחמיש
מאון :

42 לבני נפתלי תולדתהון לכרתיהון לבית אבהתהן
בבנין שבטהן כבר עסרין שנין ולעל כל נאפק חיל :

43 סניניהן לשבט נפתלי תלתחה וחמשין אלף וארבע
מאון :

44 אלין' כניניה דכנה בשה ואהרן ונסיאי ישראל
תריעסר גבר גבר אחד לשבט אחד לשבט בית
אבהתון ה[ו]ו' :

45 והוו כל כניני בני ישראל לחיליהון

46 יכבר עסרין שנין ולעל כל נפק חיל בישראל : והוו
כל מניניה שת מאון דאל[ף] ותלתחה אלפין וחמש
מאון וחמשין : ולי[אי] לשבט אבהתון לא יתכנן

47 בגוהון :

48,49 ומלל יהוה עם בשה למימר : ברם ית שבט לוי

50 לא תכני וירת סאככח לא תסב בגו בני ישראל :
ואתה חיכן ית ליואי על משכן סחדואתה ועל כל
מניו ועל כל דאית לה אנון יסבלון' ית משכנה וית
כל מניו ואנון ישבשונה וסהר לבשכנה ישרון :

51 ובאטלורת בשכנרה יעאתון יתה ליואי ובאשר[י]ו[ת
משכנה יקיבח יתה ליואי ובראי דקרב יתקטל :

52 וישרון בני ישראל גבר על בשריאה וגבר על

53 אתרה לחיליהן : וליואהי ישרון סהר לבשכן
סחדואתה ולא יהי קצף על כנשת בני ישראל

54 ויטרן ליואי ית בטרת כיבשכן סחדואתה : ועבדו
בני ישראל ככל דפקד יהוה ית בשה כן עבדו :

<sup>1</sup> ḃefore אלין on marg., .כל ק ,,.    <sup>2</sup> The ל is written over.

II. 1, 2   וכלל יהוה עם משה ועם אהרן לסיכר: גבר'
(על טכסיו בסיכנ)ין' לבית אבההון ישרן בני ישראל
3   כלקובל 'סחר לאהל כועד ישרון : ורשארין קדמאין
ככדנעה טכס כשריח יהודה לחיליהון ונסיא לבני
4   יהורה נחשח בר עמינדב: וחילה ומניניו ארבעה
5   ושבעין אלף ושרת כאת : ורשארין עמה שבט
יששכר ונסיא לבני יששכר נהנאל בר צער:
6   וחילה ומניניו ארבעה וחמשין אלף וארבע מאן :
7   Pal. 7. b.   •י[ו]שבט זבלח ונסיא לבני זבלח אליאב [ב]ר
8   חילן : וחילה ומניניו שבעה וחמשין [א]לף וארבע
9   מאן : כל סניניה למשריח יהודה מעה אלף
ותוככין אלף ושתה [א]לפין וארבע מאן לחיליהון
קדכאין יטלח :
10   סכם משריח ראובן כן דרומה לחיליהון ונסיא
11   לבני ראובן אליצור בר שדיאור: וחילה ומניניו שתה
12   וארבעין אלף וחמש מאן : ורשרין עמה שבט
שמעון ונסיא לבני שמעון שלכיאל בר צורישדה:
13   וחילה וכניניו תשעה וחמשין אלף ותלת מאן:
14   ושבט גד ונסיא לבני גד אליסף בר דעואל : וחילה
15   ומניניו חמשה וארבעין אלף ושרת כאן וחמשין :
16   כל כנינה למשריח ראובן מעה אלף ואחד וחמשח
אלף וארבע מאן חמשין לחיליהון ותנינין יטלח:
17   ונטל אהל כועד משריח ליואי בגו משריאתון כמה
דישרון כן יטלח גבר על אתרה' לטכסיהת:

' After גבר on marg. קדם בית חח.
' There has been a letter between the נ and י of בסימנך with
a line over it and the י following.
' There is a line over ח in סחר.   ' After אתרה on marg. לסדירה.

'טכס כשרית אפרים לחיליהון מן מערבה ונסיא ‏18
לבני אפרים אלישמע בר עמיהוד : וחילה ומניניו ‏19
ארבעין אלף וחמש מאן : ועליו שבט מנשה ונסיא ‏20
לבני מנשה גמליאל בר פדהצור : וחילה ומניניו ‏21
תרין ותלתין אלף ומאתן : ושבט בנימים ונסיא ‏22
לבני בנימים אבידן בר גדעוני : וחילה ומניניו ‏23
חמשה ותלתין אלף וארבע מאן : כל מניניה ‏24
למשרית אפרים מעה אלף ותובניניה אלפין ומעה
לחיליהון ותליתאין יטלון :

'°טכס משרית דן כן צפונה לחיליהון ונם[יא] ‏25
לבני דן אחיעזר בר עמישדה : וחיל[ה] ומניניו תרין ‏26
ושתין אלף ושבע מא[ן]: ודשארן עמה שבט אשר ‏27
ונסיא לבני אשר פגעאל בר עכרן: וחילה ומניני[ו] ‏28
חד וארבעין אלף וחמש מאן : ושבט נפתלי ונסיא ‏29
לבני נפתלי אחירע בר עינן : וחילה וכניניו תלתה ‏30
וחמשין אלף וארבע מאן : כל מניניה לכשרית דן ‏31
מעה אלף ושבעה וחמשין אלף ושת מאן לעקברה
יטלון לטכסיהון³ :

אלין מניני בני ישראל לבית אבהתן כל' מניני ‏32
משריאתה לחיליהון ית מאן דאלף ותלתה אלפין
וחמש מאן וחמשן : וליואי לא אתמנו בגו בני ‏33
ישראל כמה דפקד יהוה ית משה : ועבד בני ‏34
ישראל ככל דפקד יהוה ית משה כן שרו לטכסיהון
וכן נטלו גבר לכרניה על בית אבהתה :

---

¹ Before סכם on marg. סדר.
² סדר is written over סכם.
³ לסרריתן has been inserted in the text after לטכסיהון.
⁴ After כל on marg. ר, ה.

ואליך תולדת אהרן ביום דמלל' יהוה עם משה　iii. 1

בטור סיני : ואליך שכהת בני אהרן בכורה נדב　2

ואביהוא אלעזר ואיתמר : ואליך שמהת בני אהרן　3

כהניה דאכשחו דשלם אתרח לכהנה : ומית נדב　4

ואביהוא באקרבותון אש בראה לקודם יהוה

במדבר סיני ובנין לא הוה להון (וא)כהן אלעזר

ואיתמר (על אפי) אהרן אבהון :

וּמלל יהוה עם משה למימר : הקרב ית שבט'　3, 6

לוי והקים יתה לקודם אהרן כהנא וישמשון יתה :

ויטרון ית מטרתה י-[וי]ת מטרת כל כנשתה לקודם　7

אהל מועד [ל]במשמשה ית תשמיש משכנה : ויטרון　8

ית כל מאני אהל מועד וית מטרת בני ישראל

למשמשה ית תשמיש משכנה : ותתן ית ליואי　9

לאהרן ולבניו יהיבין יהיבין אנון לי 'מבני בני ישראל :

וית אהרן וית בניו תמני ויטרון ית כהנתהון וברי 'דיקרב יתקטל :　10

'וּמלל יהוה עם משה למימר : ואני אה דברת　11, 12

ית ליואי מגו בני ישראל תחות כל בכור פ[חו]ח

רחם בבני ישראל פרקניהון יהון ויהון לי ליואי :

תלא לי כל בכור ביום דקטלת כל בכור בארע　13

מצרים אקדשת לי כל בכור בישראל מן אנש עד

בהמה לי יהון אני יהוה :

'וּמלל יהוה עם משה במדבר סיני למימר : סהני　14, 15

---

[1] After דמלל on marg. ... לבה.

[2] After שבט on marg. ... סדג.

[3] This seems to have been corrected from סלו, as in ver. 12.

[4] Before וּמלל on marg. ליואי.

[5] Before וּמלל on marg. אבית אל.

ית בני לוי לבית אבהתהון לכתיהון כל דכר סבר

יח ולעל תמנינן : וכנה יתון כמשה על פימר 16

יהוה כמרה דפקדה : והוו אלין בני לוי בשכהתון 17

גרשון קהת ומררי : ואלין שמהת בני גרשון 18

לכתיהון לבני ושפעי : ובני קהת לכרניהון עמרם 19

ויצהר חברון ועזיאל : ובני מררי לכרניהון מחלי 20

ומושי אלין אנון כרני ליואי לבית אבהתהון : לגרשון 21

כרן לבנאי וכח שמעי אלין אנון כרני גרשונאי :

ומסוראתהון במנין כל דכר מבר ירח ולעל מניניהון 22

שבעה אלפין .וחמש מאין : כח גרשונאי חורי 23

משכנה ישרון מן מערבה : ונסיא בית אב לגרשונאי 24

אליסף בר .לאל :

*    *    *    *    *    *    *

גבר אי אתה אן יפרש למדר נדר נזיר לאתנזרה VI. 2

ליהוה : מן חמר וחמט' יתגזר עטי דחמר ועמי 3

דרחט לא יסתה וכ[ל] מסרח' ענבים לא ישתה

וענבין רסיב[ן] ויבישן לא ייכל : כל יומי נזרה 4

מכל דיתעבד כגפן חמרה מן אצורין ועד זג לא

ייכל : כל יומי נדר נזרה חפוף לא יעבר על רישה 5

עד אשלמות יומיה דיתגזר ליהוה קדיש יהי מרבי

פרע סער רישה : כל יומי נזרחה ליהוה על נפש 6

דמית לא ייעל : לאביו ולאמה לאחיו ולאחתו לא 7

יסתב להון במותהון הל(ה) כתר אלהה על רישה :

כל יומי נזרה קדיש חוא ליהוה : 8

---

1 There is a line in the MS. over the ח in this and the following ‏וחם.

2 The ר has been written over and ש erased between ם and ע.

9 ואן יכות מית עליו בעסף ת[רע] ויסתב' ריש
נזרה ויספר רשה ביום דכיתה ביומה שביעאה
10 יספרנה: וביומרה תמינאה ייתי תרין תורין אי
11 תרין בני יון ליד כהנה לתרח אהל מועד: ויעבד
כהנה חד לסלוח וחד לעלה ויסלח עליו מן דחטה
12 על רשה ויקדש ירת רשה ביומה ההוא: ויתגזר
ליהוה ית יומי נזרה וייתי חבאר' בר שתה לאשם
ויומיה קדמאי יבטלון הלו אסתב נזרה!
13 ודה תורות נזירה ביום אשלמות' יומי נזרה
14 ייתי יתה לתרח אהל מועד: ויקרב ית קרבנה
ליהוה אמחר בר שתה שלם חד לעלה ואמחרה
חדה ברת שתה שלמה לסלוח ודכר חד שלם
15 ב.ב.ב לשלמים: °[וק]ון פטיר סלת חלין בסיסן במשח
[ורקריקי פטיר] משחין במשח וכנחתון [ות]סוכיהן:
16 ויקרב כהנה לקודם יהוה [ו]יעבד ית סלוחה וית
17 עלתה: ית דכהה יעבד דבח שלכין ליהוה עם
קנץ פטיה ויעבד כהנה ית מנחתה וירת נסכיו:
18 ויספר נזירה בתרח אהל מועד ית ריש נזרה ויסב
ית סער ריש נזרה ויהן על אשתה דתחות דבח
19 שלמיה: ויסב כהנה ית אדרעה בשילה מן דכרה
וחלרת פטיר חד כן קנונה ורקריק פטיר חד ויהן
20 על כפי נויה בתר דאסהפר ית נזירה: וניף יהון
כהנה תנאפה לקודם יהיה קדש הוא לכהנה יהי
על ניעה דאנפיתה ועל שקה דארכיתה ובתר
21 ישחה נזירה חבר: דה תורות נזירה דידר קרבנה

---

¹ After ויסתב on marg. ושנברותה.　　² So MS.
³ After אשלמות on marg. הכרתן and underneath ,, ישח.

ליהוה על נזרה לבד דתכט ארה כפם נדרה
דידר כן יעבד על תורות נזרה:

וכלל יהוה עם משה למיכר: כלל עם אהרן כג, כב
ועם בניו לסימר אכון תברכון ית בני ישראל
אמר להון: יברכנך יהוה ויטרנך: יניר יהוה רעותה כד, כה
לידך וית[חם]נך: יתלי יהוה אפוי לידך וישוי לך כו
שלם: ושבו ית שמי על בני ישראל ואני כז
אברכנון:

והוה ביום אסכמורת משה למקבה ית משכנה א, VII
ומשח יתה וקדש יתה וית כל מניו וית מדבחה
וית כל מנוי ומשחנון וקדש יתן: ויאקרבו נסיאי ב, ג
ישראל ראשי בית אבהתהון אנון נסי(א)י שבטיה אנון
דקאמין על מניניה: ואיתו ית קרבנהון לקודם יהוה
שת עגלן דחיל ותריעסר תורין עגלה לתרין
נסי(א)יה ותור לאחד ואקרבו יתן לקודם משכנה:

ואמר יהוה למשה לסימר: סב כלותהון ויהון ד, ה
למשמשה ית תשמיש אהל פועד ותתן יתהן לליואי
אנש כלפם עביתה: ונסב משה ית עגלאתה וית ו
תוריה ויהב יתהון לליואי: ית תרתין עגלאתה וית ז
ארבעת תורידי יהב לבני גרשון כלפם עביתן:
וית ארבעת עגלאתה וית תומנת חוריה יהב ח
לבני מררי כלפם עביתן באד איתמר בר אהרן
כהנה: ולבני קהת לא יהב הלה עבידת קדשה ט
עליהון בכתפה יס(בלון): ואקרבו נסי(א)יה ית חנכת י
מדבחה ביומא (אמשח) יתה ואקריבו נסי(א)יה ית

<hr/>

בעי ברך .. Before הלל on marg. ¹
אש אנם .. After סלותן on marg. ²

ס 2

יו קרבנך לקודם מדבחה : ואמר יהוה למשה נסי(א)
חד ליום ונסי(א) חד ליום אקרבו ית קרבנון לחנכת
מדבחה :

יב והוה ד(א)קרב ביומא קדמאה ית קרבנה' נחשון
יג בר עמינדב לשבט יהודה : וקרבנה (צעה)² (ד)כסף
חדה תלתין ומאה בתקלה פינך חד דכסף שבעין
(כח)קל(ין) במתקל קדשה תריהון כלין סלת בסיס
יד במשח למנחה : פיאלי חדה עסרה דהב כליה
יה אוחדו : פר חד בר תורין דכר חד ³אמחר חד בר
יו שתה לעלה : וצפיר עזין חד לסלוח : יולדבח
שלמיה תורין תרין דכרין חמשה עורפן חמשה
אמחרין בני שנה חמשה דן קרבן נחשון בר
עמינדב :

יח ביומה תנינה הקרב נתנאל בר צוער נסי(א)
יט יששכר : הקרב ית קרבנה צח(ה)רה דכסף חד(א)רה
תלתין ומ(א)רה מתקלה פינך חד כסף שב(ע)ין
(כ)דקל במתקל קדשה רה תריהון מלין סלת בסים
כ במשח למנחה : פיאלי חדה עסרה דהב כליה
כא אוחדו : פר חד בר תורין דכר חד אמחר חד בר
כב,כג שתה לעלה : תצפיר עזין חד לסלוח : ולדבח
שלמיה תורין תרין דכרין חמשה עורפן חמשה
אמחרין בני שנה חמשה דן קרבן נתנאל בר
צוער :

כד ביומה תליתאה נסי(א) לבני ובלון אליאב בר

---

¹ After קרבנה on marg... .אביה אל.    ⁴ So MS.
² This has been altered, apparently, into אמר אחר : In this
and the following verses the ה of אמחר has been erased, but is
still legible.

חילן : וקרבנה צח(ה דכסף חדה) תלתין וכ(א)רה 25
כדקלה פינך חד כסף שבעין דקל בסדקל קדשה
תריהון פלין סלת בסים במשח לכנחה : פיאלי 26
חדה עסרה דהב מליח אחדו : פר חד בר תורין 27
דכר חד אכמר חד בר שתה לעלה : רצפיר עוין 28
חד לסלוח : ולדבח שלמיה תורין תרין דכרין 29
חמשה עורפין חמשה אכחרין בני שנה חמשה דן
קרבן אליאב בר חילן :

ביומה רביעאה נסי(א) לבני ראובן אליצור בר 30
שדיהור : וקרבנה צח(ה דכסף) חדה חלתין ום(א)ה 31
כתקלה פינך חד כסף שבעין דקל בכתקל קדשה
תריהון מלין סלת בסיס במשח למנחה : פיאלי 32
חדה עסרה דהב מליח אוחדו : פר חד בר תורין 33
דכר חד אמחר חד בר שתה לעלה : רצפיר עוין 34
חד לסלוח : ולדבח שלמיה תורין תרין דכרין חמשה 35
עורפין' חמשה אמחרין בני שנה חמשה דן קרבן
אליצור בר שדיאור :

ביומה חמישאה נסי(א) לבני שמעון שלמיאל בר 36
צורישדה : וקרבנה צח(ה דכסף חדה) תלתין 37
ום(א)ת כתקלה פינך חד כסף שבעין דקל במדקל
קדשה תריהון מלין סלת בסיס במשח למנחה :
פיאלי חדה עסרה דהב מליח אוחדו : פר חד בר 38, 39
תורין דכר חד אמחר חד בר שתה לעלה : רצפיר 40
עוין חד לסלוח : ולדבח שלמיה תורין תרין דכרין 41
חמשה עורפין חמשה אכחרין בני שנה חמשה דן
קרבן שלמיאל בר צורישדה :

¹ On marg. before ביומה, על בי אמת[?].    ² So MS.

‎42 ביום שתיתאה נסי(א) לבני גד אליסף בר דעואל:

‎43 וקרבנה צח(ה דכסף חדה) תלתין ומעה מדקלה
פינך חד כסף שבעין דקל בסתקל קדשה תריהון

‎44 כלין סלת בסים במשח לסנחה: פיאלי חדה עסרה

‎45 דהב כליה אוחדו: פר חד בר תורין דכר חד

‎46 אמאר חד בר שתה לעלה: וצפיר עזין חד

‎47 לסלוח: ולדבח שלמיה תורין תרין דכרין חמשה
ערופין חמשה אמחרין בני שנה חמשה ח קרבן
אליסף בר דעויל:

‎48 ביוכה שביעאה נסי(א) לבני אפרים' אלישמע

‎49 בר עמיהוד: וקרבנה צח(רה דכסף) חדה תלתין

‎50 וסעה מדקלה פינך חד כסף ·שבעין דקל בסתקל
קדשה תריהון כלין סלת בסים בסשח למנחה:

‎51 פיאלי חדה עסרה דהב כליה אוחדו: פר חד בר
תורין דכר אחד אמאר חד בר שתה לעלה:

‎52 וצפיר עזין חד לסלוח: ולדבח שלמיה תורין תרין
דכרין חמשה ערופין חמשה אמחרין בני שנה חמשה
ח קרבן אלישמע בר עמיהוד:

‎53 ביוטה תמינאה נסי(א) לבני כנשה גמליאל בר

‎54 פדיצור: וקרבנה צח(ה כסף עדה) תלתין וסעה
מדקלה פינך חד כסף שבעין דקל בסתקל קדשה

‎55 תריהון מלן סלת בסים בסשח למנחה: פיאלי

‎56 חדה עסרה דהב כלי(א)ה אוחדו: פר חד בר

‎57 תורין דכר חד אמאר חד בר שתח לעלה: תצפיר

‎58 עזין חד לסלוח: ולדבח שלמיה תורין תרין דכרין

---

‎¹ After אפרים on marg. כתן סה and underneath מקרה.

חמשה עשׂרפין חמשה חמרין בני שנה חמשה דן
קרבן גמליאל בר פדהצור :

ביומא תשׁיעאה נסי(א) לבני בניסים אביח בר 60
גדעוני : וקרבנה צח(ה) כסף עדה) תלתין ומעה 61
סתקלה פינך חד כסף שבעין תקל במתקל קדשׁה
תריהון מאלין סלת בסיס במשח למנחה : פיאלי 62
חדה עסרה דהב מליה אוחדו : פר חד בר תורין 63
דכר חד אמׂחר חד בר שׁתה לעלה : וצפיר עזין 64
חד לסלוח : ולדבח שׁלמיה תורין תרין דכרין 65
חמשה עשׂרפין חמשה אמׂחרין בני שנה חמשה דן
קרבן אביח בר גדעוני :

ביומא עסיראה נסי(א) לבני דן אחיעזר בר 66
עמישׁדה : וקרבנה (צחה כסף עד)ה תלתין וכ(א)ה 67
סתקלה פינך חד כסף שבעין (מ)(תקל)(ין) במתקל
קדשׁה תריהון מאלין סלת בסיס במשח למנחה :
פיאלי חדה עסרה דהב מליה אוחדו : פר חד בר 68, 69
תורין דכר חד אמׂחר חד בר שׁתה לעלה : וצפיר 70
עזין חד לסלוח : ולדבח שׁלמיה תורין תרין דכרין 71
חמשה עשׂרפין חמשה אמׂחרין בני שנה חמשה דן
קרבן אחיעזר בר עמישׁדה :

ביום חד עסר יום נסי(א) לבני אשר פגעיל בר 72
עכרן : קרבנה צח(ה דכסף ח)(דה תלתין וכ(א)ה 73
סתקלה פינך חד כסף שבעין (מ)(תקל)(ין) במתקל
קדשׁה תריהון כאלין סלת בסיס במשח למנחה :
פיאלי חדה, עסרה דהב מ(א)ליה אוחדו : פר חד בר 74, 75
תורין דכר חד אמׂחר חד בר שׁתה לעלה : וצפיר 76

¹ Before ביומא on marg. ... נן שתון.

עזין חד לסלוח : ולדבח שלמיה תורין תרין דכרין    77
חמשה ערופין חמשה אמהרין בני שנה חמשה דן
קרבן פגעיאל בר עכרן :

ביום תריעסר יום נסי(א) לבני נפתלי' אחירע    78
בר עינן : וקרבנה צח(ה דכסף ח)דה תלתין וכ(א)ה    79
מתקלה סינך חד כסף שבעין (ת)קל במתקל קדשה
תריהון מאלין סלת בסים במשח למנחה : פיאלי    80
חדה עסרח דהב מליה אוחדו : פר חד בר תורין    81
רכר חד אמחר חד בר (ע)(ת)ה' לעלה : רצפיר עזין    82
חד לסלוח : ולרבח שלמיה תורין תרין דכרין    83
חמשה ערופין חמשה אמ(א)רין בני שנה חמשה דן
קרבן אחירע בר עינן :

• [דה] חנכת מרבחה ביומ[ה רבותה] יתח    84
סלוארת' נסי(א)י ישראל צחין דכסף תרתיעסרי
פינכין רכסף תריעסר פילאן דדהב תרתיעסרי :

תלתין ומעה צח ת[ר]ה דכסף ושבעין פנך [חד]    85
כל כסף מאניה תרין אלפין וארבע מאון במתקל
קדשה : פיאלן דרדהב תרתיעסרי מאלין אוחדו    86
עסרה עסרה פילאיתה' במתקל קדשה כל דהב
פילאותה' עסרין ומעה : כל תוריה לעלתה תריעסר    87
פרין רכרין תריעסר אמהרין בני שנה תריעסר
ומנחתהן וצפירי עזין תריעסר לסלוח : וכל תור    88
רבת שלמיה עסרין וארבעה פרין דכרין שתין
ערופין שתין אמהרין בני שנה שתין דה חנבת

---

¹ After נמתלי on marg. an illegible gloss.
² So MS.

89 כדבחה בתר ר[בות]ה' יהה : ובמיעל משה לאהל
מועד לכמללה עמה ושמע ית קלה מכלל עמה כן
עלאוי כפרחתה רעל ארון סהדואתרה מביני תרין
כרוביה וסלל עמה :

viii. 1, 2 ¹וםלל יהוה עם משה למיכר : מלל עם אהרן
ותימר לה באסקותך ית בוציניה עם לקובל אפי
3 כנהרתה ינירון שבעת בוציניה : ועבד כן אהרן
עם לקובל אפי כנהרתה אסק בוציניה כמה דפקד
4 יהוה ית משה : ודן עובד מנהרתה נגר² דהב עד
כיתוביחה ועד פריחיה נגד³ היא כחזור דחזי יהוה
ית משה כן עבד ית מנהרתה :

5, 6 ⁴וכלל יהוה עם משה למיכר : דבור ית ליואי
Seu. 7 מ[ל]גו בני ישראל ותדכי יתהון : ⁴וכדן תעבד להון
לכדכאתון אדי עליה[ון] מי סלוח ויעברון עפוף על
8 כל בסרון ויריעון רקעיהון וידכון : ויסבח פר בר
תורין ומנחתה סלת בסיס במשח ופר תנין בר
9 תורן תסב לסלוח : ותקרב ית ליואי לקודם אהל
10 מועד ותכנש ית כל כנשת בני ישראל : ותקרב
ית ליואי לקודם יהוה ויסמכון בני ·· ישראל ית
11 אדירון על ליואי : ויניף אהרן ית ליואי אנאפר

---

¹ This expression occurs several times in this chapter; in
verse 1 it is impossible to decide what was the original reading, the
page being much blotted; in 10 the original word has been erased
and אמרח inserted by a later hand; in 89 the word has been
entirely erased, leaving a blank; in this place only the first and last
letters have been left, three letters apparently having been erased.

² Before וסלל on marg. ...חה רעו..

³ A letter has been erased before and after ד.

⁴ Before וסלל on marg. [נ]תר רתה.

E

לקדם יהוה כלואח בני ישראל וידון לכשבשה ית

12 תשכיש יהוה: וליואי יסמכון ית אדיהון על ריש
פרירה ויעבד ית חד סלוח ית חד עלה ליהוה

13 לכסלחה על ליואי: ותקים ית ליואי לקדם אהרן

14 ולקודם בניו ותניף יתון אנאפה ליהוה: והפרש

15 ית ליואי כלגו בני ישראל וידון לי ליואי: ובתר
כן יעאלון ליואי למשמשה ית תשכיש אהל מועד

16 וחדכי יתון ותניף יתון אנאפה: הל(ה) יהיבין יהיבין
אנח לי מ[ל]גו בני ישראל תחות כל בכור פתוח

17 רחם בבני ישראל דברת יתון לי: הל(ה) לי כל
בכור בבני ישראל באנשה ובבהכתה ביום דקטלת
כל בכור בארע כצרים וקדשת יתון לי:

18 חברית ית ליואי תחות כל בכור בבני' ישראל:

19 ויהבית ית ליואי יהיבין לאהרן ולבניו כ[ל]גו בני
ישראל למשמשה ית תשמש בני ישראל באהל
מועד ולמסלחה על בני ישראל ולא יהי בכני

20 ישראל נגף בסקרב בני ישראל לקדשה: יעבד
משה: ואהרן וכל כנשת בני ישראל לליואי ככל
דפקד יהוה ית משה לליואי כן עבדו להון בני

21 ישראל: ואסתלחו ליואי ורע רקעדהון ואניף אהרן
יתון אנאפה לקודם יהוה וסלח עליהון אהרן

22 לכדכאתון: ובתר כן עלו ליואי למשבשה ית
תשמישון באהל מועד לקודם אהרן ולקודם בניו
כמה דפקד יהוה ית משה על ליואי כן עבדו להון:

23, 24 ומלל יהוה עם משה למימר: דה דלליואי כבר

תל לחי on marg. בבני After    1
.כרת על רסר on marg. ומלל Before   2

חמש ועסרין שנ(ה) ולעל יעאל לחיל חילה בעבידת
אהל מועד: וכבר חכשין שנין יעזר מן חיל עביתה 25
ולא יעבד עד: וישמש עם' אחיו באהל מועד 26
למטר מטארה תעבידה לא יעבד (אכו)ן תעבד
לליואי במטרתן:

ויסלל יהוה עם משה במדבר סיני בשתה 1.IX.
תנינתה למפקיתון מן ארע מצרים בירחה קדמאה
למיכר: ויעברון בני ישראל ית פסחה² בזבנה³: 2
בארבעה עסר יום בירחה הדן ביני רמשיה יעבדון 3
יתה בזבניו ככל בזיריתה וככל דיניו תעבדון יתה:
ויסלל משה עם בני ישראל למעבד פסחה: ועבדו 4,5
ית פסחה בקדמאה בארבעה עסר יום ליריחה ביני
רמשיה במדבר סיני ככל דפקד יהוה ית משה כן
עבדו בני ישראל: והוו גברין דהוו מסבין לנפש 6
דאנש ולא יכלו למעבד פסחה ביום ההוא וקרבו
לקדם משה ולקודם אהרן ביומה ההוא: ויאמרו 7
גבריה האנן לה אנחנן מסבין לנפש דאנש למה
נחבצר דלא למסקרבה ית קרבן יהוה באזבניו³ בגו
בני ישראל: ואמר להון משה קומו ואשמעה סרה 8
יפקד יהוה לכון:

וסלל יהוה עם משה למימר: מלל עם' בני 9,10
ישראל למימר אנש אנש אן יהי מסב לנפש אי
באורע רחיקה לכון אי לדריכון ויעבד פסח ליהוה:
בירחה תנינה בארבעה עסר יום ביני רמשיה 11
יעבדון יתה על פטיר ומרורין יאכלונה: לא ישירון 12

---

¹ פפ is written over.      ² Before וסלל on marg. ...ות אלהן.
³ So MS.      ⁴ After פפ on marg. וסכל ממא.

E 2

כנה עד צפר וגרם לא יתברון בה ככל גזירת

13 פסחה יעבדון יתה: ואנש דהוא דכי ובאורע
לא הוה וקץ למעבד פסחא ותתעקר נפשה ההיא
כן עסיה הל(ה) קרבן יהוה לא הקרב באזבניו חובה

14 יקבל אישה ההוא: ואן יתמיר עמכן גיור ויעבד
פסח ליהוה כגזירת פסחא וכדיניו כן יעבד גזירה
חדה יהי לכון ולגיורא וליצובה דאראעה:

15 וביום דאתקם ית משכנה אכסי עננה ית'
משכנה למשכן סחדואתא וברמשה יהי על משכנה

16 כחזו אש עד צפר: כן יהי תדיר עננה יכסינה וחזו

17 איש בלילי: ולפם אסהלקורת עננה מעל משכנה
ובתר כן יטלון בני ישראל ובאתרה דישכן חסן

18 עננה תמן ישרון בני ישראל: על מימר יהוה יטלון
בני ישראל ועל מימר יהוה ישרון כל יומין דישכן

19 עננה על משכנה ישרון: ובאורכות עננה על
משכנה יומין סני ירטרון בני ישראל ית פטארת

20 יהוה ולא יטלון: ואד יהי עננה יומין במנין על
משכנה על מימר יהוה ישרון ועל מימר יהוה

21 יטלון: ואד יהי עננה כרמש עד צפר ויסתלק
עננה בצפרה ויטלון אי איכם' ולילי ויסתלק עננה

22 ויטלון: אי תרין יומין אי ירח אי יומין באורהכות'
עננה על משכנה_ למשכן עליו ישרון בני ישראל

23 ולא יטלון ובאסתחלקותה יטלון: על מימר יהוה
ישרון ועל מימר יהוה יטלון ית כטארת יהוה
נטארו על מימר יהוה באד משה:

---

[1] After יח on marg. . . . ר . .[?] חיי.
[2] Altered from יומס.          [3] So MS.

וּמַלֵּל יְהוָֹה עִם מֹשֶׁה כְּשָׁה לְמֵימַר : עֲבֵד לָךְ תַּרְתֵּין ‡ י‚א‚ב‚
חֲצוֹצְרָן דִּכְסַף נְגֵד‘ תַּעֲבֵד יָתֵין וִיהוֹן לָךְ לְכוֹעַק
כְּנִשְׁתָּא וּלְכַּמֵּל יָת כְּשִׁרְיָאתָה : וְתִתְקְעוּן בְּהֵין ג
וְיִזְדַּמְּנוּן לְוָתָךְ כָּל כְּנִשְׁתָּה לִתְרַע אֹהֶל מוֹעֵד : וְאִן ד
בַּחֲדָא יִתְקְעוּן וְיִזְדַּמְּנוּן לְוָתָךְ נְסִיֹדָה רֵישֵׁי אַלְפֵי
יִשְׂרָאֵל : וְתִתְקְעוּן אַשְׁבָּעָה רְטָלוֹ כְּשִׁרְיָאתָה דְשָׁרָין ה
מַדִּנְחָה : וְתִתְקְעוּן אַשְׁבָּעָה תִּנְיָנוּת וְיִטְלוֹ כְּשִׁרְיָאתָה ו
דְשָׁרֵין מִצִּיפוּנָה אַשְׁבָּעָה יִתְקְעוּן לְמַטְלֵיהוֹן : וּבִכְנַשׁ ז
יָת קְהָלָא תִּתְקְעוּן וְלָא תְבַעֲשׁוּן : וּבְנֵי אַהֲרֹן כָּהֲנַיָּה ח
יִתְקְעוּן בַּחֲצוֹצְרָתָה וִיהוֹן לְכוֹן לִגְזֵירַת עֲלָם לְדָרֵיכוֹן :
וְכַד תֵּיעֲלוּן לִקְרָבָה‘ בְּאַרְעֲכוֹן עַל עָקְתָה דְּמֵעִיק ט
יַתְכוֹן וְתַבְעֲשׁוּן בַּחֲצוֹצְרָאתה‘ וְתִדְּכְרוּן‘ לְקֳדָם יְהוָֹה
אֱלָהֲכוֹן וְתִתְפַּצוּן כֵּן דְּבָבֵיכוֹן : וּבְיוֹמֵי חֶדְוַאתְכוֹן י
וּבְמוֹעֲדֵיכוֹן וּבְרֵישֵׁי יַרְחֵיכוֹן ▪וְתִתְקְעוּן בַּחֲצוֹצְרָאתָה ‡ יא‚
עַל עֲלָתְכוֹן וְעַל דִּבְחֵי נִכְסַת קוּדְשֵׁיכוֹן וִיהוֹן לְכוֹן לְדֻכְרָן
לְקֳדָם יְהוָֹה אֱלָהֲכוֹן אֲנִי יְהוָה אֱלָהֲכוֹן :

וּמַלֵּל‘ יְהוָֹה עִם מֹשֶׁה כְּשָׁה לְמֵימַר סוֹבִי לְכוֹן‘ דְּאַרְן
בְּטוּרָה הָדֵין : פְּנוֹ וְטוּלוֹ לְכוֹן וְעוּלוֹ לְטוּר אֱמוֹרָאָה
וּלְכַל מַשְׁרָיו בְּבִקְעָתָה בְּטוּרָה וּבִשְׁפֵילְתָה בִּדְרוֹכָה
וּבְעוּף יַמָּה אֲרַע כְּנַעֲנָאָה וּלְבָנוֹנָה עַד נַהֲרָא רַבָּה
נְהַר פְּרָת : חֲזֵי יְהַבִּית לְקוּדְמֵיכוֹן יָת אַרְעָה עוֹלוֹ
וִירַתּוּ יָת אַרְעָה דְּאִשְׁתַּבַּעַת לַאֲבָהַתְכוֹן לְאַבְרָהָם
לְיִצְחָק וּלְיַעֲקֹב לְמִתַּן לְהוֹן לִזְרַעֲהוֹן בַּתְרֵיהוֹן :

---

¹ Before וּמלל on marg. אן בכל צ.

² A letter has been erased before and after ד.     ³ So MS.

⁴ This and the two following verses are not in the Hebrew
text, but are to be found in Deut. i. 6-8.

⁵ After לכון on marg. כנסת תאב.

יא  והוה בשתה חנינתה בירחה תנינה' בעסרין
ביחרה אסתלק ענגה מן על כישכן סהדואתה:
יב  ונטלו בני ישראל למטליהון כפדבר סיני תש[כן]
יג  ענגה במרבר פראן: ונטלו בקדמאי על מימר יהוה
יד  באד משה: ונטל [טכס] כשרית בני יהודה בקדמי
טו  לחיליהון ועל חילה נחשון בר עכינדב: ועל חיל
טז  שבט בני ישכר נתנאל בר צוער: ועל חיל שבט
יז  בני זבולן אליאב בר חילן: ואתיעח משכנה ונטלו
יח  בני גרשון ובני מר[ר]י נסבי כשכנה: ונטל [טכס]
כסרית בני ראובן לחיליהון ועל חילה אליצור בר
יט  שריאור: ועל חיל שבט בני שמעון שלמיאל בר
כ  צורישדה: ועל חיל שבט בני גד אליסף בר
כא  דעויל: ונטלו קהתאי נסבי כקדשה: ואקימו ית
כב  משכנה עד מיעלון: ונטל [טכס] כסרית בני
א.יב.ט  אפרים לחילתהן ·ועל חילה נחשון' בר עכינדב:
כג  ועל היל שבט בני מנשה גמליאל בר פדיצור: ועל
כד  חיל שבט בני בנימים אבידן בר גדעוני: ונטל
טכס כסרית בני דן מכנש לכל כשריאתה לחיליהון
כו  ועל חילה אחיעזר בר עמישדה: ועל חיל שבט
כז  בני אשר פגעיאל בר עכרן: ועל חיל שבט בני
כח  נפתלי אחירע בר עינן: אלין כטלי בני ישראל
לחיליהון ונטלו:
כט  'ואמר משה לחובב בר רעואל מדינאה חמיו
דכשה נטלין אנחנו לאתרה דאמר יהוה יתה אתן
לכן ארה עמנו וניטב לך הלא יהוה מלל טב על

30 ישראל : ואמר לה לא איתה אלהן לארעי
31 ולאתילדותי אהך : ואמר הל ני תשבק יתנו הל[א]
על כן חכמת מסרואינו במדבירה והוית לנו
32 לצורכין : ויהי כד תהך עמנו ויהי טובה ההוא
33 דייטב יהוה עמנו וניטב לך : ונטלו מטר יהוה
אורע תלתה יומין וארון קיאם יהוה נטל לקדמיון
34 אורע תלתה יומין למגאה להון מנחוה' : וענן יהוה
35 על א[פיהו]ן איכם במטלון מן מישריתה : והוה
במטל ארונה ואמר משה קומה יהוה וידבדרון
דבביך ויערקון סניך מקדמיך : ובמנותה' יתאמר
16 תובה יהוה רבואת אלפי ישראל :

xl. 1 'והוה עמה ככתנין ביש במשמוע יהוה ושכ[ע]
יחוה ואתקף רגזה ובערת בהון אש יהוה ואכלת
2 באסטר מישריחה : יתבע עמה למשה וצלי משה
ליהוה ואטפעעת' אשתה : וקר(ה) שם אתרה ההוא
3 טבעירה' הל(ה) בערת בהון אש יהוה : וספספה
4 דבבוה אתחמדו תחמדה תעזרו ובכו אף בני ישראל
5 ואמרו מן ייכלנן' בסר : אדכרנן ית נוניתה דאכלנן
במצרים כגן ית ק(שאיה) וית (הבחטיה') וית חציחה
6 וית חהומיה : וכדו נפשנ(ן) יבישה לית כל בלחוד
7 למנה סכיננו : ומנה כזרע ד(גד) הוא וחזוותה
8 כחזות ברלה : (שאט)ו עמה ולקטו וטחנו בריחים
ודכו במדוכה ובשלו בקדרה ועבדו יתה עגולין

' So MS.     ' Before יהוה on marg. an illegible gloss.

' The א of אטפעעת is written over.

' The ' is written over.

' Apparently altered from ייכלנו, as has been often done in this chapter.     ' So MS.

‏9 והוה טעכה כמעם כשר דכשחה : ובמעת טלה

‏10 על כשריתה בלילי נערה כנה עליו : וישמע משה
‏ירת עכרה בכי לכרניו אנש לתרע כשכנה ואחקף
‏רוגז יהוה שריר ובעיני משה בעיש :

‏11 ואמר משה ליהוה למה אבעשת לעבדך¹ ולכה
‏לא א(תשקעת)² חן³ בעיניך לנשבאה ית (סבל) כל
‏12 עכה הדן עלי : אנה בטנת ית כל עכה הדן אם
‏אנה ילדתה (כד)⁴ תימר לי (סבלה) בעבך כברה
‏ריסב(ל) (המאה)⁵ ירת ינקה לארעה דאשתחבערת
‏13 לאבהתה : כנען לי בסר לכתן לכל עכה הדן
‏14 הל(ה) בכו עלי לביכר הב לנ(ן) בסר וניכל : לא
‏אכול אנה לחדי לכמבל ית כל עכה הדן הל(ה)

‏15 יקיר כני : ואן (אכון) אהה עכד לי קטלני שבי קטל
‏ואן (אחשקעת רעים) בעיניך ולא אחזי בבישתי :

‏16 ⁶ואכר יהוה למשה: כנש לי שבען גבר סן
‏חכימי ישראל דחכמת הלא אנן חכימי עכה וספריו
‏והדבר יתן לאהל כועד ויתקוככין תכן עכך :

‏17 ואישרת ואכלל עכך תכן ואצל כן רוחרה דעליך
‏ואשוי עליהון ויסבון עכך בס(בל)⁷ עכה ולא תסבל⁸

‏18 אתה לחודיך : ולעכה תיכר התקדשו לכחר וחיכלון
‏בסר הל(ה) בכיתון במשבוע יהוה למיכר כן ייכלנ(ו)

---

¹ After לעבדך on marg. [1] בקות קטטה.　• So MS.

² This has apparently been altered to רים for רעים.

³ There are traces of a ל between כ and ד.

⁴ So MS., with traces of נת after, in an older hand.

⁵ Before האמר on marg. מד. על ה.

⁶ A letter has apparently been erased between כ and ם.

⁷ The ל is written over.

בסר הלו טב לנ(ו) במצרים ויתן יהוה לכון בסר
ותיכלון : לא יום חד תיכלון ולא תרין יומין ולא 19
חמשה יומין ולא עסרה יומין ולא עסרין יום : עד 20
ירח יומין עד יפק כ(אפ)כון זיהי לכון ל(ב)ר(א)ה חזו
הל(ה) אצירקתון ית יהוה דבגווכן ובכיתון לקודמיו
למימר לכה דן נפקנו כמצרים : ואמר משה שת 21
כאן דאלף רגלאי עמה דאנה בגוה ואחה אמרת
בסר אתן להון וייכלון ירח יומין : עניה ותורירה 22
יתנכס להון וספק להון אן ית כל נוני ימה יתכנש
להון וספק להון :

ואמר יהוה למשה האד יהוה ת(קצר) אתה 23
תחזי אן יערענך מלי אן לא : ונפק משה ומלל 24
עם עמה ית מלי יהוה וכנש שבעין גבר כן חכימי
עמה ואקים יתהון סחרת משכנה : ונעת יהוה בענן 25
ומלל עמה ואצל כן רוחה דעליו ויהב על שביעתי
גבר חכימיה והוה כד דשרת עליהן רוחה :

\* \* \* \*

ואפקו גבות ארעה דגשו יתרה לבני ישראל 33
למימר ארעה דעברנ(ו) בה לבנש יתה ארע אכלה
דירה היא וכל עמה דחזינ(ו) בגוה גברי פשעה :
ותמן חזינ(ו) ית גיבריה בני ענק כן גיבריה והינן 34
בעיננ(ו) כקמצין וכן הוינן בעיניהן :

ורגנ(ו) בני ישראל במשכניהון ואמרו בסנאת

1 Before ואמר on marg. נמזח יתלי.
2 This, and the following six verses, are not in the Hebrew, but are to be found in Deut. i. 27–33.
3 After ואמרו on marg. יחקי ח.

F

יהוה יתג(ו) אפקנ(ו) כן ארע מצרים לכמן יתנו באד
אבוראה לכשיצאתנ(ו) : להן אנחנ(ו) סלקין ואחינ(ו)
שפלו ית לבנ(ו) למימר עם רב וסוגי כננ(ו) ק(ריא)ן
רברבן ותלילין בעלאלרה ואף בני ענקאי חזינ(ו)
חמן :

ואמר משה לבני ישראל לא תצ[טד]ן ולא[ ]
תדחלון מנהון : יהוה אלהכון אתי לקודמיכון הוא
יגיח לכן ככל דעבד עמכון במצרים לעיניכון :
ובמדברה דחזיתה דסבלך ׳ יהוה אלהך כמה
ח[ן]סבלי גבר ית ברה בכל ארעה דהלכתח
עד כיתיכון עד אחרה הדנן : ובכמללה הח
ליתיכין מהימנין ביהוה אלהכון : אתי לקודמיכון
באורעה לכבש לכון אתר למשראתכון באש בלילי
לכ(חזא)תכון (בארעה) דתהכון בה זבעננה
באימכה :

iv. 1　ואשביאת כל כנשתה ויהבו ית קלון ובכה עמה
2　בליליה ההוא : ורנו על משה ועל אהרן כל בני
ישראל ואמרו להון כל כנשתה להוי מיתנ(ו) בארע
3　מצרים אי במדברה הדן להוי מיתנ(ו) : ולמה יהוה
fol. 17. b.　מעאל יתנ(ו) לארעה הדה לכפל בחרב ינשינן
וטפלינן יהון לבוה חלא טב לנו מעזרה למצרים :
4, 5　ואמרו גבר לאחיו נהן ריש ונעזר למצרים : ונפל
משה ואהרן על אפידהן לקודם כל קהל כנשת
6　בני ישראל : ויהושע בר נון וכלב בר יפנה כן

<hr>

¹ After לא on marg. ... עקר.

² There is an erasure, apparently of one letter, after the ס.

³ There is an erasure, apparently of one letter, before and
after the ס.

גשושיה ית ארעה בצעו רקעיהן : ואכרו לכל ‏7
כנשת בני ישראל לסיכר ארעה דעברנו בה למבש
יתה טבה ארעה שריר שריר : אן אתחרי בנ(ן) ‏8
יהוה וסמעאל יהנ(ן) לארעה הדה ויהבה לנ(ו) ארע
די כדיבה חלב חדבש : בֿם ביהוה אל המרדון ‏9
ואתון אל תדחלון מן עמה דארעה הל(ה) לחמנ(ז)
אנֿ סטה צלכה מן עליהון ויהוה עכנ(ן) אל
תדחלון : ואכרו כל כנשתה לכרגם יהון באבנין ‏10
וכבוד יהוה אתחזי באהל מעד לוֿת כל בני
ישראל :

'ואֿמר יהוה לכשה לסיכר עד אה(ן) יבתרני ‏11
עמה הדנ(ן) ועד אה(ן) לא יחיכֿנן בי בכל (סיכן)יה
דעבדֿת בגוֿה : אכ(ח)'ינה במו(ת)ר'ה (וחרבנה)' ‏12
ואעבד יתֿך ית ביֿת אבוֿך לגוי רב וחיל סנֿה :
ואֿמר משֿה ליהוה וישׁמעון כֿצראי הלה אסקֿת ‏13
בחילֿך יֿת עכה הדן כבנֿה : ויֿמרח לדיוֿר ארעה ‏14
הדה וישׁמעון הלה אֿתה יהוה בֿגו עמה הֿתֿן דחזו
בחזו מֿחחזי אֿתה יהוה וענֿנֿך קאם עלייהן ובעמוֿד
ענן אֿתֿרֿה אֿתֿי לקֿדֿמֿיֿהֿן באיֿמֿמֿה ובעמוֿד אֿש
בליֿלֿי : ותֿקטל יֿת עֿכֿה הֿדֿנ(ֿן) כֿאֿנֿש חֿד וייֿמֿרֿח ‏15
(גֿוֿא)יֿדֿה דֿיֿשֿמֿעֿוֿן יֿת שֿמֿעֿך לֿמֿיֿכֿר : כֿן דֿלֿא ‏16
יֿכֿלֿֿת יֿהֿוֿה לֿמֿעֿאֿלֿה יֿת עֿכֿה הֿדֿנ(ֿן) לֿאֿרֿעֿה
דֿאֿשֿחֿבֿע לֿהֿן וֿנֿכֿסֿן בֿסֿדֿבֿרֿה : וֿכֿדֿו יֿרֿבֿי נֿי חֿיֿל ‏17
טֿרֿי כֿמֿה דֿפֿלֿלֿת לֿמֿיֿכֿר : יֿיֿהֿוֿה רֿחֿיֿק רֿוֿגֿזֿיֿן וֿסֿוֿבֿי ‏18  ‏.ייֿ .בֿ.
(טֿוֿב) וֿחֿיֿכֿֿנֿו תֿלֿי לֿחֿוֿבֿיֿן וֿלֿפֿשֿׁיֿן וֿלֿחֿטֿאֿיֿן וֿ(דֿכֿא)יֿ[9]

---

[1] Before אֿמֿר on marg. ‏ר..נ..    [2] So MS.

[3] So, apparently, MS.

לה יזכי פקד חוב אבהן על בנין על תליתאין ועל

‏יט רביעאין : סלח ני לחוב(רת) עמה הד(נ)ן כרבות
(טוב)ך וכמה ר(סבל)ת לעמה הד(נ)ן כמצרים ועד
הכרה :

‏כ, כא ואמר יהוה סלחת כפליך : ו(אחם) חי אני'
‏כב ותמלה כבוד יהוה ית כל ארעה ! הלו כל גברי(ה)
דחזו ירת (איקר)י (וית רבות)י דעבדת במצרים
ובמדברה ונסו יתי דן עסרה זבנין ולא שמעו
‏כג בקלי : לא יחזון ירת ארעה דאשתבעת לאבהתון
‏כד לכהן להון וכל מבתרי לא יחזונה : ועבדי כלב
עקב (ד)הות רוח חורי עמה ומלי בתרי ועאלנה
‏כה לארעה דעל לתמן וזרעה יירתנה : ועמלקאה
וכנענאה דאר בעמקה מחר פנו וטלו לכן למדברה
אורע ים סוף :

‏כו, כז ומלל יהוה עם משה ועם אהרן למימר : עד"
אמת לכנשתה בישתה הרה (דאנ)ו(ז) מ(רננין) עלי
ית (רנינ) בני ישראל דאנון מ(רנין)[3] עלי שמעת :
‏כח אמר להון חי אנה מחיב(ז) יהוה אן לא כמה
‏כט דמללתון במשמעי כן אעבד לכן ! במדברה הדן
יפלון פגריכן וכל באסורתכן לכל מנינכון מבר
‏ל עסרין שנין ולעל דרנתון עלי : לא אתון תיעלון
לארעה דארמת עם אדי לכשראה יתכון בה הלא
‏לא אן כלב בר יפנה ויהושע בר נון : וטפלכן דאמרתון
לבוה יהי ועאל יתון ויעכמת ית ארעה דאציקתון
בה :

[1] After דן on marg. ייטל דן.
[2] After עד on marg. . . . וברנין נ.
[3] So MS.

‏יופגריכון אתון יפלון במדברה הד(נ)ן : ובניכון נ‏

‏יהון רען במדברה ארבעין שנין ויקבלון ית‏

‏(זנא)תכון עד יישלכון פגריכון בכדברה : במנין 34‏

‏יוכיה דגאשתון ית ארעה ארבעין יובין יום לשתה‏

‏יום לשתה תקבלון ית חוביכין ארבעין שנין ותעכבון‏

‏ית תושלכחי : אני יהוה כללת אן לא הדה אעבד 35‏

‏לכל כנשתה בישתה הדה [ד]אסידו עלי במדברה‏

‏הרן ישלכון ותכן יכותון :‏

‏וגבריה¹ דשלח כשה לכגש ית ארעה ועזרו 36‏

‏וארגו² עליו ית כל כנשתה לספקה גנו על ארעה:‏

‏וכיתו גבריה מפקי בנורת ארעה ביישה³ בכגיפה 37‏

‏לקדם יהוה : ויהושע בר נון וכלב בר יפנה 38‏

‏(אתחו)⁴ מן גבריה האנון דאזלו לכגש ית ארעה :‏

‏וכלל כשה ית פליה האלין עם כל בני ישראל 39‏

‏ואתבלו עכה שריר : ואקדמו בצפרה וסלקו לריש 40‏

‏טורה לכיכר אנן⁵ (ונסק)⁶ לאתרה דאכר יהוה‏

‏הל(ה) חטינ(ו)⁷ :‏

‏ואכר⁷ יהוה לכשה אכר להון לא תסקון ולא‏

‏תגיחון הל(ה) לית אני בגוכון ולא תתברון לקדם‏

‏דבביכון : ואכר כשה לכה דן אתון עברין ית 41‏

‏טיכר יהוה וחיא לא תצלח : אל תסקון הלו לית 42‏

¹ Before ‏ובגריה‏ on marg. ‏סן עקף רבח‏.

² The ‏א‏ is written over.    ³ The ‏ה‏ is written over.

⁴ So MS.    ⁵ A letter has been erased before ‏ן‏.

⁶ Apparently altered from the participle: ‏ק‏ is still legible after ‏ם‏.

⁷ Before ‏אכר‏ on marg. ‏אה‏..., and underneath ‏מן‏.... This verse is not in the Hebrew, but may be found in Deut. i. 42.

יהוה בגוכון ולא תתברון לקדם דבביכון: הל(ה) ‏43
עמלקאה וכנענאה חבן לקודמיכון ותפלון בחרב
חל(ה) על כן עזרתון כבתר יהוה תלא יהי יהוה
עמכון : ועצפו לכסק לריש טורא וארון יהוה ומשה ‏44
לא פסק כלגו משריתא : יונעת עמלקאה וכנענאה ‏45,44
דדאר בטורה ההוא לזיכונון ורדפו יתון כמה
דעבדי דליה ומעינין וכתנון[1] עד חרמה ועזרו
למשריחה :

וכלל יהוה עם משה לסיסר: כלל עם בני[2]
ישראל ותיכר להון כד תיעלון לארע כדוריכון
דאני יהב לכון: תעבדון קרבן ליהוה עלה או ‏3
דבח לכפרשה נדר אי רעוה אי בכיעדיכון למעבד
ריח תעוה ליהוה כן תוריה אי כן ענה : ויקרב ‏4
דמקריב ית קרבנה ליהוה כנחה סלת עסור בסיס
ברבעות אינה כשה : וחסר לנסך רבעות אינה ‏5
תעבד על עלתה אי לדבח לאמאר חד : אי ‏6
לדכרה[3] תעבד כנחה[4] סלת הרין עסורין בסיס
בכשח תלתות עינה[4] : וחסר לנסך תלתות אינה ‏7
תקרב ריח רעוה ליהוה:

וכד תעבד בר תורין עלה אי דבח[5] לכפרשה ‏8
נדר אי שלמין ליהוה: ויקרב עם בר תוריה כנחה ‏9
סלת הלתה עסורין בסיס בכשח פלגות חינה[6] :
וחסר תקרב לנסך פלגות חינה קרבן ריח רעוה ‏10
ליהוה: (כדן) יתעבד לתור חד אי לדכר חד אי ‏11

---

[1] So MS.; there is an erasure after כ.
[2] After בני on marg. קדם בי.     [3] The ה is written over.
[4] So MS.     [5] After דבח on marg. אביח אל.
[6] So MS.

לנקדה' באמאר(ה) אי בעזי(ה) : כמנינן תעבדון ‏ 12

(כת)ן תעבדון לחד במנינן : כל יצבורה יעבד ‏ 13

הכתן ית אלין לכקרבה קרבן ריח תעוה ליהוה :

ואן יתגיר (עמ)כן ביור אי דבנוכון לדריכון ויעבד ‏ 14

קרבן ריח רעה ליהוה ככרה תעבדון כן יעבד :

קהלה גזירה הדה' לכן ולגיור גזירת עלם ‏ 15

לדריכון כותכון כגיורה יהי לקודם יהוה : תורי ‏ 16

חדה ודין חד יהי לכון ולגיורה דביור עמכן :

‏ 16,17 ‏ ומלל יהוה עם משה למימר : כלל עם בני

ישראל ותימר להון במיעלכן לארעה דאני מעאל

יתכן לתמן : ויהי במיכלכם מלחם ארעה תרימון ‏ 19

אראכה ליהוה : ראשורת עצבאתכון חלה תרימון ‏ 20

אראמה כארמורת חדר כן תרימו יתה : כראשורת ‏ 21

עצואתכון' תתננון' ליהוה אראכה לדריכן : ואן ‏ 22

תשגון ולא תעבדון ית כל פקורה אלין דכלל יהוה

עם משה : ית כל רפקד לוכון באד משה לכן ‏ 23

יוכה דפקד יהוה ולרתי לדריכון : ויהי אן בעיני ‏ 24

כנשתה (אתעבדת) לשגו ויעברון כל כנשתה פר בר

תורין חד לרח רעה ליהוה ומנחתה ונסכיו כדין

וצפיר עזין חד לסלוח : ויסלח כהנה על כל כנשת ‏ 25

בני ישראל ויסתלח להון הל(ה) שגו היא ואנן

איתו ית קרבנון קרבן ליהוה וסלחון לקודם יהוה

על שבותון : ויסתלח לכל כנשת בני ישראל ולגיורה ‏ 26

דביור בנוכון הל(ה) לכל עמה בשגו :

---

¹ The ה is written over.      ³ So MS.
² Before וצלל on marg. . . . . ותה      ⁴ So MS.

כז. ‫ואן' נפש חדה תחטי בשגו ותקרב עז ברת‬
כח. ‫שתה לסלוח : וכסלח כהנה על נפשה ר(שגת‬
‫בחט)יה בשגו לקדם יהוה לכסלחה עלוי ויסתלח‬
כט. ‫לה : יצובה בבני ישראל ולגיורה דגיור בגוכון‬
ל. ‫תורו חדרה (יהי) לכון לדעבד בשגו : ונפשה‬
‫רתעבד באד רכח כן יצובה וכן גיורה ירת יהוה‬
‫הוא כגדף ותתעקר נפשה ההיא כלגו עמיה :‬
לא. ‫ירת הל(ה) מכלל יהוה אביז וית פקודיו בטל עקר‬
‫תתעקר נפשר ההיא חובה בה :‬

לב. ‫יהוו בני ישראל במדברה ואשקעו גבר מקשש'‬
לג. ‫עאין ביום שובתה : ואקרבו יתה דאשקעו יתה‬
‫מקשש עאין ליד משה ליד אהרן ליד כל כנשתה :‬
לד. ‫ואניחו יתה במטרה הל(ה) לא פרש כה יתעבד‬
לה. ‫לה : ואמר יהוה למשה קטל יתקטל גברה רגבו‬
‫יתה באבניא כל כנשתה לבר ממשריתה :‬
לו. ‫ואפקו יתה כל כנשתה לבר ממשריתה ורגמו יתה‬
‫באבנין ויתקטל כמה דפקד יהוה ית משה :‬

לז.לח. ‫ואמר יהוה למשה למימר : מלל עם בני ישראל‬
‫ותימר להן ויעבדון להן צנפן על סטרי רקעיהון‬
‫לדריהון ויתנון על צנפת סטרא שזר דתכלה :‬
לט. ‫ויהן לכון לצנפן ותחזון יתין ותדכרון ירת כל‬
‫פקודי יהוה ותעבדון יתון ולא תתורין' בתר‬
מ. ‫לבכן ובתר עיניכך דאתן זנין בתרן : בדיל‬
‫תדכרון ותעבדון ית כל פקודי ותתהן קדישין‬

¹ Before ואן on marg. ‫סבל סטאן‬.
² After מקשש on marg. ‫..תרין‬.
³ After בני on marg. ‫ו[?] בתר לבה‬.　　⁴ So MS.

לאלהכון: אני יהוה אלהכון דאפקת יתכון מן 41
ארע מצרים למהי לכון לאלהים אני יהוה
אלהכון :

ודבר קרח בר יצהר בר קהת בר לוי ודתן' xvi. 1
ואבירם בני אליהב ואון בר פלת בר ראובן: וקמו 2
לקודם משה וגברין מבני ישראל חמשין ומאתין
נסיחי כנשתה זמיני (סהדו) גברי שכ(ה)ן: ואתכנשו 3
על משה ועל אהרן ואמרו להון סגיו לכון הל(ה)
כל כנשתה כל(ון) קדשין ובגו(נן) יהוה ומכרה
תתרברבון על קהל יהוה: ושמע משה ונפל על 4
אפיו: ומלל עם קרח ועם כל כנשתה למימר 5
fol. 92 b. יצפר ויעכם יהוה ית דלה וית קדישה' יקרב
לירה וית דיבחר בה יקרב לידה: דה עבדו וסבו 6
לכון מחתיא(ן) קרח וכל כנשתה: והבו בהין אש 7
ושוו עליהין אטורו לקודם יהוה מחר וידי אישה
דיבחר יהוה הוא קדישה סגיו לכון בני לוי:

ואמר' משה לקרח שמעו ני בני לוי: וזעור 8, 9
מנכון הל(ה) אפרש אלהה דישראל יתכון מכנשת
ישראל למקרבה יתכון לידה למשמשה ית חשמיש
משכן יהוה ולמקם' לקודם כנשתה למשמשתון:
ואקרב יתך וית כל אחיך בני לוי עמך ובעיתון אף 10
כהנה: לא שפיר אתה וכל כנשתך דכסידין על 11
יהוה ואהרן מה הוא הל(ה) תרנן עליו: ושלח 12

---

' After דום on marg. an illegible gloss.
' The ת is written over.
' Before חמר on marg. ברמה דאלהה.
' So MS.; a letter has been erased after כ.

משה לסוֹעק לדתן ולאבירם בני אליאב ואמרו לא

13 נסק : הזעוּר הל(ה) אסקתנ(ו) כן ארע כ(ד)יבה
חלב ודבש למקטלנ(ו) במדברה הל(ה) אתרברבת

14 עליני אף (אתרברבת) : אף לא לארע כ(ד)יבה חלב
ודבש עאלתנ(ו) ויהבת לנ(ו) פלנת עקל או כרם

15 העיני בברירה האנן תעטט לא נסק : ו(א)תרגז'
למשה שריר ואמר ואסר·ליהוה אל ת(סתכל) לסמנחתון לא
חמדרה דחד מנהן נסבת ולא אבעשרת (ית) חד
מנהון :

16 'ואמר משה לקרח אתה וכל כנשתך הוו לקודם

17 יהוה אתה ואנן ואהרן כחר : וסבו נבר כחתיתה
ותתנון עליהן חואדו' ותקרבון לקודם יהוה גבר
כחתיתה חכשין וכאתין כחתיאן ואתה ואהרן גבר

18,... כחתיתה: ונסבו נבר כחתיתה ויהבו בהין אש
ושוו עליהין חואדו וקמו בתרע אהל מעד ומשה

19 ואהרן: וכנש עליהן קרח ירת כל כנשתה לתרע
אהל מועד ואתחזי כבד יהוה לכל כנשתה :

20 וּמלל יהוה עם משה ועם אהרן לסימר :

21 התפרשו' כלגו כנשתה הדי ואסכם יתן בעטף :

22 ונפלו על אפיהן ואמרו אל אלהין דרוחירה לכל
בסרה הא אנש חד יחטי ועל כל כנשתה תרגז :

23,24 וּמלל יהוה עם משה לסימר : מלל עם כנשתה'
לסימר אסתלקו כן סהר' למשכן קרח דתן ואבירם :

---

[1] The ה is written over.
[2] Before אמר on marg. כבד ....     [3] So MS.
[4] After חתפרש on marg. . ק בעות.
[5] After כנשתה on marg בעי אלהה.
[6] There is a line over ה.

וקם משה ואזל ליד דתן ואבירם ואזלו בתרה 25

חכימי ישראל: וכלל עם כנשתה לכימר סטו ני 26

מעל משכני גבריה רשיעיה אלין ואל תקרבון בכל

דלית דלא תסתחפון בכל חוביהון: ואסתלקו מן 27

(על) משכן קרח דתן ואבירם מן סחר חדתן

ואבירם נפקו קאמין בתרע משכניהון ונשיהון

ובניהון וטפליהון :

ואמר משה בהדה תעכמון הל(ה) יהוה שלחי' 28

למעבד ית כל עובריה אלין הל(ה) לא מלבי : אן 29

כמות כל אנשא ימותון אלין תסורת כל אנשה

יתמסר עליהן לא יהוה שלחי : ואן בריה יברי 30

יהוה ותפתח ארעה ית פמה ותבלע יתהן וית כל

דלון וייתתן חיין לשיול ותתחכבון הל(ה) באתרו

גבריה האלין ית יהוה:

וחוה כאסכמותה למללה ית כל מליה האלין 31

ואבקעת אדמתא דתחותיהון: ופתעת ארעה ית 32 fol. &c.

פמה ובלעת יתהן וית בתיהון וית כל אנש דלקרח

וית כל עותרה: ונעתו אנן וכל דלון חיין לשיול 33

וכסיאת עליהן ארעה ואבדו מלגו קהלה: וכל 34

ישראל דסחרתון ערקו לקלון הלה אמרו דלא

תבלענע ארעה: ואש נפק מלואת יהוה ואכלת ית 35

חמשין ומאתין גבר מקרבי אודותה':

ומלל יהוה עם משה למימר: אמר לאלעזר 36,37

בר אהרן כהנא וירים ית מחתיאתה מביני יקידיה

וית אשתה ברא יתה להל הל(ה) קדשו: ית 38

¹ After שלחי on marg.. אלהה על.  ² So MS.
³ Before ומלל on marg. כל רחמי. In the Heb. text chap. xvii
begins here.

מחתיאת (חוביה) אלין בנפשתהון ועבדו יתין רקועי
טסין חפוי למדבחא הלה אקרבונין לקדם יהוה
<sup></sup> ואקדשו' ויהן לסימן לבני ישראל : ונסב אלעזר
בר אהרן כהנא ית מחתיאת נחשא דאקרבו יקידיה
<sup></sup> ורקרק אנין חפוי למדבחה: דוכן לבני ישראל
בדיל דלא יקרב גבר ברי דלא מזרע אהרן הוא
לכוחדה אוהדו' לקודם יהוה, ולא יהי כקרח
וככנשתה ככה דמלל יהוה באד משה לה :
<sup></sup> ורנו² כל כנשת בני ישראל כן בתר על משה
ועל אהרן למימר אתון קטלתון ית עם יהוה:
<sup></sup> והוה בכנש כנשתה על משה ועל אהרן וא(סתכלו)
לאהל כועד והא כסיאה עננא ואתחזי כבד יהוה:
<sup></sup> ועל משה ואהרן לקודם אהל כועד :
<sup></sup> ⁴ומלל יהוה עם משה למימר : התראמו מלבו
כנשתה הדה ואסכמיתן כעסף ונפלו על אפיהן :
<sup></sup> ואמר משה לאהרן יסב ית מחתיתה והב עליה
אש כן על מדבחה ושוי אחדז ואזל בפר לכנשתה
וסלח עליהן הל(ה) נפק קצפה כלקדם יהוה שרי
<sup></sup> נגפה : ונסב אהרן כמה דמלל משה וחט לבו
קהלה והא שרי נגפה בעמה ויהב ית חואדותה
<sup></sup> וסלח על עמה : וקם בין סיתיה ובין חייה
<sup></sup> ואתעצרת מגיפתה: והוה דמיתו במגיפתה
ארבעדסר⁵ אלפין ושבע מאה לבר מן דמיתו על
<sup></sup> מסלל קרה : ועזר אהרן לית⁵ כשה לתרע אהל
מועד ומגיפתה אתעצרת :

---

¹ The א is written over.        ³ So MS.
² Before חדו on marg. כבבוד ...
⁴ Before נפל on marg. ך ...        ⁵ So MS.

ומלל יהוה עם משה לסימר : סלל עם בני[1]  2 ,1 .xvii
ישראל וסב סלותא עוטר עוטר לבית אב סלות
כל נסיחיהא לבית אבהתא תריעסר עוטרין גבר
ירת שמה תכתב על עוטרה : וירת שם אהרן  3
תכתב על עוטר לוי הל(ה) עוטר חד לריש בית
אבהתם : ותניחנן באהל מועד לקדם סחדואתה  4
דאזדמן לך תמן : ויהי אישה דיבחר[2] בה עוטר(ה)  5
יפרח ואנכ מן עלי ירת (רנינ)י בני ישראל דאנן
ס(רננ)ין עליכא : ומלל משה עם בני ישראל ויהבו  6
לה כל נסיחיהא עוטר לנסיח חד עוטר חד
לבית אבהתא תריעסר עוטרין ועוטר אהרן בגו
עוטריהא : ואנ(יח) משה ית עוטריה לקדם יהוה  7
במשכן סחדואתה : הוה מן דבתר ועל משה  8
למשכן סחדואתה והא פרח עוטר אהרן לבית לוי
ואפק פרח ואנכ נץ וחסל לוזין : ואפק משה ירת  9
כל עוטריה מלקדם יהוה לות כל בני ישראל וחזו
ונסבו גבר עוטרה :

ויאמר[3] יהוה למשה חזר ית עוטר אהרן לקדם  10
סחדואתה למטארה לסימן לבני מריה ואסכם (ית
רנינ)ח[4] מן עלי ולא ימותן : ועבד משה כמה  11
דפקד יהוה יתה כן עבד : ואמרו בני ישראל  12
למשה למימר הא שלמנ(ו) אבדנ(ו) כלנ(ו) אבדנ(ו) :
כל קרוב דקרב למשכן יהוה יתקטל דימנ[ן][4]  13
דש(למנ)ו למשלם :

<hr>
[1] After בני on marg. אלוה בעי.   [2] So MS.
[3] ...בין Before ואמר on marg.
[4] So MS. apparently.

ואמר ' יהוה לאהרן אתה ובניך ובית אבוך עמך    xviii. 1

תקבלון ית עוב מקדשה ואתה ובניך עמך תקבלון

ית חוב כהנתכון : ואף ית אחוך שבט לוי שבט    2

אבוך הקרב עמך ויסתמכון עליך וישכשונך ואתה

ובניך עמך לקודם משכן סהדותא : ויטרון מטרתך    3

וכטרת כל משכנא ברן למני קדשה ולמדבחה לא

יקרבון ולא ימותון אף אנון אף אתון : ויסתמכון    4

עליך ויטרון ית מטארת אהל מועד לכל עבידת

משכנא ובראי לא יקרב לידכון : ותטרון ית    5

מטארת קדשה וית מטארת מדבחה לא יהי עוד

קצף על בני ישראל : ואני אה דברית ית אחיכון    6

ליואי כלבו בני ישראל לכון מתנה יהיבין ליהוה

למפשרה ית חשמיש אהל מועד : ואתה ובניך    7

עמך תטרון ית כהנתכון לכל ממלל מדבחה

ולמלגאב לפרכתה ותשמשון תשכיש מתנה אתן

ית כהנתכן ובראה(ה) דקרב יתקטל :

וטלל ' יהוה עם אהרן ואני אה יהבת לך ית    8

מטארת ארמותי לכל קדשי בני ישראל לך יהבתון

לרבו ולבניך לחולק עלם : חן יהי לך מקדשי    9

קדשיה מן אשתה · כל קרבנון לכל מנחתון ולכל

סלחון ולכל אשכם דיתחבון לי קדש קדשין לך

הוא ולבניך : בקדש קדשיה תיכלנה כל דכר ייכל    10

יתה קדש יהי לך : ודן לך ארמות מתנן לכל    11

אנאפות בני ישראל לך יהבתון ולבניך ולבנתך

עמך לחולק עלם כל דכי בביתך ייכל יתה : כל    12

---

¹ Before ואמר on marg. ... אה ביתא

² Before וטלל on marg. .... קיאם

דמח (רטיב) וכל דמח ד(יבש) וד(גין) ראשותח
דיתנח ליהוה לך יהבתח :

13 כל וֵי בכירי כל דבארעון דייתח ליהוה לך יהי'
14 דכי בביתך ייכלנרח : כל חרם בישראל לך יהי :
15 כל פ(תו)ח רחם לכל בסר דיקרבון ליהוה באנשה
ובבהכתרה יחי לך ברן אפרקרה תפרק ירת בכורי
16 אנשה וית בכורי בהסחה מסבחה תפרק : ופרקנה
מבר ירח תפרק בשיאם(ה) כסף חמטרה מדקלין'
17 בכתקל קדשה עסרין ג(רה) הוא : ברן בכור תור
או בכור אמאר או בכור עז לא תפרק קדש אנון
ירת אדמון תזרק על סדבחרה וירת חרבון תוחד
18 קרבן ריח רעוה ליהורח : ובסרון יהי לך כניערה
19 דאנאפותה וכשק ימינה לך יהי : כל ארמות קדשיה
רירימון בני ישראל ליהוה יהבת לך ולביך ולבנתך
עמך לחולק עלם קיאם מלח עלם הוא לקדם
יהוה לך ולזרעך עמך :

20 ואמר יהוה לאהרן בארעון לא תפלגי וחולק
לא יהי לך בנחהון אני חולקך ופלגתך בגו בני
21 ישראל : ולבני לוי הא יהבת כל מעסר בישראל
לפלגה חלב תשמישון דאנן משמשין ירת תשביש
22 אהל מועד : ולא יקרבון עוד בני ישראל לאהל נב ו.ב. מ.
23 סעד למקבלה חטי למפ(ו)ת : וישבש ליוּאה הוא
ית תשמיש אהל מעד ואנן יקבלון חוביהון בזירת
עלם לדריכון ‌ובגו בני ישראל לא יפלגח פלגה :

¹ After יהי on marg. לבה שחר.
² The ס is written over.
³ After תפלני on marg. [1]על אנח.

הל(ה) ית מעסר בני ישראל דיריסון ליהוה אראסה 24
יהבתה לליואי לפלגה על כן אמרת להון בגו בני
ישראל לא יסלגון פלגה :

וסלל יהוה עם מסה לסיסר : ועם ליואי תמלל 15, 16
ותיסר להון כד תסבון מלות בני ישראל ית מעסרה
דיהבת לכון מלותון בפלגיכון ותרימון מנה ית
אראסות יהוה (מעסר) מסעסרה : ויתחסב לכון 17
אראסתכון כדגנה סן אדרה וכסליתה מן מעצרתה :
כן תריסון אף אתון ית ארמות יהוה מכל מעסריכון 18
דתסבון מלות בני ישראל ותתנון מנה ית ארמות
יהוה לאהרן כהנה : מכל מתנתכן תריסון ית כל 19
ארמות יהוה מכל דמחה ית אקרסה (בנה) : ותיסר 20
להון בארמותכון ירת דמחרה סנה ית תחסב ללואי
כעללת אדהר וכעללת מעצרה : ותיכלון יתה בכל 21
אתר אתון ובתיכן הל(ה) אגר הוא לכן חל(ף)
תסמיסכן באהל מועד : ולא תקבלון עליו חטי 22
בארמותכון ירת דמחה סנה ירת קדסי בני ישראל
לא תחללון ולא תמותון :

וסלל יהוה עם מסה ועם אהרן למיסר : דה 1, 2 xix.
גזירת תורותה דפקד יהוה למיסר מלל עם בני
ישראל ויסבון לך פרה סמוקה סלמה תלית ברה 3
מום ידלא סלק עליה ניר : ותתנון יתה לאלעזר
כהנה ויפק יתה לבר ממסרחה ויכוס יתה לקדמוי : 4
ויסב אלעזר כהנה סן אדמה באצבעה וידי עם

' Before וסלל on marg. על לואי .
' Altered, apparently, in MS. to אקרסתה.
' Before וסלל on marg. כל סלך .

לקובל אפי אהל כועד כן אדמה שבעה זבנין:
ויוקד ית פרתה לעיניו ית (משכה) ית בסרה וית ⁵
אדמה על פרדה יתוקד: ויסב כהנה (קיסם ד)אע ⁶
ואזוב חעורי צביעה וירמי לגו יקידת פרתה: וירע ⁷
רקעיו כהנה ויסעי ית בסרה בטין ובתר ייעל
למשריתה ויסתב כהנה עד רמשה: ודכוקד יתה ⁸
ירע רקעיו בטין ויסעי ית בסרה, בטין ויסתב עד
רמשה:

ויכניש גבר דכי ית קטם פרתה ויניח לבר¹ ⁹
כמשריתה באתר דכי ותהי לכנשת בני ישראל
למטרה למי נדה סלוח היא: וירע דסכנש ית ¹⁰
קטם פרתה וירע רקעיו ויסהב עד רכשה ותהי
לבני ישראל ולגיורה דגיור בגוכן לנזירת עלם:
דיקרב במית לכל נפש דאנש יסהב שבעה יומין: ¹¹
הוא יסתחלח בה ביוכה תליתאה וביוכה שביעאה ¹²
וידכי ואן לא יסתלח ביוכה תליתאה וביוכה
שביעאה לא ידכי: כל דקרב בכית בנפש דאנש ¹³
דימות ולא יסתלח ית משכן יהוה (סי)אב ותתעקר
נפטרה ההיא כישראל הלה כי נדה לא זריק עליו
כסב יהי עוד סובתה בה:

ורה תורותה אנש אן יכות במשכן כלי דעלל ¹⁴
למשכנה וכל דבמשכנה יסתב שבעה יומין: וכל ¹⁵
סאן (קיסם) דלא צניק רשזיר עליו כסב הוא: וכל ¹⁶
דיקרב על אפי ברה, בקטיל חרב או בכית או
בגרם דכן אנש יאו בקבר יסתב שבעה יומין: א. ⁵ ⁵

¹ After לבר on marg. וסכל סטוא.
² After כל on marg. וסד....

17 ויסבון לד(ת)סחב מן עפר יקידת סלוחה יתנון עליו
18 סין חיין על סהן : (וי)סב אזוב ויטבל בסין גבר
דכי וידי על משכנה ועל כניה ועל נפשתה דהו(י)
חמן ועל דקרב בגרם אי בקטיל אי במירת אי
19 בקבר : וידי דכיארה על סםבארה ביומה חליתאה
וביוכרה שביעאה ויסלחנדה ביומה שביעאה וירע
20 רקעיו ויסעי בסין וידכי ברמשה : ואנש דיסתאב ולא
יסחלח ותתעקר נפשה ההיא סלגו קהלדה הל(ח)
(ירת) מקדש יהוה (סיא)ב מי נדה לא זריק עליו
21 כסב הוא : ותהי לכון לגזירת עלם וכדי סי נדה
22 ירע רקעיו ודקרב בסי נדה יסתב עד רמשה : וכל
דיקרב בה כסברה יסתאב ונפשרה דקרב(ה) יסתאב
עד רמשה :

1 22. ועלו בני ישראל כל כנשתה כדבר צן ביחה
קדמאה ודר עכה בקדיש ומיתת חכן כרם
2 (וא)קברת חכן : ולא הוה סין לכנשתה ואתכנשו
3 על משה ועל אהרן : ואתינר עסה עם משה ואמרו
למיסר ולוי שלמנ(ו) במשלם אחינו לקודם יהוה :
4 ולסה היתיחון ית קהל יהוה למדברה הדן לכבות
5 חכן אנחנו ובעירנו : ולכה אסקתנ(ו) מכצרים למעלה
יתנ(ו) לאתרה בישה הדן לא אתר זרע תינה גפן
6 ורסן וכין לית למשתי : ועאל משה ואהרן מקודם
קהלה לתרע אהל כועד ונפלו על אפיהן ואתחוי
כבד יהוה להון :

---

1 Before תלו on marg. קטמה ר׳ , מ.
2 So MS.; a letter has apparently been erased after ב.
3 ב has been written over.    4 ו is written over.

וכלל' יהוה עם משה לסימר: סב ית עוטרה 8 ,7.
וכנש ית כנשתה אתה ואהרן אחוך 1יתמללון 11. &c.
עם כיפה לעיניהון ויתן סכיו' ותפק להון מין מן
כיפה וחשקי ית כנשתה וית בעירון: ונסב משה 9
ית עוטרה מלקחדם יהוה כמה דפקדה: וכנשו 10
משה ואהרן ית קהלה לקדום2 כיפה ואמר להון
שמעו ני כמריה הא מן כיפה הדנן' נאפק לכון
מין: וארם משה ית אדה ומחא ית כיפה בעוטרה 11
תרן זבנין ונפקו מין סגי ושחת כנשתה ובעירון:
ואמר יהוה למשה ולאהרן חזו לא6 היכנתון בי 12
למקדשתי לעיני בני ישראל לכן לא תעאלון ית
קהלה הדנן' לארעה דיהבת להון: אנון מי תיגרה 13
דאתיגרו בני ישראל עם יהוה וקדש בהון: ואמר'
משה מאר' יהוה אתה שרית למחזאה ית עבדך
ית רבותך וית אדך תקיפתה דמן אל בשומיה
ובארעה דיעבד כעובדיך וכ(נבוראת)ך: אעבר ני
ואעזי ית ארעה טבתה דבעבר ירדנה טורה טבה
הדן ולבנונה:

ואמר יהוה למשה סובי לך אל תוזף' סמלל
עמי עוד במללה הדן: סק לריש סכיתה ו(תלי)
עיניך למערבה ולצפונה ולדרומה ולמדינחה וחזי

---

בעיניך הלו לא תעבר ירת ירדנה הדן : ופקד ירת
יהושע ותקפה ועיצה הלא הוא יעבר לקדם עכה
הדן ורוא יפלג יתון ית ארעה דתחזי :

ומלל יהוה עם משה למיכר סוגי לכון' סחרין ית
טורה הדנ(ן) פנו לכון צפונה‏ : וית עמה פקד למיכר
‏ יאתון עברין בתעום אחיכון בני עשו דדארין בגבלה
וידחלון מנכון ותתנטרון שריר : אל תגיחון בהון
הל(ה:) לא אתן לכון מן ארען ירתה עד כדרם
כף רגל הל(ה) יורתה לעשו יהבת ית טור גבלה :
כזון תזונון כלותון בכסף ותיכלון ואף מין תחכון
כלותון בכסף ותישתון :

14   ושלח‏ כשרה שלחין בקדש ליד מלך אדום
(כדנ)ן אמר אחוך ישראל אתה חכמת ירת כל
15   ליעותרה דאשקעתנ(ו) : ונעתו אבהתנו לכצרים
חדרנ(ו) במצרים יומין סגי ואבאשו לנ(ו) מצראי
16   ולאבהתנ(ו) : וצבענ(ו) ליהוה ושמע קלנ(ו) ושלח
שליח ואפקנ(ו) ממצרים והא אנחנ(ו) בקדיש קרתה
17   דבאיסטר תחוכך : נעבר ני בארעך לא נעבר בחקל
ובכרם ולא נשתי כי גוב אורע כלכה נהך לא
18   נסטי ימין וסמאל עד דנעבר תחוכך : ואמר לה
אדום לא תעבר בי דלא בחרב אפק ל(זימונך) :
19   ואמרו לה בני ישראל בחומר נסק ואם ממיך
נשתה אנה וקניני ואתן דמיהון ל(וד)‏ לית ממלל
20   ברגלי אעבר : ואמר לא תעבר ונפק אדום לזימונה
21   בעם יקיר ובאר תקיפה : ומהי אדום יהב ירת

<hr>

‏ After לבן on marg...חר.      ‏ ל ל is written over before ע.
‏ Before ושלח on marg.‏...ו...      ‏ So MS.

ישראל עבר בתחומה ו(ארכן) ישראל בן עליו :
ונטלו פקדיש ועלו בני ישראל כל כנשתה ל(טור) 22
טורה :

ואמר יהוה למשה ולאהרן ב(טור) טורה על 23
תחום ארע אדם לסיכר : ית(כנש) אהרן על עמה 24
הל(ה) לא ייעל לארעה דיהבת לבני ישראל יעל 25
דכריתון ית סיכרי למי חיגרה : דבור ית אהרן 26
וית אלעזר ברה ותסק יתהן לטור טורה : ותישלע 26
סן אהרן ית רקיעו ותלבשנון ית אלעזר ברה
ואהרן ית(כנש) ויתות חכן : ועבד משה כמה 27
דפקד יהוה ואסקה לטור טורה לעיני כל כנשתה :
ואשלע משה כן אהרן ית רקיעו ואלביש יתון ית 28
אלעזר ברה ומית אהרן תכן בריש טורה ונעת
משה ואלעזר סן טורה : וחזו כל כנשתה הל(ה) 29
שלם אהרן ובכו ית אהרן תלתין יום כל בית
ישראל :

ושמע כנענאה סלך ערד (די)אר דרומה[1] הלה 1.XXI
(אתי) ישראל אורע גישושיה ואביע בישראל ושבה
סנה שביה : ונדר ישראל נדר ליהוה ואמר אן 2
מחן תתן ית עמה הרנן[2] באדי וחרם ית
ק(רית)חון : ושבע יהוה בקל ישראל ויהב ית 3
כנענאה באדרה וחרם יתהן ית ק(רית)הון וקרא
שמה אתרה חרמה :

ונטלו סטור טורה אורע ים סוף[3] למסחר ית 4

[1] After דרומה on marg. רחצתה.
[2] The ן is written over.
[3] After סוף on marg. ..וסבתם.

5 ארע אדום וקצר(ת)¹ נפש עמה באורחה: וכלל
עמה באלהים ובמשה לסה אפקתנן ממצרים למכת
במדברה הלה לית להם² ולית כין ונפשנן מעיקה

6 בלחמה (ראקלק)ל: ושלח יהוה בעמה ית (נחשי)ה
דמוקדין וגכתו ית עמה ומית עם סגי מישראל:

7 ואתא עמה ליד משה ואמרו חטינן הלה כללן
ביהוה ובך צלי ליהוה ויסטי כן עלינו ית נחשה
וצלי משה בדיל עמה:

8 ⁸ואמר³ יהוה למשה עבד לך יקיד רשוי יתה
9 על סכי' ויהי כל נכית ויחזי יתה ויחי: ועבד משה
נחש דנחש ושויאה על סכי' והוה אן נכת (נעט)ה
10 ית אנש ואסתכל לנחשה דנחשה וחי: ונטלו בני
11 ישראל ושרו באבות: ונטלו מאבות ושרו בכפרני
עבראי במדברה דעל קודם כואב כדנח שימשה:

ואמר⁴ יהה למשה אל תיצר ית כואב ואל
תניח בה הל(ה) לא אתן לך כן ארעה יורתה
12 הל(ה) לבני לוט יהבת ית עורשה יורתה: מתבן
נטלו ושרו בנחל זרד:

ומלל⁵ יהוה עם משה למימר: אתה עבר יומן
ית תחום סואב ית עורשה: ותקרב לקובל בני
עמון אל תיצרנון ואל תגיח בהון הל(ה) לא אתן

¹ Another ת is visible at the end of the word.
² So MS.　³ Before ואמר on marg. רע על ל ר. ...
⁴ A letter, apparently ס, has been erased before ס.
⁵ Before ואמר on marg. שׂר... This verse is to be found in Deut. ii. 9.
⁶ Before ומלל on marg. אלהא בעי אתח. These three verses are to be found in Deut. ii. 17-19.

כן ארע בני עמך לך יורתה הל(ה) לבני לוט
יהבתה יורתה : ונטלו מנתל זוד ושרו בעבר ארנון 13
דעל מדברה דנפק מתחום אמוראה הל(ה) ארנון
תחום מואב בין מואב ובין אמוראה : על כן יתאמר 14
בספר קרביא יהוה עם רעבה בסופה תעם (פא)לגי
ארנון : ודמלגנין ודראם לסדור קר(י)ה ואתמצין 15
לתחום מואב : ומתמן בארה היא בארה דאמר 16
יהוה למשה כנש לי ית עמא ואתן להון מין :

הדח' אשיר ישראל ית שירתה הדה סקי בארה ענו 17
לה : באר חפרוה רבנין עמאה נחירי עמה יב(נוד 18
ובטני)ן : כמדברה למהנתה וכמנתתה' לפביאל 19
ומן פלגיאל' לבאמתה : ומן באמתה לגיאה דבחקל 20
מואב ריש סכיתה דמ(דיקה) על קודם הישמון :

ואמר' יהוה למשה קומו וטלו ועברו ית' נחל 21
ארנון חזי יהבית בידך ית סיחון מלך חשבון
אמוראה וית ארעה שרי ירת וסדר בה קרבה :
יוכר' הד(נ)ן שרי יהב חיכחך דחלחך על אפי 22
עמכיה דתחורת כל שוכיה דישמעון ית שמע
וישרעון ויתלחלון מקדמיך :

ושלח ישראל שלחין ליד סיחון מלכא' אמוראה 21
מלי שלם למימר : אעבר בארעך באורח מלכה 22
אהך לא אסטי ימין ומסמאל לא ארום בחקל
וכברם : בזון' בכסף תמברני ואיכל ומין בכסף

תתן לי ואשתי לחוד אעבר ברגלי : ככה דעבדו
לי בני עשו דדארין בגבלה וכואבי דדארין בעורשה :
כג ולא יהב סיחון ית ישראל עבר בתחומה :
ואמר[1] יהוה למשה חזי שרית יהב[2] לקודכך ית
סיחון וית ארעה שרי ירת לסירת ית ארעה ; וכנש
סיחון ית כל עמה תפק לוזמן ישראל למדברה
כד וא(תי) ליחצה ואגיח בישראל : וקטלה ישראל וית
בניו וית כל עמה לפם חרב וירתו ית ארעה
כארנון עד יבק עד בני עמון הל(רה) תקיף תחום
כה בני עמון ; ונסב ישראל ית כל ק(ריה)רה האלין
ודר ישראל בכל קורי אמוראה בחשבון ובכל
כו בנתה : יהל(ה) חשבון קרתה דסיחן כלכה חמוראה
היא הוא דאגיח במלך כואב קדמאי ונסב ית כל
כז ארעה מן אדה עד ארנון : על כן ייכרון שליטיה
כח עאלי חשבון תבנה ות(תכו)נן קרתה דסיחון : הל(ה)
אש נפק(ת) כן חשבון לתבה מקרית סיחון אכלה
כט עד כואב כסחני במות ארנון : ויל כואב אבדת
עסך[3] (כ)ספש יהב בניו פליטיה ובנתה בשבי[4]
ל לכלכה חמוראה סיחון : ו(ארחכנן כאבד)רה
חשבון עד דיבן ושוינן סחד נפח אש על
מידבא :
לא,לב ודר[5] ישראל בקורי חמוראה: ושלח משה
לכללה ית יעזיר וכבשו בנתה וערבו ית חמוראה

---

[1] The words from אמר to ארעה are to be found in Deut. ii. 31.
[2] After יהב on marg. ובר ישלם.    [3] So MS.
[4] ה is written over after י.
[5] Before חר on marg. יאותה רבעה. ..

דתסן: (ואתפ)נו וסלקו לארע (בת)נין ונפק עוג 33
כלך בתנין לויכ( ונ)ן) הוא וכל עמה לקרבה
לאדרעי: ואסר יהוה לכשה אל תחל מנה 34
הל(רה) באדך יהבת יתה ויה כל עמה וית ארעה
ותעבד לה ככה רעבדת לסיחון מלכה חמוראה
דיאר בחשבון: וקטלו יתה וית כל עמה עד דלא 35
אשתיר לרה שיור וירתו ירת ארעה: ונטלו בני 1 XXII
ישראל ושרו בבקעת מואב מעבר ליורדנה יריחו:

וחזה' בלק בר צפור ית כל דעבד ישראל 2
לאמוראה: ודחל מואב מקודם עמה שריר הלו 3
סיני הוא ואציק מואב מקדם בני ישראל: ואמר 4
מואב לסבי מדין כרו ילחך קהלה הד(נ)ן ית כל
סחרתנ(ו) כלחך תוחה ית ירק ברה ובלק בר צפור
כלך למואב בזמן ההיא: וישלח שלחין ליד בלעם 5
בר בעור (חרש)ה' דעל נהרדה לארע בני עמח
לכזעק לה למימר הא עם נפק ממצרם הא כסי
ית חזות ארעה והוא יתב כלקובלי': וכדו אתה 6
שו להט לי ית עמה הד(נ)ן הל(ה) תקיף הוא כני
להוי אכיל (קטל) בה ואטרדנה כן ארעה הלה
חכמת ית דתברך פביך וית דתלוט ליט:

ואולו (סא)בי' סואב ו(סא)בי' מדין' וקסמיהון 7
בידון ואתו ליד בלעם ומללו עמה מלי בלק:
ואסר להון אביתו הכה לילק וחזר יתכון כפלל 8
ככה ריסלל יהוה עמי ויתבו רבני מואב עם

I

בלעם : וא(תר) אלהים ליד בלעם ואמר מה    ۹

גברייה האלין עמך : ואמר בלעם לאלהים בלק    ۱۰

בר צפור סלך ‐מואב שלח לידי : הא עמה נפק    ۱۱
ממצרים וכסי ית הוות ארעה וכדו אתה לוט לי
להוי אכול למגחה בה ואטרדינה :

ואמר אלהים לבלעם לא תיזל עמהון' ולא    ۱۲

תלוט ית עמה הל(ה) בריך הוא : וקם בלעם    ۱۳
בצפרה ואמר לרבני בלק אזלו לארעכון הל(רה)

מאי יהוה למתנני' למהך עמכון : וקעמו' רבני    ۱۴
מואב ואתו ליד בלק ואמרו מסאי בלעם אתי

עמנ(ז) : ואוזף עוד בלק שלח שלחין רברבין    ۱۵

ויקירין מן אלין : ואתו ליד בלעם ואמרו לה    ۱۶
(אכון) אמר בלק בר צפור אל ני' תתכלי כיתי

לידי : הל(ה) איקר אוקרתך שרר וכל דתימר לי    ۱۷

אעבד' ואתה שוי לאוט לי ית עמה הד(נ)ן : וענה    ۱۸
בלעם

| | |
|---|---|
| א    אן יתן לי בלק כלו | ואמר לעברי בלק |
| ח    לא אוכל למעברה י | ביתה כסף אי דהב |
| למעבד זעורה אי רבה | מיסר יהוה אלהי |

וכדו חבו ני בדן    אף ארון ליין ואענכם    ۱۹
מה יוזף יהוה כמלל עם

ואתה' כלאך אלהים ליד בלעם בלילי ואמר    ۲۰

---

1 After עמהן on marg. לאורן ו.
2 Apparently altered from לסח לי.
3 The final ו is written over.
4 Altered into סבי.
5 Before אתה on marg. לפן מכל בר ...

לה אן למזעק לך אתו גבריה קם אזל עמהון

וכח ית ממללה דאבלל עסך יתה תעבד : וקם 11.
בלעם בצפרה ושוי ית אתנה ואזל עם רבני מואב :

ותקף חבו יהוה הל(ה) אזל הוא ואתקוכם מלאך 11.
יהוה באורעה לעשרה' לה והוא רכב על אתנה

וחרין רביז עמה : וחזת אתנה ית מלאך יהוה 11.
קאם באורעה וחרבה שליפה בידה וסטרת אתנה
סן אורעה והלכת בחקלה וכעה בלעם ית אתנה
למטוחה אורעה : וקם מלאך יהוה בשויל כרמין 11.

ד(רגה) מדן ו(דרנה) כרן : וחזת אתנה ית מלאך 11.
יהוה תלחצת (לגו)' כותלה ולחצת ית רגל בלעם

(לגו)' כותלה ואחף לספסיה : ואחף כלאך יהוד 16.
עבר וקם באתר לחיץ דלית אורע לכסטי ימין
וסמאל : וחזת אתנה ית מלאך יהוה ורבעת 11.
תחות בלעם ותקף רוגז בלעם ומעה ית אתנה
בעטר :

ופתח' יהוה ית פכה דאתנה ואמרת לבלעם 11.
כדה עברת לך הל(ה) סעיתני דן תלתה רגלין :

ואמר בלעם לאתנה הל(ה) שקרת בי אלו אית חרב 19.
בידי הל(ה) כדו קטלתיך : ויאמרת אתנה לבלעם 30. 31.
הלא אנה אתנך דרכבת עלי סן דהויך עד יומה
הדן אסכלו אסכלת למעבד לך הכאן ואמר לא :
וגלי יהוה ית עיני בלעם וחזה ית מלאך יהוד 11.
קאם באורעה וחרבה שליפה בארה וחקד וסגד

---

' ס apparently has been erased between ל and ע.
' Altered, apparently, from ל.
' Before חחה on marg. ולבל עובר.

לב. לאפיו: ואמר לה מלאך יהוה על מה מעית ית
אתך דן תלתה רגלין הא אנכי נפקת לעטרה(ת)ך¹

לג. הל(ה) ב(י)שה אורעך לקובלי: וחזתי אתגה וסטת
קלקדמי דן תלתה רגלין אלולי סטותה כלקדמי

לד. הל(ה) כדו אף יתך קטלת ויתה חיאית: ואמר
בלעם למלאך יהוה חטית הל(ה) לא חכמת הל(ה)
אתה קאם לזמני² באורעה וכדו אן בעש ב(עיני)ך
חזרה לי:

לה. ואמר מלאך יהוה לבלעם אזל עם גבריה³
תשבוק ית כמללה דאמלל עמך יתה חטר למכללה:

לו. ואזל בלעם עם רבני בלק ושבע בלק הל(ה) אתי
בלעם ונפק לזבונה לקרית מואב דעל תחום

לז. ארנן דבאיסטר תחומה: ואמר בלק לבלעם הלא
שלחא שלחת לידך למזעק לך לכה לא אתית

לח. לידי הא[יכנון] לא אוכל מקירתך: ואמר בלעם לבלק
הא אתית לידך כדו (הם)(כו)כל¹ א(כו)ל מכלל מדעם
ממללה דישוי אלהים ב(פ)מי יתה אטר לכמללה:

לט. ואזל בלעם עם בלק ועאלה ל(מדינ)ת חיו:

מ. ו(נכס) בלק תורין וען ושלח לבלעם ולרבניה

מא. דעמה: והוה בצפרה ודבר בלק ית בלעם ואסקה
לבמת בעל וחזה מחכן ית סטר עמה:

xxiii. ז  ואמר בלעם לבלק עבד לי בדן שבעה מדבחין

ב.ג. וכן לי בדן שבעה פרין ושבעה דכרין: ועבד
בלק כמה דמלל בלעם ואסק בלק ובלעם פר

ג. ודכר במדבח: ואמר בלעם לבלק התקיים על

---

¹ Altered apparently from למעשׂרה לך.   ² So MS.
³ After נבריה on marg. an illegible gloss.   ⁴ So MS.

עלהתך ואהך להוי יזדמן אלהים לויכוני ואסלל
כרה יחזיני ורוי לך ואזל כלשם : ואשקע כלאך 4
אלהים ית בלעם ואמר לה ית שבעת מדבחיה סדרת
ואסקת פר ודכר במדבח: ושוי כלאך יהוה כמלל 5
בפם בלעם ואמר חזר ליד בלק ו(כדנ)ן תכלל: וחזר 6
ליה והא קאם על עלהתה הוא וכל רבני כואב :

'(וחלה מתלה) ואמר מארם (נגד)אי בלק מלך 7
כואב מן טבארי מנח' אתה לאוט ליעקב ואתה
סכוף לישראל :   כה אלוט דלא לאטרה .אל ומ ד 8
אסכף דלא סכף יהוה: הל(רה) כן ריש טורין 9
אחזינה וכן גלבן אשבעננה הן עכה' לתודיו ישרי
וב(נוא)יה לא יתחשב : כן [כני] עפר יעקב מנין 10
כרבעת ישראל תמות נפשי מות(י)ן כשבעין ותיחד
חרא(יתי) כותה :

| | | | |
|---|---|---|---|
| ואמר' בלק לבלעם | כה עבדת ל | 11 | |
| לכלאם דבבי דברתך | והא ברכת ברי | ך | |
| וענה ואמ | ר | הל(ה) ית' דרישי יהוה בפמי 12 | |
| יתה אטהר לכמללה | ואמר לה' בלק אתה ני 13 | | |
| עמי לאתר שר | ן | תחזינה מן תם | ן |
| שבוק סטרוה תחמי | וכלה לא תחז | | ' |
| ולוטה לי מתם | ן | ודבחה לחק | ל 14 |
| צפי | ם | לריש סכית | ה |
| ובנה שבע | ה | מדבחי' | ן |
| ואסק פר ודכר על | מדבח | | ח |

¹ Before וחלה on marg. אסארן ...    ³ So MS.
⁵ ח is written over, as a correction of ו.
⁴ Before ואמר on marg. עדתך ....    ⁶ ית is written over.

| | | |
|---|---|---|
| ה | אתקומם על עלהתך ואנ | ‫‫ואמר לבלק‬ ‫15‬ |
| י | חעק מלאך יהוה לבלעם ושי | אורסן הכרה ‫16‬ |
| ז | ואמר חזר לית בלק ו(אכו) | מסלל בפסה |
| | ואתה ל ידרה והא הוא קאעם | תמסלרל ‫17‬ |
| ה | ורבני מואב עמה ואמר ל | על עלהתה |
| | בלק כה סלל יהוה : | |

| | | |
|---|---|---|
| ע | קום בלק ושם | (ותלה סתלה) ואמר ‫18‬ |
| ב | לא אנש אל ויכר | אצית סחדי ברה צפור ‫19‬ |
| ר | ההוא אמר ולא עבר | ובר אנש ויתו(ח ) |
| | הא לסברכרה (נסבתך) מ | כסלל ולא סקאי ‫20‬ |
| | לא אסתכלת עובה ביעקב ה | אברך ולא חזרנ ‫21‬ |
| | ל יהוה אלהרה עמה | ולא חזית תורעה בישרא |
| | אל ראפפקנן ממצרים | וא(פריאות) מלכיה ב ה ‫22‬ |
| | הל(רה) לא נחש ביעקב | (כעפרות) רוצה ל ה ‫23‬ |
| | כובן יתאמר ליעקב ל | ולא קסם בישרא |
| | הן עם(ה) (כלב)יה יק(ו)ם ל | ולישראל מה פעל א ‫24‬ |
| | לא י(שכב) ער יסכם ב | וכאריה (יח)רבר |
| ד | | קטל חדם קטליח יאג |

‫25‬ ואמר בלק לבלעם אף (לו)אט לא תלטנה ואף
‫26‬ ברוך לא תברכנה : וענה בלעם ואמר לבלק הלא
סללת עכך למיכר כל כסלל ריסלל האלהים יחה
‫27‬ אעבר : ואמר בלק לבלעם אתה ני אדברנך לאחר

---

1 So MS.   2 After שמש on marg. ‫שמח בפס פו‬.
3 The ה is written over.   4 So MS.
5 After אף on marg. ‫...חסבת‬.
6 There is a trace of ה after ‫סללת‬.

עוֹק לוי אתכסר בחזות האלהים ולוטה לי מתמן :
חדבר בלק ית בלעם לריש פעור דם(דיק) על קדם 18
הישמן :

ואמר בלעם לבלק בהני לי בדן שבעה' מדבחין
וכן לי בח שבעה פרין ושבעה דכרין ועבד בלק
ככה דסלל בלעם ואסק פר ודכר על מדבחה :

וחזה בלעם הל(ה) טב בחזות יהוה למברכה
ירת ישראל ולא אזל כזבן בזבן לוימן (נחשו)יה'
ושוי למדברה. אפיו : ותל(רה) בלעם ירת עיניו
וחזה ית ישראל (שכן) לשבטיו וחות עלאוו רוח
אלהים :

| | | |
|---|---|---|
| ס[ח]ימן בלעם בריה' בעור ₃ | | (ותלה סתלה) ואכר |
| דכחי (בר)ה יחוי ₄ | חז | (וכח)יסן נברה דב(שוי חז)ו : |
| מרה טבין משכניך יעקב ₅ | ו | ספל וגלי חז |
| כנחלין נציבי ₆ | ל | (וסארו')ך' ישרא |
| כבסכנן ד(רוב)ם יהוה | ר | כגנין (ע)ל(ו)י נה |
| ידל(לי) סין כדלי ₇ (ה) | ן | כארזין (ע)ל(ו)י כי |
| ויכס כגואה כלכ ה | י | ויזדרעך בטין סב |
| אל דאנגדה ממצרים ₈ | ה | ותת(אלי) מלכות |
| יסיף (גו)י'ן דלחצוי | | כ(עפראו)ת רוכה לה |
| ופלגיו יפל נ | | וגרמיהון יגר ם |
| וכנמרה מן יקומן ה ₉ | | כר(עי) דמך כאר ה |

---

¹ After שבעה on marg. ...לא.

² So MS. apparently.

³ Before וחלה on marg. ..יתסן רשותה.

⁴ The ה is written over.

⁵ Apparently badly altered from ומשכנך.

מברכיך בריכי    ז    ולאטיר אלוט :    ותקף    י
חגז בלק לבלע    ם    ושקף ית כפי    ו
ואמר' בלק לבלעם לסלאט דבבי זעקת לך והא

ברכת בחד דן תלתה רגלין : וכדו חקיר לך    יא
לאתתך אמרת איקר אוקרנך והא כליתך יהוה סן

איקר : ואמר בלעם לבלק הלא אף לשלחיך    יב

דשלחת לידי כללת למיסר : אן יתן לי בלק מלוא    יג
ביתה כסף אי דהב לא אכול למעברא ית מימר
יהוה למעבד טבה אי בישה מלבי דימלל יהוה עמי

יתה אמלל : וכדו אנה אזל ל'עמי אתה ואב[נ]ל'כנך    יד
ית דיעבד עמא הד(נ); לעמך בעקב יומיה :

יונסב' כן ש(לטנ)ה ואמר כחימן בלעם ברה' בעור'    טו

וסחיכן נברדה ד(מ)שי')    עזו    כחיכן שבע מיכרי אל    טז
ו(חכם) דעת עליו    ז    כחזי    (בר/ה)    יחזי

סטל וגלי חזוה    ז    אחזינה ולא כד    ו    יז
אשבענה ולא קר'    ב    (א/ר/ח)' כוכב מיעק ב
וקאם שבט מישרא    ל    וכעי פאתי כוא    ב

ורום כל בני ש    ת    ויהי אדום ירת    ה    יח
ויהי זרהרה עשו רבבי    ו    וישראל עבד חיל

ו(ישלט) מיעק    ב    (וי)אבד דאתשר מקרתה    יט

וחזה ית עמל    ק    ונסב כן ש(לטנ)ה ואמר    כ
ראשות גואיה עכל    ק    וחראיתה סחדה יאבר

וחזה ית קינא    ה    ונסב כן ש(לטנ)ה ואמר    כא

---

1 .... מתחשב Before אמר on marg.
2 ותלה מחלה is written over.
3 The ח is written over.
4 ... בעור on marg. ב תרע.
5 There is a line over ר.

עסיק מדור          ך          וכשיר בכיפה קג          ך

הלא אן יהי לבער קין     סחדה כן (אשר) תתובתך .יי

ונסב מן ש(לטנה) ואמר     וילה כן דיהי משם     (ה) יי.

אל דאפקגין כן אד כתאי לבט(נה) אשו     ר יִ.

(וי)לבס(נה) עב          ר ואף הוא סחדרה יבד

וקם בלעם ואזל וצזר לאתרה ואף בלק אזל יי

לאורעה :

ודאר ישראל בשטים ושרי עמה למזורנאה' עם י .יויי.

בנת מואב : וזעקי לעמרה לדבחי אלהיהן ואכלו .

עמו' וסגדו לאלהיהן : ואצטמד' מבני ישראל לבעל ו

פעור ותקף רוגז יהוה בישראל : ואמר יהוה למשה י

אמר ויקטלון ית גבריה דאצטמכדו לבעל פעור ויתוב

חרון רוגז יהוה מישראל : ואמר משה לדיאני' י

ישראל קטלו גבר ית אנשיו דאצטמכדו לבעל פעור:

והא גבר מבני ישראל אתה וקרב' ליד אחיו ית י

כדינאיתה לעיני משה ולעיני כל כנשת בני ישראל

ואנון בכין בתרח אהל מועד : יחזא פינחס בר י יו. יו.

אלעזר בר אהרן כהנה וקם מלגו כנשתה ונסב

מסה בארה : ועל בתר גברא ישראלאה לגו י

(קבה) ודקר ית תריהון ית גברה ישראלאה וית

א(תה)ה על רקיתה ואתעצרת מגיפתה כן על בני

ישראל : והוו דמיתו במגיפתה ארבעה ועסרין י

אלף :

¹ After למזורנאה on marg. . . . . ית.          ² So MS.

³ A letter, probably ו, appears to have been erased at the end
of אצטמד.

⁴ The א is written over.

⁵ א has apparently been erased before p.

K

וסלל¹ יהוה עם משה למימר: פינחס בר אלעזר    ‏10,11
בר אהרן כהנה חזר ית חמתי מן על בני ישראל
בקנואה ית קנאתי בנההון ולא אסכבת ית בני
ישראל בקנאתי: לכן אמר האנה יהב לה ית ברתי    ‏12
שלם: ותהי לה ולזרעה בתרה בריה³ כהנה לעלם    ‏13
תחות דקני לאלהה וסלח על בני ישראל: ושם    ‏14
גברה ישראלה קטילה דקטל עם כדינאיתה זמר
בר סלוא נסיח בית אב לשטעונאי: ושם א(תת)ה    ‏15
קטילתה מדינאיתה כזבית ברת צור ריש אומה
בית אב במדין הוא:

ומלל¹ יהוה עם משה למימר: אעיקו ית מדינאי    ‏16,17
ותקטלון יתה: הלה אעיקו⁴ אנון לכון בנכליהון    ‏18
דנכלו לכון על כמלל פעור ועל מכלל כזבי ברת
נסיח מדין אחתה (ראקט)ל(ח) ביום מגיפתה על
מכלל פעור: וחה בתר מגיפתה    ‏XXVI. 1

ומלל¹ יהוה עם משה ועם אלעזר בר אהרן
כהנה למימר: סבו ית סכום כל כנסת בני ישראל    ‏2
מבר עסרין שנ(ה)⁵ ' ולעל לבית אבהתון כל נפק
חיל בישראל: ומלל משה ואלעזר כהנה עמהון    ‏3
בבקעת מואב על ירדן ירחו לסימר: יסכבר עסרין    ‏4 fol.
שנין ולעל כמה דפקד יהוה ית משה ובני ישראל
דנפקו מן ארע מצרים: ראובן בכור ישראל ובני    ‏5
ראובן חנוך כח חנוכאי לפלוא כח פלואהי:

---

¹ Before וסלל on marg. . . הלא בעות.    ³ So MS.
² Before וסלל on marg. . . . . מקשה    ⁴ Altered into אעיקו.
⁵ Before וסלל on marg. an illegible gloss.
⁶ Originally שנין.

לחצרון כח חצרונאי לכרכי כרן כרכאי: אלין 6, 7

כרנאי ראובנאי והוו כניניהון תלתה וארבעין אלף

ושבע מאן ותלתין:

בני פלוא אליאב: ובני אליאב נכואל׳ דתן 8, 9

ואבירם הוא דתן ואבירם זמיני כנשתה דאסידו

על משה ועל אהרן בכנשת קרח באסדותן על

יהוה: ופתחת ארעה ית פמה ובלעת יתן ארעה 10

במות כנשתה במיכל אשתה ית קרח וית חכשין

ומאתין גבר והוו לעִרוק: ובני קרח לא מיתו: 11

בני שמעון לכרן שמעונאי לנמואל כרן נמולאי 12

ליכין׳ כרן יכינאי׳: לזרח כרן זרחאי לשאול כרן 13

שאולאי: אלין כרני שבעונאי תרין ועסרין אלף 14

ומאתין:

בני גד לכרניהון לצפון כרן צפונאי לחגי כרן 15

חגאי לשוני כרן שונאי: לאזני כרן אזנאי לעדי 16

כרן עדאי: לארודי כרן ארודאי לאחלי כרן 17

ארואלי׳׳: אלין כרני גד לכניהון׳ ארבעין אלף 18

וחמש מאן:

בני יהודה ער ואונן ומית ער ואונן בארע כנען: 19

והוו בני יהודה לכרניה[ון] לשלה כרן שילאני 20

לפרץ כרן פרצאו[ן] ׳לזרח כרן זרחאי: והוו בני 21 & 22 MS.

פרץ לחצרון כרן חצרונאי לחמואל כרן חמואלי׳:

אלין כרני יהודה לכניניהון שתה ושבעין אלף 22

וחמש מאן:

בני יששכר לכרניהון לתולע כרן תולעאי לפואה 23

¹ After נמאל ou marg. ר. על מלה.

² So MS.

K 2

‫,י כרן פואהי: ליושב כרן יושבאהי לשכרון כרן‬
‫,כ שמרחנאהי: אלין כרני ישׁשכר למניניהון ארבעה‬
‫ושתין אלף ותלת מאן:‬
‫,כו בני זבלון לכרניהון לסרד כרן סרדאי לאלון כרן‬
‫,כז אלונאי ליחלאל כרן יחלאלאי: אלין כרני זבלון‬
‫למניניהון שתין אלף וחמש מאן:‬
‫,כח,כט בני' יוסף לכרניהון מנשה ואפרים: בני מנשה‬
‫למכיר כרן מכיראי ומכיר הולד ית גלעד כרן‬
‫,ל גלעדאי: אלין בני גלעד אחיעזר כרן חוראי לחלק‬
‫,לא כרן חלקאי: ואשרואל כרן אשראלהי ושכם כרן‬
‫,לב שכמאי: ושמידע כרן שמידעאי וחפר כרן חפראי:‬
‫,לג וצלפחד בר חפר לא הוד לה בנין אלה אן בנן‬
‫ושם בנת צלפחד מחלה ונעה תגלה מלכה ותרצה:‬
‫,לד אלין כרני מנשה לסניניהון תרין וחמשין אלף ושבע‬
‫מאן:‬
‫,לה ואלין² בני אפרים לכרניהון לשותלח כרן שותלחי‬
‫,לו לבכר כרן בכראי לתחם כרן תחסי: אלין בני‬
‫,לז שותלח לעזן כרן עדאי: אלין כרני בני אפרים‬
‫למניניהון תרין ותלתין אלף וחמש מאן אלין בני‬
‫יוסף לכרניהון:‬
‫,לח,לט,מ,מא ⁰בני בנימים לכרניהון לבלע כרן בלעאי לאשביל‬
‫,לט כרן אשבילהי לחירם כרן חירמאי: לשופם כרן‬
‫,מ שופמאי לחופם כרן חופמאי: לארד כרן ארדעי‬
‫,מא לנעמן כרן נעמאי: אלין בני בנימים לכרניהון‬
‫וסנינידון חמשה וארבעים אלף ושת מאן:‬

---

¹ Before ‫בני‬ on marg. ‫ריש‬....  
² Before ‫ואלין‬ on marg. an illegible gloss.

וֹ⁴² ²אלין בני דן לכרניהון לשוחם כה¹ שוחמאי

⁴³ אלין כרני דן לכרניהון: כל כרני שוחמאי ומנינידון

ארבעה ושתין אלף וארבע מאן:

⁴⁴ בני אשר לכרניהון ליכנה כה ימנאי לישוה כרן

⁴⁵ ישוהי לבריעה כה ברעהי: לחבר כרן חבראי

⁴⁶ לכליאל כה כלכיאלי: ושם ברת אשר שרח¹

⁴⁷ אלין כרני בני אשר לכניניהון תלתה וחמשין אלף

וארבע מאן:

⁴⁸ בני נפתלי לכרניהון ליחצאל כרן יצחאלהי¹

⁴⁹ לגוני כה גונאי: ליצר כרן יצרחי לשלום כרן

⁵⁰ שלומאי: אלין כרני נפתלי לכתיהון ומנינידון חמשה

⁵¹ וארבעין אלף וארבע מאן: אלין מניני בני ישראל

שת כאן דאלף ואלף ושבע כאין ותלתין:

⁵², ⁵³ וכלל יהוה¹ עם כישה לכיכר: לאלין תחפלג

⁵⁴ ארעה בפלגה בכנכ שכהן: לסוגן¹ן] תסבי פלגתה

לתורה תוער פלגה[ה] אנש לפם כניניו יתיהב

⁵⁵ ⁵⁶ ⁵⁵ פלנתה: [ברן] בנכז יפלג ית ארעה ילשטחרת

⁵⁶ שבטי אבהתון תפלגן: על כיכר נבזה יפלג

פלנתה בין סובי לוועור:

⁵⁷ ואלין⁴ מניני ליואי לכרניהון לגרשון כרן גרשונאי

⁵⁸ לקהת כה קהתאי לכרדי כה כרדהי: אלין כרני

בני לוי כה לבנהי וכה חברונאי וכה כחלהי וכה כרן

קרחהי וכה כרשהי וקהת הולד ית עכרם: ⁵⁹ ושם

אתת עכרם יוכבד ברת לוי דיל(ידה) יתה ללוי

בכצרים וילדת לעכרם ית אהרן וית כישה וית

¹ After כה on marg. . . . וחיצן.    ² So MS.
³ Before ואלין on marg. לואי.

כרין אחתהן ; ואתיליד לאהרן ית נדב וית אביהוא ⁶⁰

ית אלעזר וית איתמר : וכית נדב ואביהוא ⁶¹

באקרבותהן אש בראה לקדם יהוה : והוו כניניהון ⁶²
תלתה ועסרין אלף כל דכר מבר ירח ולעל הל(ה)
לא התמנו בגו בני ישראל הל(רה) לא יהיב לון
פלגה בגו בני ישראל :

אלין מניני מישה ואלעזר כהנא דמנו ית בני ⁶³

ישראל בבקעת מואב על ירדן יריחו : ובאלין לא ⁶⁴
הוה אנש ממניני מישה ואהרן כהנא דמנו ית בני

ישראל במדבר סיני : הל(ה) אמר יהוה להון מית ⁶⁵
ימותון במדברה ולא (א)תותר מנהון גבר אלה
אן כלב בר יפנה ויהושע בר נון :

וקרבי בנת צלפחד בר חפר בר נלעד בר ¹ xxvii.
[מ]כיר בר כנשה: לכת מנשה בר יוסף [וא]לין
שמהת בנתה מחלה ונעה תגלה [מלכה] ותרצה:

וקמי לקדם משה ולקדם [אלעזר] כהנא ולקדם ²
נסיהיא וכל [כנשתה] בתרח אהל מועד למימר:

אבונן מית במדברה והוא לא הוה בגו כנשתא ³
דאסידו על יהוה בכנ(שת) קרח הלו בחטא[י]ה מית

אבונן ובנין לא הוה לה : לכה יובצר שם אבונן ⁴
מלגו כרנת הלו לית לה בר הב לנו סעתת פלגה

בגו אחי אבונן : ואקרב משה ית דינך לקדם ⁵
יהוה :

ומלל יהוה עם משה למימר : שפיר בנת ¹ ⁶,⁷
צלפחד כמללן [כת]ן חתן להין מחנת פלגה בגו
אחי אבוהין ותעבר ית פלגת אבוהין להין : ועם ⁸

_____

¹ After בנת on marg. .נפשה יתל.

בני ישראל תמלל למיסר אנש אן ימות ובר לית
לה ותתנגן ית פלגתה לברתה : ואן לית לה ברה  ,
ותתנגן ית פלגתה לאחוי : ואן לית לה אחים  ,,
ותתנגן ית פלגתה לאחי אביו : ואן לית אחין  ,,
לאביו ותתנגן ית פלגתה לעמירה דקריב לה
מכרנה ויירת יתה ת[ת]הי לבני ישראל לגזירת דין
כמה דפקד יהוה ית משה :

ומלל יהוה עם משה למימר סק לטור עבראי  ,,
הדין וחזי ית ארעה דאנ['] יהב לבני ישראל :
ותחזי [י]תה ותת[כנש] על עמך אף אתה, כמה  ,,
דאתכ[נש] אהרן אחוך : דמריתון ית מימרי במדבר  ,,
צן בתגרנות כנשתה למקדשחי במיה לעיניהת אנון
מ' תיגרנות קדש מדבר צן : ומלל משה עם יהוה  ,,
למימר : יפקד יהוה אלהין דרוחיה לכל בסרה  ,,
גבר על כנשתה : דיפק לקודמיהת ודיעל לקדמיהון  ,,
ודיפ[קנון] ודיעאלנון ולא תהי כנשת יהוה [כענה]
דלית לון רעי :

ויאמר ' יהוה למשה דבור לך ית יהושע בר נח  ,,
[גברה] דרוחה בה ותסמך ית אדך עליו : ותקים  ,,
יתה לקודם אלעזר כהנה ולקודם כל כנשתה
ותפקד יתה לעיניהון : ותתן מן שורך עליו ובדיל  ,,
ישמעון כל כנשת בני ישראל : תלקודם אלעזר  ,,
כהנה יקום וישול לה בדיל (נה)יריה לקודם יהוה
על מימרה יפק ועל מיכרה ייעל הוא וכל בני
ישראל עמה תכל כנשתה : ועבד משה כמה דפקד  ,,
יהוה יתה תדבר ית יהושע ואקימה לקודם אלעזר

כהנה ולקודם כל כנשתה : וספך ית ארה עליו ‏ כג

ופקדה כמה דמלל יהוה באד כשה : 'ואמר לה

עיניך חזי ית דעבד יהוה לתרין מלכיה האלין כן

יעבד יהוה לכל מלכואתה דאתה עבר תמן : לא

תדחל כנהון הלו יהוה אלהכון הוא דכגיח לכון :

ומלל יהוה עם משה למימר : פקד ית בני    xxviii. 1, 2

ישראל ותימר להון ית קרבני לחמי לקרבן ריח

רעותי תטרון למקרבה לי ב[זבנ]יו : ותימר להון זן    ג

קרבנה דתקרבון ליהוה אמרין בני שנה שלמין

תרין ליום עלת הדיד : ית אמהרה חדה תעבד    ד

בצפרה וית אמהרה תנינה תעבד ביני רמשיה :

ועסור סאתה סלת למנחה [ב]סיס במשח רבועת    ה

אינה : עלת תדיר עבדוה בטור סיני לריח רחוה    ו

קרבן [לי]הוה : ונסכיו רבועת אינה לאמהר [חד    ז

ב]קדשה שפי מ_שפי רחט ליהוה : וית [אמהרה    ח

תנינה תעבד ביני רמשיה יכמנחת צפרה וכנסכוה '    ט, ...

תעבד קרבן ריח רחוה ליהוה : וביום שובתה    ט

תרין אמהרין בני שנה שלמין ותרין עסורין סלת

למנחה בסיס במשח ונסכיו : עלת שובה בשובה    י

על עלת תדירה ונסכיהון :

ובראשי ירחיכון תקרבון עלה ליהוה' פרין בני    יא

תורין תרין ודכר חד אמהרין בני שנה שבעה

שלמין : ותלתה עסורין סלת מנחה בסיס במשח    יב

לפר חד ותרין עסורין סלת מנחה בסיס במשח

לדכר חד : ועסור עסור סלת מנחה בסיס במשח    יג

---

לאכהר חד עלה ריח רעוה קרבן ליהוה: ונסכיהון 14
פלגות אינה חמר לפר חד ותלתות אינה לדכר
ורבעות אינה לאכהר חד חמר דה עלת ירחה
בחדתותה לירחי שתה: וצפיר עזין חד לסלוח 15
ליהוה עם עלת תדיהה יתעבדון ונסכיהון:
ביחרה קדמאה בארבעה עסר יום ליחרה פסח 16
ליהוה: ובחמשתחר עסר יום ליחרה הדן חג 17
שבעה יומין פטיר תיכלון: ביומה קדמאה זימון 18
קדש כל פלען עבידה לא תעבדון: ותקרבון קרבן 19
עלה ליהוה פרין בני תורין תרין ודכר חד ושבעה
אכהרין בני שנה שלמין יהון לכון: ומנחהון סלת 20
בסיסה בכשח הלתה עסורין לפר ותרין עסורין
לדכר תעב[דון]: ועסור עסור לאכהר חד לשבעה 21
אכהר[יה]: וצפיר עזין חד לסלוח לכפר[ה עליכון]: 22
לבר מן עלת צפרה דלעלת תדיה[ה] •תעבדון ית 23
אלין: כאלין ליום תעבדון שבעת יומיה יוכסיה לחם 24
קרבן לריח רחוה ליהוה עם עלת תדיה יתעבדון
ונסכיהון: וביומה שביעאה זימון קדש יהי לכון כל 25
פלען עבידה לא תעבדון:
ביום[1] בכוריה באקרבותכן מנחה חדתה ליהוה 26
בשבעיכון זימון קדש יהי לכון כל פלען עבידה לא
תעבדון: ותקרבון עלה ריח רחוה ליהוה פרין 27
בני תורין תרין ודכר חד אכהרין בני שנה שבעה
שלמין יהון לכון: וסנחתון סלת בסיסה במשח 28
חלתה עסורין לפר חד ותרין עסורין לדכר חד:
ועסור עסור לאכהר חד לשבעת אכהריה: וצפיר 29, 30

עזין הד לסלוח לכסלחה עליכון : לבר מן עלת
חדירה ומנחתה תעבדון שלכין יהון לכון ונסכיהון :

וביררחר שביאארה בחד ליררחה זימן קדש יהי
לכון כל פלען עבידה לא תעבדון [י]ום אשתערה

יהי לכון : ותעבדון עלה [ל]ריח רחוה ליהוה פר
בר תורין חד דכר [ח]ד אבהרין בני שנה שבעה

שלמין : [ו]מנחתון סלת בטיסרה בכשח תלתה
[ע]סורין לפר ותרין עסורין לדכר : תעסור [ע]סור

לאמהר חד לשבעת אבהרירה : וצפיר [עז]ין חד
לסלוח לכסלחה עליכון : לבר [מן ע]לת ירחה

ומנחתה תעלת תדירה [ומנחת]ה ונסכיה כדינן
לריח רחוה קרבן ליהוה : ¹ובעסרה לירחה

שביאארה הדינן זימן קרש' יהי לכון וח(לבעט)ון
ית נפשתכון וכל עבידה לא תעבדון : ותקרבון

עלה ליהוה ריח רחוה פר בר תורין חד דכר חד
אבהרין בני שנה שבעה שלמין יהי לכון : ומנחתון

סלת בסיסרה בכשח תלתה עסורין לפר ותרין
עסורין לדכר חד : ועסור עסור לאמהר חד לשבעת

אבהרירה : וצפיר עזין חד לסלוח לבר מן סלוח
סלחיה תעלת תדירה ומנחתה ונסכיה :

²ובחמשתה עסר יום לירחה שביאאה הדינן' זימן
קרש יהי לכון כל פלען עבידה לא תעבדון ותיחגון

חג ליהוה שבעה יומין : ותקרבון עלה קרבן ריח
רחוה ליהוה פרין בני תורין תלת עסר דכרין תרין

אבהרין בני שנה ארבעסר שלמין : ומנחתון סלת

¹ After קרש on marg. ‎מבחד ר[ינה].
² After הרנן on marg. ‎..ח.

בסיס בפסח תלתה עסורין לפר חד לתלתת עסר

15 פריה ותרין עסורין לדכר חד לתרין דכריה : ועסור

16 עסור לאמהר חד לארבעה עסר אמהריה : וצפיר

עזין חד לסלוח לבר כן עלת תדירה ומנח(תה]

ונסכיה :

17 וביומא תנינה פרין בני תורין תרי עס[ר] דכרין

18 תרין אמהרין בני שנה ארבעס[ר]' שלמין : ומנחתון

ונסכיהון לפרי[ה] לדכריה ולאמהרי במנין כדין :

19 וצפ[יר] עזין חד לסלוח לבר כן תדירה וכנ[חתה]

ונסכיה :

20 וביומא תליתאה פרין חד עסר דכ[רין] תרין

21 אמהרין בני שנה ארבעה עס[ר] שלמין : ומנחתון

א.ב. ונסכיהו[ן] ‏ילפריה לדכריה ולאמהריה במנין

22 כדין : וצפיר עזין חד לסלוח לבר כן עלת תדירה

וסנחתה ונסוכיה :

23 וביום רביעאה פרין עסרה דכרין תרין אמהרין

24 בני שנה ארבעה עסר שלמין : וכנחתון ונסכיהון

25 לפריה לדכריה ולאמהריה במנין כדין : וצפיר

עזין חד לסלוח לבר כן עלת תדירה וסנחתה

ונסכיה :

26 וביום חמישאה פרין תשעה דכרין תרין אמהרין

27 בני שנה ארבעה עסר שלמין : ומנחתון ונסוכיהון

28 לפריה לדכריה לאמהריה במנין כדין : וצפיר

עזין חד לסלוח לבר כן עלת תדירה ומנחתה

ונסוכיה :

29 וביומא שתיתאה פרין תומניה דכרין תרין

אמהרין בני שנה ארבעה עסר שלמן : ומנחתון ₃₀
ונסוכיהון לפריה לדכריה ולאמהריה בכנינון כדין :
רצפיר עיזן חד לסלוח לבר מן עלת תדירה ₃₁
ומנחתה ונסוכיה :

וביומה שביעאה פרין שבעה דכרין תרין אמהרין ₃₂
בני שנה ארבעה עסר שלמן : ומנחתון ונסוכיהון ₃₃
לפריה לדכריה ולאמהריה במנינון כדין : רצפיר ₃₄
עיזן חד לסלוח לבר מן עלת תדירה : ומנחתה
[ו]נסוכיה :

[ו]ביומה תמינאה (עצר)ה תהי לכון [כל פ]לען ₃₅
עבידה לא תעבדון : ותקרבון [עלה ק]רבן ריח ₃₆
רחוה ליהוה פר חד דכר [חד אמה]רן בני שנה
שבעה שלמן : ומנחתהן ונסוכיהון לפרה לדכרה ₃₇ ⁵ ,₃₇
לאמהריה' במנינון כדין : רצפיר עיזן חד לסלו[ח] ₃₈
לבר מן עלת תדירה ומנחתה ונסוכיה : אלין ₃₉
תעבדון ליהוה במועדכון לבר מנדריכון ורחותכון
לעלתכון ולמנ[חתכון]² ולנסכיכון ולשלמיכון : ואמר ₁
משה לבני ישראל ככל דפקד יהוה ית משה :

ומלל משה עם ראשי שבטיה לבני ישראל ²
למימר' דן מכללה דפקד יהוה : גבר [אן] ידר ₃
נדר ליהוה או השתבע שבועה למיסר אסר על
נפשה לא ישרי כליו ככל דיפק כפמה³ יעבד :
ואתה [אן] תדר נדר ליהוה ותיסר אסר בבית אבוה ₄
ברביותה : וישמע אבוה ית נדריה ואסריה ₅
דאסרת על נפשה וישת[ק]⁴ לה אבוה ויקמן' כל

נדריה ואסריה דאסרת על נפשה יקומן: ואן 6
כב[ע יכב]ע אבוה יתה ביום משמעה כל נדריה
ואסריה דאסרת על נפשה לא יקומן ויהוה יסלח
לה הלו כבע אבורה יתה: ואן הוי תהי לגבר 7
ונדריה על[ה] אי פרוש ספאבותה' דאסרת על
נפשה: ושמע גברה ביום משמעה וישתק לה 8
ויקומון כל נדריה ואסריה דאסרת על נ[פשה
יקומן]: ואם ביום שמע גברה כבע יתה ויב[טל 9
ירת] נדריה דעליה אי פרוש סבאבותה' דאסת[ה]
על נפשה ויהוה יסלח לה :

ונדר ארמלה ו[משבק]ה כל דאסרת על נפש[ה] 10
יקום עליה: ואן אבית' גברה נדרת [אי] אסרת 11
אסר על נפשה בשבועה: ושמע [גברה] (וי)שתק 12
חז. 33, 8 לה לא כבע יתה יוקובון כל נדריה וכל אסריה
דאסרת על נפשה יקומן: ואן בטול יבטל יתון 13
גברה ביום משמעה כל מפוק ספאבותה לנדריה
ולאסר נפשה לא יקומן גברה בטלון [ויהוה] יסלח
לה: כל נדר וכל שבועת אסר לכבלא[ט]ה נפש 14
גברה יקימנה וגברה יבטלנה: ואן משתק ישתק 15
לה גברה מיום ליום ויקים ית כל נדריה אי ירת
כל אסריה דעליה [ה]קים יתון הלה שתק לה
ביום מש[מעה]: ואן בטול יבטל יתון בתר משמעה 16
ויקבל ירת שובה: אלין בזירירה דפקד יהוה ית 17
משה בין גבר לאתתה ובין אב לברתה ברביאותה
בבית אבוה :

ומלל יהוה עם משה למימר: נקם נקמת בני 2, 1 .xxxi

¹ So MS.

ישראל כן עם מדינאי ובתר תתכנש על עמך:

3 וטלל משה עם עמה למיכר זינו מנכון גברין
לחילה ויהון על מדין למתן נקמת יהוה במדין:

4 אלף לשבטה אלף לשבטה. לכל שבטי ישראל
תשלחון לחילה: וא[תכס]רו מאלפי ישראל אלף

5

6 לשבטה תריעסר אלף מאזיני חיל: ושלח יתהון
משה אלף לשבטה לחילה יתהון [ית פינח]ס בר
אלעזר כהנא לחילה [וכאני] קדשה וחציצרת תרועה

7 בירה: ואתחילו על מדין ככה דפקד יהוה ית
משה וקטלו כל דכר: וית מלכי מדין קטלו על

8 קטליהון ית אוי. וית רקם [ו]ית צור וית עור וית
רבע וחמשתת מלכי מדין וית בלעם בר [בעור] קטלו

9 בחרב: ושבו בני ישראל ית נשי מדין וית
טפלהון' וית כל בהכתון וית כל קנינהון וית כל

10 חלק בזו: וית כל קריתאון במדורתהון וית כל

11 [טירזו]הון אוקדו בנור: ואנסבו ית כל חנאיתה

12 וית כל מסאבה באנשה ובבהכתה: ואתו ליד
משה וליד אלעזר כהנא וליד כל כנשת בני ישראל
ית שביה וית מסאבה וית חנאיתה למשריתה
לבקעת מואב דעל ירדן יריחו:

13 ונפק משה ואלעזר כהנה וכל נסיחי' כנשתה

14 לוזמנון לבר כמשריתה: ורגז משה על מ(הים)ני'

15 חילה רבני אלפיה ורבני מאותה דחתו'.מן חיל

16 קרבה: ואמר להון משה למה חואיתון כל נקבתה:

¹ After טפלהון on marg. .. תל מר.
² After נסיחי on marg. .. אלמ.
³ There is a line over ים in מהימני.     ⁴ So MS.

א(ל)ין אנין הוי לבני ישראל במכלל בלעם לממסר
שקר ביהוה על ככלל פעור והות כניפה בכנשת
יהוה: וכדו קטלו כל דכר בטפלה וכל אתה דחכמת 17
גבר למשכב דכר קטלו: וכל טפלרה בנשיה דלא 18
חכמו כשכב דכר חאו לכון: ואתון שרו לכון לבר 19
מסריתה שבעה יומין כל דקטל נפש וכל דקרב
בקטיל תסתלחון ביוכה תליתאה וביוכה שביעאה
אתון ושביתכון: וכל לבוש וכל כאן כשך וכל 20
עובד ד(חזין)' וכל כאן ד(קיצ)ם תס(ח)לחון:

ואמר משה לאלעזר כהנה אמר לגברי חילרה 21
דעלו לקרבה דרה גזירת תרות[ה] דפקד יהוה:
ברן ית דהבה רת כספה ת[ית] נחשה ית פרחלה 22
וית קסיטרה [וית] אבארה: ·כל כמלל דעלל 23 אבא
בנורה תעברון בנורה וידכי ברן בסי נדה
יסתלח וכל דלא עלל בנורה תעברון במיה:
ותרעון רקעיכון ביומה שביעאה ותדכון ובתר 24
תיעלון למשריתה:

ואמר· אלעזר כהנה לגברי חילה דעלו לקרבה
דרה גזירת תרויתה דפקד יהוה ית משה: ברן
ית דהבה וית כספה וית נחשה וית פרחלה וית
קסיטרה וית אבארה: כל כמלל דעלל בנורח
תעברון בנורה וידכי ברן בסי נדה יסתלח וכל
דלא עלל בנורה תעברון במיה: ותרעון רקעיכון
ביומה שביעאה ותדכון ובתר תיעלון למשריתה:

---

¹ So MS. apparently.
² The words from here to verse 25 are not in the Hebrew.

25, 26 ואמר' יהוה למשה למימר: סב ית סכום
מאסב שביה באנשא ובבעירה אתה ואלעזר
27 כהנא וראשי אבהת כנשתה: ותפלג ית סאבה
בין אהידי קרבא דנפקו לחילה ובין כל כנשתה:
28 ותרים מכס ליהוה מלות גברי קרבא תפקו
לחילה חדה: נפש כן חמש מאון כן אנשא וכן
29 תוריה וכן חמריה מן ענה וכל בהמיה: כפלגתון
30 תסבון ותתן לאלעזר כהנא ית ארכות יהוה: וכן
פלגת בני ישראל תסב חד אהיד כן חבשיתה
וכן אנשא וכן תוריה וכן חמריה וכן ענה בכל
בהמתה ותתן להון לליואי נטרי מטרת משכן
31 יהוה: תעבד משה ואלעזר כהנא ככה דפקד יהוה
32 ית משה: [ו]הוה מאסבא מותר בזתא דבזו עם
[חילא] (ענין) שת כאן ראלף ושבעין אלף [וחמש]ה
33, 34 אלפים: יותורין תרין ושבעין אלף: וחמרין חד
35. 39. ושתין אלף: ונפש דאנש כן נשיה דלא חכמי
35 ושתין אלף: ונפש דאנש כן נשיה דלא חכמי
36 משכב דכר כל נפש תרין ותלתין אלף: והות
פלגתה חולק כל נפש תרין ותלתין אלף: והות
פלגתה חולק נאפק(י) בחילה מנין דען תלת מאן
דאלף ותלתין אלף ושבעה אלפין וחמש מאן:
37 והוה מכסה ליהוה מן ענה שת מאן חמשה
38 ושבעין: ותורין שתה ותלתין אלף ומכסן ליהוה
39 תרין ושבעין: וחברין תלתין אלף וחמש מאון
40 ומכסון ליהוה חר ושחין: ונפש דאנש שתת עסר
41 אלף ומכסון ליהוה תרין ותלתין נפש: ויהב משה

---

1 Before ואמר on marg. an illegible gloss.
2 The ח is written over.
3 ו has apparently been erased after י.

ירת סכם ארמות יהוה לאלעזר כהנא כמה דפקד
יהוה ית משה :

וכפלגת בני ישראל רפלג משה מן' גבריה ‏42
חיליה : הות פלגת כנשתא מן ענא תלת תלת מאון ‏43
דאלף ותלתין אלף ושבעה אלפין וחמש מאון :
ותורין שתה ותלתין אלף : וחברין תלתין אלף ‏44,45
וחמש מאון : ונפש ראנש שתת עסר אלף : ונסב ‏46,47
משה מפלגת בני ישראל ית אהד חד כן חמשיתה'
וכן אנשה וכן בהמתה ויהב יתון לליואי נטרי
מטרת משכן יהוה כמה דפקד יהוה ית משה :

וקרבו ליד משה כחיכניה דלאלפי חיל רבני ‏48
אלפיה ורבני כאותה : ואכרו למשה עבדיך נסבו ‏49
ית סכום גברי קרבא דבידנו ולא אתעשד כננו
גבר : ונקרב ית קרבן יהוה גבר דאשקע כאן ‏50
דה[ב] קעמלה ושיר עסקא גיכן וספוד לכסלחרה
על נפשתנו לקודם יהוה : *ונסב משה ואלעזר ‏51,52,b
כהנא ית דהבא סלותון כל מהן עובד : והוה ‏52
דהבא דארטותא דאריכו ליהוה שתת עסר אלף
ושבע כאן וחמשין דקל מלות רבני אלפיה ומלות
רבני מאותה : גברי חילה בזו גבר לה : ונסב ‏53,54
משה ואלעזר כהנא ית רהבא כלות רבני אלפיה
ומאותה ואיתו יתה לאהל מועד דוכרן לבני ישראל
לקודם יהוה :

וקנין‏3 סגי הוה לבני ראובן ולבני גד ולפלגות ‏xxxii. 1

---

‏1  After מן on marg. ...בק.
‏2  The ח is written over.
‏3  Before קנין on marg. ...‏ בריל צ.

שבט מנשה חיול שריר וחזו ית ארע יעזיר וית

3 ארע גלעד והא אתרא אתר קנין: ואתו בני גד

ובני ראובן ופלגות שבט מנשה ואמרו לכטה

3 לאלעזר כהנא ולנסיחי כנשתה למיכר: עטרות

חדבון ויעזיר ונטרה וחשבון ואלעליה ושבם ונבו

4 ובען: ארעא דכבש יהוה לקודם כנשת ישראל

5 ארע קנין היא ולעבדיך קנין: ואמרו אן אש(חקע)נ(ן)

רחים' בעיניך יתיהב ית ארעה הדה לעבדיך

לסחנה ואל תעברנן ית ירדנה:

6 ואמר מיטה לבני ראובן ולבני גד ולפלגות שבט

מנשה אחיכון ייעלון לקרבה ואתון תתבון הכה:

7 ולכה תשפלון ית לב בני ישראל מן עבר לארעה

8 דיהב להון יהוה: א[כו]ן עבדו אבהתכם בשל(ו)חי

9 יתון מקדש ברנע לםחזי ית ארער: וסלקו עד

נחל תכאלה וחזו ית ארעה ושפלו ית לב [בני]

ישראל דלא מיעל לארעה דיהב להון יהוה:

*     *     *     *     *

Fol. 49.
XXXIII.
19, 20

[בכם]געדה בה הוא יקטלנ[ה: וא]ן בסנה דח[פה

11 א]י רמה עליו בכמנ[ה וסית] : אי בדבבו [כח]תה

באדה וסית [קטל] יקטל מעיה [ק]טיל הוא גא[ול

13 אדמה] יקטל ית קטולה במפגעה בה: וא[ן בעסף]

דלא בדבבו דחפה או רכה [עליו כל] כהן דלא

13 בכמנה: או בכל אבן דיכ[ית בה] בדלה' חזי

ואפל עליו וסית והוא לא דבוב לה' ולא [כ]בעי

בישא[ה]:

---

' The ' is written over.      ' So MS.

' So MS., apparently.

[ו]ידונון כנשתה בין סעיה ובין גאול' אדכה על 24

דיניה האלין : ויפצון כנשתה ית סעיה מן אד גאול 25

אדכה ויעזרון יתה כנשתה לקרית' מקלטה דערק

לתמן וידור בה עד מות כהנה רבה דמשח יתה

במשח קדשה : ואן מפק יפק קטולה [מן] תחום 26

קרית' מקלטו דערק לתמן : וישכע יתה גאול 27

אדמה לבר מתחום קרית' מקלטה ויקטל גאול

אדכה ית קטולה לית לה אדם : הל(ו) בקרי[ת] 28

מקלטה יזור עד מות כהנה רבה ובתר מות כהנה

רבה יעזר קטולה לארע סחנת[ה] :

ויהן אלין לכן לגזירת דין לדריכ[ו]ן] בכל 29

מדוריכן : כל קטל נפש למיכ[ו]ר] סחדין יתקטל ית 30

קטולה וסחד ה[ד לא] יאני בנפש למתקטלה : ולא 31

תסבון [סלוח] לנפש קטול דהוא חיב למתקטלה

[הלא] קטל (ית)קטל : ולא תסבון סלוח [לערוק] 32

לק(ורי) מקלט(ה) למעורה למדאר ב[ארעה] עד מות

כהנה רבה : ולא (ת)חנפון [ית] ארעה דאתון 33

דארין בה הל(ו) [אדם] הוא יחנף ית ארעה

ולארעה לא [יסתלח] לאדם דשפיך בה ה[לא] אן 34

באדם שפכה : [ולא הס]יבון ית ארע[ה] דאתון

דארין ב[ה ד]אני] שרי בנוה הל[א] אני יהוה שרי

ב[גו בני י]שרא[ל] :

וקרבו' ראשי אבהתה לכן [בני ג]לעד בר 1 xxxvi.

---

1 After גאול on marg. . . אפיץ לח.

2 Altered apparently into קור.

3 Altered apparently into קרד.

4 Before וקרבו on marg. וסקומה.

מכיר בר מנשה מכח בני י[וֹסֵף] וּכללו לקודם
משה ולקודם נסיחזה ראשי אבהתה לבני ישראל :

2 ואמרו ית רבי פקד יהוה לכתן ית ארעה בפלגה
בנאבו לבני ישראל ורבי מפקד ביהוה למתן ית

3 פלגת צלפחד אחונן לבנתה : ויהן לחד מבני
שבטי בני ישראל לנשין ויתבצר פלגתהין מן פלגת
אבהתנ(ו) ותתחף על פלגת שבטה דיהן להון

4 וכנאבז פלגתנ(ו) יתבצר : ואן יהי יבולה לבני
ישראל ותתחף פלגתהין על פלגת שבטה דהן להה
ומן פלגת שבט אבהתנ(ו) יתבצר פלגתהין :

5 ופקד משה ית בני ישראל על מימר יהוה

6 למימר שפיר שבם בני יוסף מַמַללין : ח [מַם]לללה
דפקד יהוה לבנת צלפחד למימר [לטב] בעיניהן
יהן לנשין בח לכח [שבט] אבוהין יהן לנשין :

7 ולא תסז(הר)' [פלגה] לבני ישראל משבט לשבט
הלא (גבר) [בפלג]ת שבט אבהתה ידקבון' בני
ישראל :

8 [וכל ב]רה ירתה פלגה כן שבטי בני ישראל
[לחד כ]כח שבט אבוה תהי לאתה בדיל [דיירתו]ן
9 בני ישראל אנש ית פלגת [אבהתה] : ולא תסז(הר)'
פלגה מן שבט לשבט עורק

●        ●        ●